MY FRIEND MICHAEL

MY FRIEND MICHAEL

AN ORDINARY FRIENDSHIP
WITH AN EXTRAORDINARY MAN

FRANK CASCIO

with Hilary Liftin

wm
WILLIAM MORROW
An Imprint of HarperCollins*Publishers*

MY FRIEND MICHAEL. Copyright © 2011 by Frank Cascio. All rights reserved. Printed in the United States of America. No part of this book may
be used or reproduced in any manner whatsoever without written permission except in the case of brief quotations embodied in critical articles and
reviews. For information address HarperCollins Publishers, 10 East 53rd
Street, New York, NY 10022.

HarperCollins books may be purchased for educational, business, or sales
promotional use. For information please write: Special Markets Department, HarperCollins Publishers, 10 East 53rd Street, New York, NY 10022.

FIRST EDITION

Designed by Jamie Lynn Kerner

Library of Congress Cataloging-in-Publication Data has been applied for.

ISBN 978-0-06-209006-5

11 12 13 14 15 OV/RRD 10 9 8 7 6 5 4 3 2

To Michael, my teacher—thank you for being a father, a brother, a mentor, and a friend, and for the greatest adventure I could ever have imagined. I love you, and I miss you every day.

With all my love,
Frank

To Paris, Prince, and Blanket—I love and adore all three of you. When you came into this world, one by one, you brought new light, energy, and purpose to your father. You made him the happiest person in the world. Nothing was more important to him than you. You have always been as smart, beautiful, and well-mannered as he wanted you to be. I see him in each of you, and watching you grow makes me happy on his behalf. I hope that reading this book brings back good memories of your father and his love for you. Please know that I will always be there for you.

To Frank "Tookie" DiLeo—first and foremost I want to thank you for loving and protecting Michael for all those years. He loved you very much. I miss our lunches by the pool at the Beverly Hilton Hotel and hearing your crazy stories and life experiences. Thank you for being a mentor and father figure to me. I miss you and I love you so much.

To the fans of Michael Jackson—I wrote this book to show you a personal side of Michael that you may or may not know. I hope you can appreciate the human being that he was behind his enormous gifts and talents. For over twenty-five years, my family and I were blessed to experience the world from his perspective. Through Michael's eyes, the world was a very different place. He was the innocent.

We were all very fortunate to have been blessed by his presence in this world. He wasn't only my friend Michael; he was our friend Michael.

CONTENTS

PROLOGUE

AS I DROVE MY CAR THROUGH THE DARK COBBLE-stone streets of Castelbuono, Italy, I turned my phone on. Text messages started rolling in, one on top of another, so fast that I couldn't read them. Flashes of phrases like "Is it true?" and "Are you okay?" piled on top of one another on the screen, layers of questions and concern. I had no idea what news they were talking about, but I knew it wasn't good.

In Castelbuono, my family's hometown, many people have two homes, one in the town, where they work, and a summer retreat up in the mountains, where they plant vegetable gardens and tend fig trees. I had spent the evening at the summer home of the man who had rented me a house down in the town. He had invited me to a dinner party with six or seven other people, and I was the guest of honor, because in Castelbuono, having flown in from New York is reason enough to be warmly and widely welcomed.

It was June 25, 2009. There weren't many of us at the table, but as at any good Italian dinner party, there was more than enough food, wine, and grappa. During the dinner, I turned off my phone. Having spent years of my life tethered to a cell phone, I've grown to love those moments when good manners force me to shut it down. The other guests and I lingered in the balmy night, then finally said our good-byes to our host, and around midnight I headed with a few friends back to the house I'd rented, following my cousin Dario's car down the dirt mountain roads into the city.

Now, as the stream of text messages flooded my phone, my cousin Dario's car swerved suddenly to the side of the road and came to an abrupt stop. As soon as I saw him pull over, I knew that what I was starting to glean from the texts had to be true. I rolled to a stop behind Dario. He ran toward my car, shouting, "Michael's dead! Michael's dead!"

I got out of my car and started walking down the road, with no plan or destination. I was numb. Shocked.

I don't know how much time passed before I finally dialed one of Michael's most loyal employees, a woman I'll call Karen Smith. Was this one of Michael's schemes? A prank on the press or an ill-conceived attempt to get out of a concert? Sadly, Karen confirmed that what I had heard was true. We cried on the phone together. We didn't say much. We just cried.

After I hung up the phone, I just kept walking. My friends were still waiting back in my car. My cousin was following behind me saying, "Frank, get in the car. Come on, Frank." But I didn't want to be around anyone.

"I'll meet you at home," I called out as I walked away from them. "I just want everyone to get away from me."

And then I was alone. I walked up and down the cobblestone streets, under the streetlights, late into the summer night. Michael, who was a father, a mentor, a brother, a friend. Michael, who was the center of my world for so long. Michael Jackson was gone.

I'd first met Michael when I was five years old, and it hadn't taken long for him to become a close friend of my family's, visiting our home in New Jersey, spending Christmases with us. As a child, I'd spent many vacations at Neverland, both with the rest of my family and alone. As teenagers, my brother, Eddie, and I had joined Michael to keep him company on the *Dangerous* tour. When I was eighteen, having grown up with Michael as a mentor and friend, I went to work for him, first as his personal assistant, then as his personal manager. To be honest, I didn't ever have a clear title for my position, but it was always personal. I conceived the idea for a network television special honoring his thirty years in show business. I was alongside him as he made the *Invincible* album. And when Michael was falsely accused of child molestation for the second time, I was named as an unindicted co-conspirator. The pressure of that trial was more than any friendship should be expected to bear. For nearly all of my life, until Michael's death—over twenty years in all—I was with him in one capacity or another, through ups and downs, struggles and celebrations, always as a close friend and confidant.

Knowing Michael was both an ordinary and an extraordinary experience. From the very beginning (almost—after all, I was only five), I knew that Michael was special, different, a visionary. When he walked into a room, he was captivating. There are plenty of special people in the world, but Michael had a magic about him, as if he were chosen, touched by God. Wherever he went, Michael created experiences. His concerts. His Neverland estate. His midnight adventures in far-flung cities. He entertained stadiums full of people, and he enthralled me.

But at the same time, he was a regular, expected presence. I always appreciated the moments we shared. But I never looked at him as a superstar. He was my friend, my family. I knew I wasn't living a traditional life. Not compared to what my friends were doing. I knew this was not normal. But it was my normal.

It was no accident that when I heard the news of Michael's death, I walked away from my friends and family. From the very beginning, I kept my relationship with Michael to myself; his fame required that his friends be discreet. When I was a kid, it was easy enough to just compartmentalize. I had one life at home in New Jersey, going to school and playing soccer, occasionally bussing tables and cooking at my family's restaurants, and another with Michael, having adventures and hanging around. The two never intersected. I did my best to keep them separate.

When I started working for Michael, I moved into a completely confidential world and the rest of my life took second place. I didn't talk about what happened at work, not the everyday details of what had to get done, not the darkest moments of false accusations and insane media spectacle, not the joyful moments helping children and making music.

Living in Michael's world was a rare and special opportunity, of course, and that was why I stayed there. But, without my realizing it, the discretion affected me. From a very young age, I trained myself not to talk freely. I kept everything inside and suppressed most of my reactions and emotions. I was never one hundred percent open or free. That's not to say I lied—except, I'll admit, when I was working for Michael and told people I'd just met that I was a door-to-door Tupperware salesman and that I was very proud of the plastic we manufactured. Or that my family was from Switzerland and was in the chocolate business. With my close friends and family, I never lied, but when it came to my experiences with Michael, I chose every word I said carefully. Michael was a private person, and so am I. I didn't want to call attention to myself or to have people look at me differently because of my connection to Michael, and I certainly didn't want to be the source of any gossip about him. There was plenty of that already. Speaking is revealing. It's still hard for me to talk freely: I always think, and think again, before speaking.

Over the course of our relationship, Michael played many roles. He was a second father, a teacher, a brother, a friend, a child. I look at myself, and I see the way my experiences with Michael have shaped and molded who I am, for better and for worse. Michael was the greatest teacher in the world—to me personally and to many of his fans. At first I was a sponge. I agreed with all of his thoughts and beliefs and signed on to them. From him I learned the values of tolerance, loyalty, truthfulness.

As I got older, our relationship evolved, and I began to see more clearly that he wasn't perfect. I became a protector of sorts, helping him through the hardest times. I was there for him when he needed a friend—to talk, to brainstorm and conceptualize ideas, to just hang out. Michael knew he could trust me.

When Michael and I had free time at Neverland Ranch, his 2,700-acre fantastical home/amusement park/zoo/retreat near Santa Barbara, we liked to kick back and relax. Sometimes he would ask me if we should just get some movies, stay in, and "stink." (Michael had a particular affinity for juvenile jokes about body odor.) On one of those days, when the sun was just about to set, Michael said, "Come on, Frank. Let's go up to the mountain." Neverland was nestled in the Santa Ynez Valley, and mountains surrounded the property. He named the tallest one Mount Katherine, after his mother. The property had numerous paths that led up to the peaks, where the sunsets were extraordinary. We drove up one of those paths on a golf cart, sat down, and watched the sun flame out behind the mountains, shadowing them in purple. It was there that I finally understood the "purple mountain majesties" of "America the Beautiful."

Sometimes helicopters flew over the property, trying to take pictures. Once or twice they saw us up in the mountains, and we sprinted away from them, trying to hide behind trees. But this time all was still. Michael was in a reflective mood, and he started talking about the rumors and accusations that plagued him. He found it all both funny and sad. At first he said he didn't think he should have to explain himself to anyone. But then his tone changed.

"If people only knew how I really am, they would understand," he said, his voice tinged with equal parts hope and frustration. We sat there in silence for a bit, both of us wishing there were a way for him to reveal himself, to have people truly understand who he was and how he lived.

I think about that night often as I mull over the roots of Michael's predicament. People fear or are intimidated by what they don't understand. Most of us lead familiar lives. We do what our parents or the other role models around us have done. We follow a safe, comfortable, easily categorized path. It's not hard to find other people who lead lives similar to those we chose. This was not the case with Michael. From the very first, alongside his family and later on his own, he forged a completely original path. Innocent and childlike as he was, he was also a complicated man. It was hard for people to know him because they hadn't seen anyone like him before, and, in all likelihood, never would again.

Michael's life ended abruptly and unexpectedly. And when it did, he was still misunderstood. Michael Jackson the superstar—the King of Pop—will be remembered for a long, long time. His work endures—a testament to his deep and powerful connection with millions of people—but somehow the man became obscured and lost behind the legend.

This book is about Michael Jackson the man. The mentor who taught me how to make a "mind map." The friend who loved to feed candy to animals. The prankster who donned a disguise and pretended to be a wheelchair-bound priest. The humanitarian who tried to be as great and generous in his private life as he was in public. The human being. I want Michael to be seen as I saw him, to be understood with all the silly, loving, challenging, imperfect beauty that I loved.

My greatest hope is that, as you read this book, you can put aside all the scandals, all the rumors, all the cruel jokes that surrounded him later in his life, and come to know him through my eyes. This is our story. It's the story of growing up with a guy who happened to have one of the most recognizable faces in the world. It's the story of an ordinary friendship with an extraordinary man. It started simply; it shifted and evolved as we both grew and changed; it struggled for a footing when people and circumstances came between us . . . and most of all, it endured. Michael was a rare being. He wanted to give greatness to the world. I want to share him with you.

PART ONE

THE APPLEHEAD CLUB

CHAPTER ONE

A NEW FRIEND

ONE COLD DAY, IN THE AUTUMN OF MY FIFTH year, I sat in my family's living room playing with a die-cast toy limousine. I was obsessed with that limo, the way five-year-olds tend to be with favorite toys, and when my father told me I would be going to work with him that day in order to meet a friend of his, my first concern was that I be allowed to keep that car clutched tightly in my little fist. I had never heard of Michael Jackson, so when my father told me the name of the person we were to meet, I didn't really care. I was just happy to get out of the house and proud to accompany my father to work. As long as I had my toy limo in tow.

Of course I had no idea at the time how important that meeting would prove to be—that it was a turning point in my life. Still, for some reason I remember the day clearly, right down to what I was wearing: dark blue pants, a blue sweater, a bow tie, and mini brown dress shoes with little holes in the front. I know, not exactly typical duds for a five-year-old—at least within the past hundred years. I was always dressed immaculately—my father was from Italy, the fashion capital of the world. I had short, straight hair. A neat, stylish, limo-loving kid.

At the time, my father was working at the Helmsley Palace in Manhattan. The Palace was an exclusive five-star hotel with an elite clientele. My father was the general manager of the towers and the suites—the luxurious quarters catering to the hotel's VIPs. To me, the hotel was always a magical place. Maybe it was the vibrant energy of the people passing through, each with a unique and grand purpose. Back then I couldn't begin to fathom everything that was going on, but I could sense the excitement pulsing through the air. To this day I still remember the smell of that lobby and the surge of excitement that it brought me. I love hotels.

My father and I went up an elevator and walked toward a guest room, in front of which we were greeted by a guy I would later know as Bill Bray, who at the time was Michael Jackson's manager and head of security. Bill Bray was a father figure of sorts to Michael. He had worked with him since his Motown days and would stay with him as a trusted adviser for many years.

Bill was an African American man with a beard who stood about six foot two, and when we showed up that day, he was wearing a fedora-type hat. He had multiple rolls of skin at the back of his neck, and a "country" way about him. In the coming years I would often see Michael walk behind him, imitating his laid-back swagger. Bill greeted my father warmly. It seemed to me that he and my father were already friends.

Bill led us into the hotel room. It was pristine, as if nobody were staying there. In fact, given what I now know about Michael's habits, it's clear that the suite was not, in fact, the one he was using: he had gotten this room specifically for this meeting because he didn't know us well enough to invite us to his suite. Though Michael often reached out to others, he always created layers of protection between himself and the people he met.

Michael rose from a chair to greet us. He didn't look exceptional to me. At five, the only real distinctions I drew between people were whether they were grown-ups, big kids, or kids like me.

"Hey, Joker," Bill said. "We have Dominic and his son here to see you." Later I would understand that Bill called Michael "Joker" for the obvious reason that Michael was always playing jokes on people. Michael gave me a big smile, took off his sunglasses, and shook my hand. He was, at twenty-seven years old, a world-renowned entertainer, and his most recent album, *Thriller,* was the best-selling album of all time—a record it still holds as of this writing.

Once we were settled in, Bill Bray exited, and my father, Michael, and I were left in that rather empty room, just talking.

"You have such a wonderful father," Michael told me. He would repeat this many times in the years ahead, and I know that it was because of the special impression that my father had made on him that he wanted to meet the rest of his family. People are always immediately comfortable around my father. His honesty and sincerity radiate from his core.

Then Michael and I started talking about cartoons. I told him I loved Popeye, and I had the dubious honor of introducing him to the Garbage Pail Kids—my brother and I collected the trading cards. Michael knew how to talk with kids—he was genuinely interested in my small world—and I must have liked him because I remember driving my toy limo over his head, his shoulders, and down on his arms. He took the car from me and made it fly over my head like an airplane, making airplane sounds.

"What do you want to be when you grow up?" Michael asked.

"I want to be like Donald Trump," I said, "but with more money."

My father laughed. "Can you believe it?" he said.

"Donald Trump doesn't have that much money," Michael said.

Then my father asked to take a picture of me and Michael. I climbed into his lap and curved my arm around his chin. I smiled, and we took a picture.

So that was the first time I met Michael. Years later, he would show that picture off to people, saying, "Can you believe that's Frank?" The relaxed casualness of the image—our smiles, a lock of dark hair escaping down the middle of Michael's forehead—foretold the momentousness the occasion would assume for me in retrospect.

We spent about an hour with Michael that day, and as we left he told us he would call us the next time he was in New York, and that he would love to see us again.

On the car ride back to New Jersey, my father glanced at me in the backseat and said, "You have no idea who you just met."

THAT FIRST MEETING BETWEEN MICHAEL AND ME HAD taken place because of Michael's appreciation for my father: whenever he stayed at the Palace hotel, my father always took care of him. That was my dad's job at the Palace, and he was good at it. He made sure that when Michael came, his favorite suite was available for him. If Michael wanted a dance floor in his room, my father made sure it was installed. When Gregory Peck was staying at the hotel and Michael wanted to meet him, my father made it happen. He oversaw security for Michael's comings and goings from the hotel. He was attentive to even the smallest requests, like special food. He went out of his way to make sure Michael got everything he needed or wanted.

Michael knew that my father was handling this stuff, and eventually he told Bill Bray that he wanted to get to know Dominic. Bill Bray arranged for them to spend some time together. As they got to know each other better, my father found Michael extremely warm, gracious, and humble. At the same time I'm sure my father made Michael feel at home in a way that demonstrated he wasn't drawn to

Michael because of his celebrity status. He wasn't starstruck. People have always been drawn to my father because of his sincerity. His whole manner reflects the fact that he sees people as people. He listens without judgment and helps without wanting anything for himself.

That kind of treatment was rare in Michael's world, and he started looking at my father as a friend. He didn't ask for the regular list of amenities that celebrity guests requested. He wanted to talk to my father. To get to know him as a person. My father didn't seek out such intimacy with the VIPs who stayed at the hotel. It was Michael who initiated the friendship, and certainly my father was flattered, though not unduly so. The friendship grew and flourished into what would become a lifetime of camaraderie, loyalty, and trust.

Obviously, meeting Michael Jackson didn't mean much to me as a five-year-old. I had no idea who he was. I had no idea what *Thriller* was, or the moonwalk, or the Jackson 5, and I wouldn't have cared if anyone had told me. I was not especially into TV or music, except whatever my mother played in the car. I was a normal New Jersey kindergartner, occasional bow tie excepted. My friend Mark Delvecchio and I built forts near the road and squirted water guns at passing cars. I loved to kick around a soccer ball, play in the woods, climb trees, and get dirty. I loved the outdoors. I was just happy and free.

I liked any new person who showed interest in my interests. I didn't have preconceptions, and I didn't make judgments. Michael was my father's friend and decades my senior, but when he addressed me, it wasn't as an adult speaks to a child. It was as a friend speaks to a friend. We played, and for a good long time this childlike foundation was a sufficient basis for our friendship.

Two or three weeks after our first meeting, my father brought me, my younger brother, Eddie, and my pregnant mother back to the hotel to see Michael again. Those were the only two times I had met him before the night at our house in Hawthorne, New Jersey, when the doorbell rang long after I'd gone to sleep. Hawthorne was a modest town, and our house was small. My brother and I shared a room with single beds separated by a little dresser. I remember lying in bed wondering who could be ringing the doorbell in the middle of the night. I heard the side door open, and moments later, my parents came to the door of our bedroom to wake us up. They were with two men. One was Bill Bray, and the other was Michael Jackson.

A nighttime visitor was a rare and exciting event. My brother and I sprang out of bed to greet him, and I scrambled off to get our impressive collection of Cabbage Patch dolls and Garbage Pail Kids trading cards and show them to Michael. Then my parents told us to show him how we were learning to play the piano. I was not especially eager to play, but I pounded out the *Star Wars* theme song and "Für Elise." My brother, Eddie, who, though he was only three was already a more accomplished musician than I, played the theme from *Chariots of Fire*. Michael was delighted by the performance.

It's probably an overstatement to say that at that age I already recognized something different about Michael, something that distinguished him from the other grown-ups I knew, but the next time he came over I bestowed upon him what I considered to be a great gift, one of my most valued possessions: my Garbage Pail Kids card collection. At first he refused to accept them, saying, "No, I can't take your cards!"

But I saw how delighted he was with the collection and insisted: "No, no. I want you to have them." That was the first present I gave to Michael, and he kept it for the rest of his life (in his mess of a closet at Neverland).

From then on, Michael's visits became a frequent occurrence. At the time, he was on tour with the Jacksons for the *Victory* album, so he was in New York a lot, and on each of his visits he made a point of seeing us. Why did Michael do this? Why did the busiest man in entertainment start to make time for our outwardly unremarkable family? I think, for him, we represented something that he, for all his fame, didn't have, and maybe in a way wished he did. Being a close friend of my family meant that he could escape to the green calm of suburban New Jersey, and, at least for a little while, live an ordinary life with an ordinary family.

As for hanging around children and being interested in toys and cartoons, it wasn't a sexual thing for Michael. When he was with children, he could be himself. He'd been in the spotlight his entire life, and people looked at him differently because of that. But children didn't care who he was. I certainly didn't.

On that tour, the Jacksons did three concerts at Giants Stadium, and my parents took me and Eddie to all of them. At the beginning of the first concert, when Michael began to sing, I looked up at my father and asked, "Is that the same Michael Jackson who comes to the house?" It was the first time I really grasped that there might be something truly singular about this nice man who shared my love of cartoons, Cabbage Patch Kids, and toys in general. Onstage, he was transformed. This didn't seem like our friend Michael. This was Michael the superstar.

Those were late nights for such a young boy, and my parents, especially my mother, weren't laid-back about such things. But obtaining box-seat tickets to a Michael Jackson concert didn't happen every day, and my parents wanted to give Eddie and me as many memorable experiences as possible. Maybe Michael was the biggest star in the world, and maybe it made them feel special to be on intimate terms with him, but this kind of thinking didn't drive their decisions as parents. They weren't dazzled by Michael. Yes, it was a cool experience to know him and spend time with him, and that was important. But mostly, going to the concerts, and all the other times we would eventually share with Michael, were simply the kind of things my parents did with someone they loved. What my father thought was special about Michael was not his fame or stardom. It was his smile, his sincerity, his humanity. He was touched that Michael, a megastar in the world of entertainment, had formed a real friendship with the whole of our family. My mother is a supportive, loyal person, and as she got to know Michael, she felt maternal toward and protective of him, the way she would feel toward any trusted and beloved friend. She was there for him, especially as time went on and she felt that he needed her loyalty and support.

My parents believed in actively participating in life. Their doors were open to the world, and anyone who walked into their house found warmth and comfort awaiting them. That was just the way they were. Dominic Cascio, my father, grew up in southern Italy. He lived between Palermo and Castelbuono, the small town I referred to earlier. It's a little village, a special place where people don't have to make a lot of money to appreciate the better things in life. Love, family, religion, food—these are the pleasures that count in Castelbuono. I know this all sounds like one of those clichéd movies about food and romance in sunny, picturesque Tuscany, but it really exists. My father was raised there, and though my mother was born in Staten Island, her family came from Castelbuono, too.

As I was growing up, our Sunday-night dinners always included more guests than our immediate (albeit rapidly expanding) family. Even before all five of her children were born, it wasn't unusual for my mother to be cooking for almost twenty people. Our house in New Jersey was like a hotel: there were always people showing up, staying for dinner, staying for days, weeks, even months. No wonder my father was so successful at the Helmsley Palace: he'd been running the Cascio Palace for years. My parents were the center of their families, and they were the ones who made sure everyone came together to congregate, which usually meant eating together. Family was a top priority to them, and they raised their children to feel the same way.

I think Michael recognized our values from the very start. He already felt comfortable with my father, and when he met the rest of us, he must have realized that we were basically warmhearted, honest people who had no particular motives or agenda beyond living life and being happy. That's my best theory of why Michael fell in love with my family: it was because we never saw him as Michael Jackson, the superstar. My parents didn't raise their kids to think about people in those terms. We recognized and respected Michael's talent and success, and the kind of demands they placed on him, so we accommodated ourselves to his unconventional schedule, compromising on logistics, not on who we were or how we saw him. I mean, frankly, what mattered most to me was that he was an adult who liked Cabbage Patch Kids and cartoons. Megastardom be damned: *that* was impressive.

FOR THE NEXT FEW YEARS, THAT'S THE RELATIONSHIP that we had with Michael. The doorbell would ring late at night and Eddie and I would know it was Michael. We'd wake up, run to give him hugs and show him whatever new toys we had and tricks we had learned, the whole family talking at the same time, greeting him like a beloved relative from far away whose plane had arrived late.

I was never a big sleeper. Many nights I wandered around our house, spying on my parents, reveling in the dark mystery of the grown-ups' world. But every so often I made up for the lost hours by crashing heavily. It must have been one of those nights when the doorbell failed to wake me up. Instead I opened my eyes to find a chimpanzee making noises right in my face. I assumed, with a calmness and confidence that it surprises me to recall, that I was dreaming as I watched the chimp jump over to Eddie's bed and wake him up as well. Then I realized that Michael, Bill Bray, my parents, and another man I would later know as Bob Dunn, the chimp trainer, were crowded in my small bedroom. It was past midnight and the chimp currently freaking out my brother was the legendary Bubbles, Michael's beloved pet.

As Michael became a more familiar presence in my life, I learned bits and pieces about him and his music. In the early days, soon after I met him, I told my kindergarten teacher, Mrs. Whise, "I can play the piano. I'm going to play 'Thriller.'" I started banging on the keys, certain I could play the piano and that my rendition of "Thriller" would impress the class. But Mrs. Whise just said, "Get away from that piano, you're going to break it."

A year or so later, when I was in the first or second grade, I was supposed to bring in something meaningful to class for show-and-tell. I had no idea what to bring until my mother suggested a snapshot of Michael. Although I still thought of him as my friend Michael, I was beginning to realize that people knew him as someone bigger, the person whom I'd seen perform on the huge stage at Giants Stadium, with all the lights and applause. So I brought the picture to school—the photo that had been taken on the first day I met him.

The kid who took his turn before me had gone around the classroom showing a teddy bear to his classmates. He told us his teddy's name and what was so special about him. (Forgive me if I don't remember the details.) Then I stood up and said, "This is a picture of Michael. He's a friend of mine. He's a singer and an entertainer."

My teacher, who was probably in her late fifties, called me up to her desk and asked to see the snapshot I was holding. She looked a little amazed.

"Is this real?" she asked.

"Yes, it's real," I replied.

Then she said, "Class, this is Michael Jackson. He's a very, very famous singer." And although I didn't totally understand why, I felt a surge of pride.

WHEN HE STAYED WITH US, ONE OF MICHAEL'S FAVORite activities was to help my mother clean the house. He loved to vacuum. He told us that as a child, he and his siblings would clean and sing at the same time. One brother would sing the first verse, another would make up the B section, and a third would have to come up with the chorus or, as Michael called it, the hook. Then someone would do the second verse, and someone else the bridge.

He said they used to come up with some really good stuff while they cleaned. Or so he said . . . I always suspected the story was a clever way of motivating my brother and me to help.

My mother used to make our beds and clean our rooms. We were a little spoiled that way. But Michael always urged us to help her.

"You have no idea how special your mother is," he'd tell us. "One day you'll see."

Michael told us that our mother, Connie, reminded him of his own mother, Katherine, and I'll never forget the time when I got mad at my mother and screamed at her. Michael reprimanded me harshly, saying, "You never speak to your mother that way, ever. She gave birth to you. You would not be here if it weren't for her. And she would die for you. You must respect your mother."

As an Italian, I already knew to respect my mother. But hearing it from Michael gave the familiar admonition extra weight, and I took his words to heart.

One of the things Michael enjoyed most about my mother, in addition to her warm and nurturing heart, was her cooking. Every time he came to our house, he begged her to make a turkey dinner, complete with mashed potatoes, stuffing, yams, and cranberry sauce. Michael loved cranberry sauce. And always peach cobbler for dessert: the way Michael used to talk about peach cobbler, you'd think it was the Second Coming.

My uncle Aldo and my father owned a restaurant called Aldo's. When we brought Michael there, we ate in a private room so he could feel comfortable, enjoying a meal without having to deal with people staring at him.

But whether we were eating at home or at Aldo's, it felt totally natural to be around Michael. The funny thing was, none of us ever really talked about him with other people. We loved him, but at the same time we always protected him.

He was one of us.

CHAPTER TWO

THE RANCH

THOSE EARLY GRADE SCHOOL YEARS PASSED WITH
Michael as a regular, if often unannounced, visitor to my
family's home in Hawthorne.

In 1987, when I was seven, his seventh album, *Bad*, came out.
Michael mailed us a copy of the album before it was released, we
went to the concert, and my family watched the "Man in the Mirror"
video on MTV when it first came out (and I watched it a million
times afterward—this was back in the glory days when MTV ran
nonstop music videos).

Bad went on to sell over thirty million copies and was a massive
worldwide success. Michael was on top of the world.

Over the next few years, whenever we'd see Michael, he'd play
us songs that he was currently working on, ask us for our opinions,
and let us listen to the new directions he was taking musically. When
Dangerous arrived in our mailbox four years after *Bad*, I was surprised

to find that some of the new songs Michael had been playing for us weren't included on the album—for example, a track called "Turning Me Off" and another called "Superfly Sister" (which was later released on the album *Blood on the Dance Floor*). *Dangerous* sold even better and faster than *Bad*. As Michael cemented his worldwide following, my knowledge of his music was expanding all the time, but my friends remained mostly unaware of Michael Jackson. We were still at the age when most of us adopted our parents' musical preferences, and my friends' parents weren't into Michael. But it was a different story with my parents; as far as they were concerned, Michael was a part of our family, and I was proud of his every success.

Then, in 1993, my relationship with Michael reached a new level when, for the first time, he invited my family to visit him at his home, Neverland Ranch.

For years we'd known that Michael had been building a residence in California. Often, as he was overseeing the construction of the ranch, he would say, "You should come to Neverland. There's a movie theater, a zoo, some amusement park rides. There are no rules at Neverland. You can do whatever you want, just relax and be free."

I had no idea what I was in for. No. Idea. The reality was something I could never have imagined. I was twelve when my family took its first trip to Neverland over spring break. All my siblings had been born by then—my parents brought me, Eddie, my brother Dominic, my sister, Marie Nicole, my youngest brother, Aldo, who was just a baby, and my two cousins, Danielle and Aldo. Our family traveled regularly—even with all those kids—because my parents made a point of taking frequent trips back to Italy to see our extended family, but this was our first time in California. I didn't have a concept of what exactly California would be like—Michael had said, "I have a Ferris wheel," so as the plane banked to land, I, in my innocence, looked out the window expecting to see it down there on the tarmac. I had no idea the ranch was over two hours north, near Santa Barbara.

We arrived in Los Angeles and spent a day at Universal Studios, but the ordinary tourist itinerary stopped there. Late the next morning, Michael's superstretch black limousine picked us up at our hotel to take us up to Neverland. As an adult, I would become very familiar with that drive, but as a kid, all I knew was that it seemed to take forever. We kids (except baby Aldo) were zipping around the interior of that fancy limo like a bunch of fireflies caught in a jar.

When we finally arrived at the gate to Neverland, we were met by security. The driver said, "We have the Cascio family here," and the security guard opened the gate.

As if the drive from Los Angeles hadn't been enough of an endurance challenge for six young children, once we entered the gate we still had to travel the long road up to the house. Now, though, we were, at last, in Neverland, and it truly was another world. Beautiful classical music alternating with the soundtracks from Disney movies like *Peter Pan* and *Beauty and the Beast* played throughout the property. There were sycamore trees, flowers, fountains, and acres and acres of some of the most beautiful landscapes in America. The driveway curved past a train station on the right, a lake on the left. There were bronze statues of children playing, and we were surrounded by mountains on all sides. It was stunning. Neverland was by far the most magical place I'd ever been. It still is.

The entrance to the Tudor-style house was filled with statues and paintings, and grand red carpets flowed across the gleaming hardwood floors. The house manager, Gail, led us in, past a gleaming wood staircase and the hallway to Michael's wing, and down a corridor into the sitting room.

"Mr. Jackson will be right out to greet you," Gail said.

Moments later, Michael arrived. "Welcome to Neverland," he said simply. Then he added, "Just be free." In one way or another, all of his guests were given this same instruction.

We were led into the dining room, where the staff brought us lunch, and we all ate together, catching up. After lunch, Michael gave us a tour of the property. We visited the animals in the zoo, rode the train, and took a spin on the Ferris wheel. Throughout the ranch, everything was in perfect working order and fully staffed: there were animal handlers and ride operators, all of whom seemed to emerge, as if magically conjured into being, at the exact moment their help was needed.

The rides at Neverland were fun, but I was always more impressed by the zoo. It is an amazing thing to visit a private zoo. Michael had several specialists who looked after the animals: there was a reptile handler, someone else for the bears, lions, and chimps, another person for the giraffes and the elephant, and so on. The handlers would bring out the animals for us, letting us feed them and telling us about their habits. In the reptile house there were anacondas, tarantulas, a spitting cobra, rattlesnakes, piranhas, and crocodiles. The crocodiles ate only every week or so, and they would consume whole, fresh chickens. There were four or five giraffes. Michael was allergic to them, and to horses; he had to take medicine if he wanted to touch them, but I loved to pet the giraffes—up close, for some reason, their breath smelled like mint.

The chimps and the orangutans were my favorites. They were always walking around fully dressed in diapers, shirts, and OshKosh overalls. The chimps, for some reason, were obsessed with small details. If, for example, I had a hangnail, the chimps would notice it right away, study it, fiddle with it, and kiss it. They drank juice straight out of juice boxes with straws. And their favorite candies were Jujubes and Nerds. They'd hold up each piece of candy and fully examine it before eating it. Now, I can't swear that candy was the most nutritious, animal-rights-approved option for any of these animals, but I can tell you that the baby bear absolutely loved Skittles. He'd lick at his cage, asking for more. Oh, and the elephants loved to drink sodas and eat Starbursts. Much as pets are said to look like their owners, the animals at Neverland appeared to have developed tastes in food that were remarkably similar to those of Michael himself.

The approach to the Neverland movie theater was remarkable

for its elegance. Visitors strolled up a cobblestone walkway, passing a beautifully lit fountain with dancing water while gorgeous music played in the background, as it did throughout the ranch. After passing through two sets of double doors, they entered the theater, where, on the left of the entryway, they saw an animatronics display of the characters from *Pinocchio* that Michael had had custom-made by the people at Disney. It included a life-size, animatronic Michael, dressed in his attire from the "Smooth Criminal" video. In the little skit that accompanied the display, a voice would say, "Look, there's Michael," and the animatronic Michael would spring to life, moon-walking in a circle.

On the right, across from Pinocchio and Michael, was an ani-matronic version of the Big Bad Wolf. And straight ahead was the ultimate candy counter, with every type of candy known to man. The concession stand also had a soft-ice-cream machine, a popcorn machine, and every drink you could want. Back home in New Jersey, if my siblings and I had been lucky enough to have free access to a soft-ice-cream machine for a couple of hours on a Saturday afternoon, it would have been cause for great celebration. Here, it was just one small element in a full-blown dream come true.

A red carpet led into the theater. There were about a hundred plush red seats. On future visits, we would get Graveyard the orang-utan all dressed up and take him to the movies with us. He'd sit between me and Michael, chomping popcorn and sipping his own soda. There were also two private bedrooms, one on each side of the theater, so you had the option of watching in the comfort of an adjustable hospital bed, if that should be your fancy. Over the years there would be many times when I went to watch a late movie and ended up sleeping in the theater all night.

Neverland may have been a truly magical place, but it didn't change my feelings about Michael. He was as humble at his home as he was at ours. I didn't equate the splendor of the place with riches or power—I'd already seen Michael in concert, where his transformation to a megastar was far more dramatic.

It may have been during that trip—certainly it was during one of them, and there were many—that while driving me around in a golf cart, Michael started talking about how his Neverland was going to be like Elvis's Graceland. In a deliberately nasal tour guide's voice, he began to narrate: "If you look to the right, you will see the water balloon fort. Michael won many a battle on that field . . ."

"When do you plan on making this happen?" I asked.

"I am planning it right now," he responded. "But it won't be opened until I'm dead."

DURING THAT TRIP, WE SPENT THREE OR FOUR DAYS AT Neverland, staying in what were known as the guest bungalows—a ranch-style house divided into four separate units. They were simple but elegant, with dark wooden floors and furniture and white linens on all the beds. The bathrooms had custom-made soaps engraved with the Neverland logo: a boy in the moon. (DreamWorks film studio has a similar logo, but Michael designed his boy-in-the-moon years before DreamWorks was an entity. Steven Spielberg must have been inspired when he came to visit the ranch.) The Elizabeth Taylor suite had a king-size bed. If I remember correctly, on that first trip my brother and I stayed in Bungalow Two, which had two double beds. That was one of the few times that I stayed in the bungalows; for every subsequent childhood visit, I stayed in the main house.

In the morning, when we woke up, the chefs made whatever we wanted for breakfast, which they would either bring to our rooms or serve in the kitchen. They were on call twenty-four hours a day. Creeks bubbled across the land. The music played on. We used golf carts to get around the property—from the movie theater to the amusement park to the zoo.

My parents loved the ranch. My father said it was like "walking through the gates of heaven," and that it called forth the youth and innocence that lurked in all of its visitors. He would walk around the property happily smoking his cigar. Meanwhile, my mother, who was ordinarily one of those superwomen who never stop doing from morning till night, would finally slow down. Neverland was the only place in the world where she could relax and enjoy herself—especially at the movie theater. My parents were even known to take part in our water balloon fights from time to time.

During the day, everyone wandered off on his or her own, but each night we reconvened for a big family dinner. One night we had dinner in the tepees. Michael had created a little Indian village with tepees and a big bonfire. We sat on the floor, wearing blankets, talking and watching the fire. It was so much fun that on every subsequent trip we made a point of having at least one dinner in the tepees.

Another favorite tradition was taking early morning rides in the hot air balloon. For some reason—it must have had to do with the weather—we had to wake up at the crack of dawn. Still sleepy, but excited, we'd drive to a point on the property and climb aboard the balloon. Soon we would be floating high over Neverland, looking down at the lush landscape.

Eddie and I spent most of our time at the ranch with Michael. It was a place where every visitor could experience complete freedom and be completely on his own, but there was no question that being able to experience Neverland with its creator, beside him and through his eyes, compounded the magic. We wanted to hang out with him. He was the spirit of the place.

In *Peter Pan*, Neverland is a place where children never have to grow up. As a child, Michael had lived in an adult world—he worked from the age of five. He toured. His time was not his own. When he overheard the sounds of children at play, he wanted more than anything to join them, but it was not an option. As an adult, as he himself put it, Michael was drawn to the childhood he had never had. He'd say, "I'm ten years old. I never want to grow up." Sure, growing up is a part of life, but Michael was determined to rediscover the best elements of his lost boyhood and to keep them alive. He loved the idea that we can hold on to innocence, joy, and freedom. Neverland was a world unto itself, where children could be free and any visitor could let go of his worries and be a child again. Once you passed through its magic portals, the world outside didn't matter anymore.

Michael designed every aspect of Neverland, and it was always a work in progress. He was a man of vision—sometimes crazy visions—and whenever he had an idea, he didn't hesitate to move ahead with making it a reality. If he wanted tree houses, he planned tree houses. If he thought there should be a whole island filled with flamingos for guests to enjoy as they drove in, he would build an island and stock it with flamingos.

In later years, when it was just the two of us on the property, we'd walk around and check on every detail. Sometimes we'd peek in on the guest units, and if the potpourri wasn't to his liking, Michael would have it replaced. He'd move a clock two inches to the left to place it perfectly. He'd move furniture around. He liked the flowers to be freshly picked. He wanted the landscaping to be neatly pruned. As we ambled along, he'd get on the walkie-talkie, saying, "We need more flowers over here. Turn the music up" or letting management know if he couldn't hear the bird soundtrack chirping its continuous melodies. This was his fantasy brought to life. He knew exactly how he wanted every element to be placed and maintained. He was an artist and a perfectionist in everything he did.

Michael built Neverland to share with people, especially children, and as it became a more public place, visited by schools and orphanages, he set up magical experiences for his guests. Every moment was choreographed, from the instant guests hit the first gate. He would have the entire house staff line up on the stairs to greet new arrivals and welcome them to Neverland. They might be having breakfast and suddenly they'd see elephants, including Gypsy, a gift from Elizabeth Taylor, walking past the window or a llama walking around.

That trip I took to Neverland with my entire family brought us all even closer to Michael than we'd been before. Until then, he'd been the family friend whose surprise visits were always welcome. Now, on his turf, we saw Michael's true self. Neverland embodied Michael's heart and soul, and we felt honored and privileged to be there in his company. As we all piled back into the limo and went down the long road back to the airport, it was simply unimaginable to think that one day a dark shadow would cast a pall over all its beauty.

Not surprisingly, once I'd gotten a taste of Neverland, all I wanted to do was to go back and visit it again. But I had important things to do, like finishing seventh grade. Only when summer vacation rolled around did my parents finally say that my brother Eddie and I could return, this time all by ourselves, for a week or two. When Eddie and I stepped off the plane at LAX, a driver named Gary was waiting for us, holding a sign that said "The Cascios."

"Mr. Jackson is expecting you," he said, and asked if we were hungry—we could stop and pick something up on the way. Maybe we were, maybe we weren't. Either way, we said no. We just wanted to see Michael.

The 1993 American Music Awards were scheduled for that night, and Michael was receiving the first-ever International Artist Award, so instead of taking us directly to the ranch, Gary drove us to a secret apartment that Michael kept in Century City called "The Hideaway."

The Hideaway was a three-story apartment that was a mini-Neverland of sorts. There was a whole floor of video games—Michael's private arcade. On the walls were pictures of Michael's idols—the Three Stooges, Charlie Chaplin, Laurel and Hardy—and images of Disney characters. There was music playing, of course. Michael loved to have music playing, wherever he was, at all times.

When Michael met us, he seemed to feel bad about the fact that he would be busy receiving an award the very night we arrived, and told us that instead of leaving us with no one but his security guys for company, he'd invited a cousin to come over and hang out with us. (Michael, by the way, called anyone who was close to him a cousin, or a second cousin—as if he wanted to be surrounded by one big, extended family.) This "cousin" turned out to be a kid named Jordy Chandler, who was about my age.

I went up and shook Jordy's hand; he seemed like a nice kid. This wasn't the first time I'd met another kid through Michael. Like my own, Jordy's family was one of many families Michael befriended, although the Cascios were the only ones he called his "second family." We Cascios were a big family ourselves, and we were more than happy to embrace Michael's friends. There was always room for more. To me, Jordy and his family seemed pleasant and unexceptional.

Right before Michael left that evening, he turned to me and said, "Applehead, what do you think I should wear to the show?" We'd seen an episode of the Three Stooges where Curly or Moe called somebody "Applehead." From then on we called each other, and everyone else, Applehead. Everyone was an Applehead. We were the Applehead Club.

I looked into Michael's closet and picked out a white V-neck T-shirt, black pants, boots, and a jacket that he'd worn to a photo shoot for the "Remember the Time" video. When he walked out the door wearing the whole outfit I'd picked out for him, I could feel myself beam. He hadn't changed a single thing.

After Michael's departure, Eddie, Jordy, and I were left to entertain ourselves, which wasn't hard to do given the full arcade we had at our disposal. I got along with Jordy—he was into science and puzzles and I thought that was cool. Eventually we took a break from the arcade, and Jordy and I went out on the balcony to throw water balloons and try to hit the cars that were parked below. This was good fun for a while. Then Jordy was fooling with a slingshot. I don't know what he put in it, but it definitely wasn't a water balloon because before I realized what was happening, whatever he had fired with that slingshot hit a parked car's window and shattered it.

Yikes. We ducked out of view, and then sneaked back inside the apartment. We didn't tell security what had happened. Poor Jordy was a wreck. He, like me and Eddie, was an adventurous, fun-loving boy, not a troublemaker. He paced back and forth, terrified that the police would come, fretting that Michael would be angry. He was shaking with fear. I tried to calm him. I said, "Just relax, don't worry. It's not a big deal, nobody's going to be upset." Finally, he went into the bathroom to wash his face. When he came back, we played more video games, the ultimate tonic for a freaked-out teenage boy.

Later that night, when Michael came home and we were all together, we actually told him what had happened. I thought it was the right thing to do.

"Are you guys okay? Did anyone get hurt?" Michael asked. We told him we were fine—but we weren't so sure about the car. He wasn't angry. He just said, "Let's go out and see if it's still there. If it is, we'll tell the owner what happened, and we'll find a way to replace his window." We went out onto the balcony, but by now the car was long gone, and none of us heard anything else about the matter. That night my brother, Jordy, and I spread sleeping bags all over the floor, watched movies, and fell asleep. Slingshot antics aside, Jordy was a likable kid who seemed a lot like me. I didn't notice anything unusual or disturbing in his relationship with Michael.

The next day Michael took us to Disneyland with Jordy; Jordy's mother, June; and his sister. I had never been to Disneyland before, but even so it wasn't hard to see that because of our host we were getting VIP treatment. We went on every single ride without having to wait on a line.

Michael, of course, was recognized by every person in the entire park. He made absolutely no attempt to disguise his identity. In fact, he was wearing his regular outfit: sunglasses, a hat, a red corduroy shirt, black pants, and penny loafers. He wore this almost every day. Later, when I knew him better, I would make fun of him as he got dressed. He'd stand in front of his closet, which was a sea of red shirts and black pants, saying, "Hmm, I wonder what I'm going to wear today. Mmm, maybe black pants and a red shirt. Maybe I'll wear a fedora, just to change things up."

And I would say, "Hey, I've got an idea. Why don't you go crazy today and wear something totally different?" Then I'd take out . . . a different type of red shirt and a different type of black pants from those he usually wore.

Anyway, as we walked through the park, the members of the Disneyland security force formed a protective circle around us because the park visitors were going nuts over Michael, seeking autographs and trying to take photos. A couple of times we had to take a car across the park and enter rides through side doors so we wouldn't have to deal with the commotion the fans were causing. I was beginning to get a firsthand sense of how Michael was treated in the world at large. It didn't mean too much to me. It was kind of like his job—that was just what Michael did when he was in public.

At the end of the day we left in a white limousine, and if we thought the day's fun was over, we were wrong. On the way home we got into a massive Silly String fight. Eventually we had to open the car windows because the fumes were becoming a bit much. Back then, I didn't notice that Michael's behavior wasn't exactly what people expected to see in an adult. He'd been this way as long as I'd known him, and—maybe because of his example—I wasn't in the habit of drawing precise distinctions between adult and childlike behavior. Even now, I have my childish moments. We all do; we all should.

That night Michael brought Eddie, me, Jordy, and Jordy's mother and sister up to the ranch. In his limo there were always movies playing, but we were all still too excited and too busy talking about the day we'd had to pay much attention to them. We had all bonded that day. It was clear to me that Jordy and his whole family loved

Michael as much as my family did. They were like another family to him, and I felt like we had that in common. I didn't feel jealous of the relationship. I'm not the jealous type. Truth be told, it was nice to have another kid around, particularly one who didn't seem either especially impressed by or dubious about my relationship with Michael.

Remembering my earlier visit, I expected the drive to feel like a long one, but soon enough we were at the ranch. This time we arrived at night, so I had a chance to see the way the trees and water features were beautifully lit. The music was playing. The train, most likely empty, was chugging along its cheerful way. And dinner was waiting for us.

Since we weren't there with our parents, my brother and I asked Michael if we could stay with him in his room. That's what we would have done at a regular sleepover with kids our own age, and we thought of Michael as one of us. Of course we knew he was a grown-up, but he felt like a best friend. A kid, but a kid with amazing power and resources. He had an amusement park in his backyard, for heaven's sake. We wanted to hang out with him, and Michael couldn't say no, not to us or to anyone else he cared for.

Michael, Eddie, and I stayed up late that night talking. We lay on the floor in front of the fireplace, flipping through magazines while Michael filled us in on some entertainment-world gossip, telling us how he'd gone to Eddie Murphy's house for dinner and how Madonna tried to seduce him. Mindful of our ages, he delicately tried to explain Madonna's invitation to accompany her to her hotel room without resorting to words like "seduce."

"She . . . she asked me to join her in her bedroom." He put his hands over his face. "I was so shy—I didn't know what to do," he confessed.

"You should have gone for it. I would have done anything for one night with Madonna," I told him. I was young, but already girl-crazy. Michael was the opposite, though. He wasn't used to being put into these situations where he was supposed to feel or be romantic. He wasn't gay. He was definitely interested in women, and anyone who saw him dance couldn't help but recognize his powerful sexuality. But he was inhibited.

This inhibition was, in part, a result of the road life Michael had had to live when he was young. That night, Michael told us about how, starting when he was five, he'd been on tour with the Jacksons. Sometimes the act before the Jackson 5 was a burlesque show. Michael, watching from the side of the stage, saw that the female performers were often badly treated by the men. After the show, he and Randy would hide under a bed while their older brothers brought girls back to the room. When Michael would start giggling, Jermaine would drag him and Randy out from under the bed and throw them out of the room. But not before Michael had seen and heard more than a kid his age probably should.

Michael was always telling stories about his brothers. He told us some of these stories as if they were funny, but it's now clear to me that they weren't funny at all. Michael had been exposed to sex at too young an age, and the experience had deeply scarred him. As a result, when it came to women, it was as if he was frozen in time.

Later on, after his brothers were married, the family members stopped being as close as they once were, and gradually this pulled the Jackson 5 apart. On top of his fears of intimacy, Michael didn't want to fall into the trap of allowing something to distract him from his music.

Starting from a very young age, work was Michael's first priority. He was very professional. He was on point all the time. I think it's because when he was working, he felt most comfortable, most in control. Even when his older brothers would be playing basketball or some other sport, he would just sit around and watch and sing melodies. He never joined in (and I can only assume he would have been welcome, even if it would have meant a two-on-three game). One reason was that his father never really wanted him to participate. He was more protective of Michael than he was of the other siblings. Of course, this might have been because Michael was, as I saw many times, shockingly bad at sports. I never could understand that. Here was the guy with the most extraordinary sense of rhythm in the world . . . and he couldn't even dribble a basketball properly. He said he was even worse at baseball. But the point is, Michael didn't want anything—not sports, and not women—to affect his work. As he got older, Michael would stay home to rehearse and choreograph dance routines. When his brothers came back, Michael would teach them the routines. He was the youngest of the Jackson 5, but also the most serious.

Later that night our conversation turned to Jordy, who was staying with his mother and sister in the guest bungalows. I said, "Oh, he's really really nice. Next time you come to New York, you should bring him to our house."

"Yeah, we should bring him to New York—he's never been there," Michael replied.

"Why isn't Jordy staying with us?" I asked.

"I don't know—Jordy never stays in my room," Michael answered. "I like it to be just us so we can catch up."

So that night the three of us talked in front of the fire until around two in the morning, at which point we decided to raid the refrigerator. We went to the kitchen and warmed up vanilla pudding (one of Michael's favorite snacks) in the microwave, gathered chips, orange Creamsicles, vanilla wafers, and juice boxes, brought them back to the room, and stayed up until four in the morning talking and listening to Michael's fascinating stories.

As he would do again in future visits, Michael offered the bed to me and Eddie and said he'd sleep on the floor, but we ended up all sleeping on the floor. I loved to fall asleep near the dying crackle of the fire. From that visit until I was old enough to want privacy, whenever I went to Neverland I made my bed right next to the fireplace. Let me be absolutely clear: odd as it may seem for an adult to have "sleepovers" with a couple of kids, there was nothing sexual about them—nothing that was apparent to me then, as a child, and nothing that I can see now, as a grown man scrutinizing the past. They were harmless. Michael was truly just a kid at heart.

The next day we slept until midday. Michael's chef, Buckey, was famous for his burgers. We had Buckey burgers and fries for lunch. Then Michael said, "You have two thousand seven hundred acres. Be free. Do what you want." He urged us to explore on our own, but what we wanted most of all was to be around him and to have him show us what to do. So we spent the day playing in the arcade and running around Neverland together. Michael was game for anything.

That night, Michael suggested that we all go to Toys "R" Us. I wondered if his chauffeur was going to take us, but Michael said, "No, I'm going to drive."

So we piled into an ugly brown Dodge Caravan. I sat in the front, and my brother, June, Jordy, and his sister sat in the back. Michael Jackson, wearing a fedora, drove us to the store.

I said, "I can't believe you're driving." I had never seen Michael drive a car. It was quite a sight.

When we arrived at Toys "R" Us, the lights were on, but the doors were locked. My heart sank, but then several of the staff members hurried to the door, unlocked it, and said, "Hello, Mr. Jackson, come on in!" They had clearly been awaiting our arrival.

The store was completely empty of other shoppers. It felt like Christmas. Michael grabbed an empty cart and said, "Go ahead, get whatever you like." We knew that this meant that we had the run of the whole store. There was no limit to what we could buy. But my brother and I weren't comfortable just filling up a cart with toys. Jordy seemed to feel the same way. We zoomed through the aisles, relishing the feeling that the store was open for *us*. It was *ours*. But when it came down to making actual purchases, we just selected a handful of small items, nothing too crazy. We were extremely respectful. Besides, there would be plenty to enjoy when we got back to Neverland. Michael, meanwhile, had quickly stacked three carts full of toys that he wanted.

Michael loved to collect toys. He didn't necessarily play with them, or even take them out of their packages. But he sure loved to buy them. At Neverland he had a toy room full of unopened toys that he was saving as collector's items. He also paid close attention to whatever new toys were coming onto the market. He was interested in what was popular—what kids were playing with, and why they were drawn to those particular toys.

Michael approached most of popular culture with the same intense curiosity he brought to trends in toys. He studied the Top 10 music lists and he also followed the *New York Times* best-seller list for books. It was part of how he developed a remarkably broad—even universal—sense of what people wanted to see, hear, and experience.

I was learning from Michael. He taught me to pursue knowledge. He encouraged me to study. He told me to be humble and to respect my parents, especially my mother. He warned me away from partying and using drugs and cigarettes, saying, "Have a drink, enjoy yourself, but if you can't walk out of a place on your own two feet, you're a bum." He inspired me to be the best that I could be. Because he connected with me, I was receptive to his influence. At school, I was not a good student. Ever since kindergarten, I had been a daydreamer, lost in my own world. But Michael made me see that school wasn't the only way to learn. He said that some of the most successful people in the world, like Thomas Edison and Albert Einstein, hadn't done well in school. I could teach myself whatever I needed to know in order to become a master of my chosen craft. No matter what I did, Michael believed in me. I could be a leader and a creator. My parents saw the influence Michael had on me, and it was one of the reasons why they encouraged our relationship.

As summer came to a close, Eddie and I returned to New Jersey. I was starting eighth grade. Eddie was starting sixth. Our parents had moved over the summer, and we came home to a new house in a new town. Meanwhile, Michael flew to Bangkok. Over the past year he had been touring internationally for his album *Dangerous,* and after a short break it was now time for him to go back on the road. Eddie and I said our good-byes, but we had no idea how long it would be before we would see our friend again, how far away from home we would be, and what unhappy circumstances Michael would be in.

CHAPTER THREE

GOOD-BYE NORMAL

AT OUR NEW HOUSE IN FRANKLIN LAKES, NEW Jersey, Michael's influence was increasingly apparent. My father liked the stone statues that graced Neverland, so he went out and bought similar statues to decorate our backyard. My father loved the classical music that played constantly across Neverland, so he had a sound system installed in that same backyard, complete with outdoor speakers shaped like rocks. Michael made a Neverland CD for us, and soon our life began to be lived with a classical soundtrack in the background. It would have been nice if my father had brought home a chimp for a pet, but he never took it that far.

According to my parents, we had moved to Franklin Lakes for the school system, but as far as I was concerned, it was all about the soccer team. Growing up, I was considered one of the best soccer players in Hawthorne. Another guy, Michael Piccoli, was the best player in Franklin Lakes. Throughout my childhood, Michael Piccoli's and my teams propagated a theoretical rivalry between him and me—we hadn't met, but we knew we didn't like each other. Now I'd moved to his turf, and even though I was only entering the eighth grade, the coach had recruited me to play soccer with the high school. Mike, who was in the same grade, would be doing this as well. We would be on the team together. It was the talk of the soccer world. The soccer world of northern New Jersey, at least.

These were my biggest problems in my world. And then, just before school started, news arrived that completely eclipsed whatever soccer concerns I had. When I poked my head into the laundry room one afternoon looking for a shirt, my mother, who was in there, started to say something, stopped, then finally spoke.

"Do you know a guy named Jordy?" she asked.

"Yeah, he's a really nice kid. I hung out with him at Neverland," I said. She took that in for a moment and I could see her hesitation. Finally she blurted out:

"Well, he is accusing Michael of child molestation."

The words came out awkwardly, as if she'd never uttered them before. It's quite possible she hadn't. I could see that my mother was upset, but I didn't even know what "molestation" meant. When I asked, my mother turned back to the laundry and, avoiding the question, quickly said, "Did Michael ever do anything inappropriate to you or to anyone else that you know of?"

"What are you talking about?" I asked, suddenly realizing that she was crying.

"I feel so bad for Michael," she said.

Seeing the look on her face, I understood that my friend was being accused of doing something wrong to Jordy. I was beyond shocked: the idea didn't even make sense to me. I had spent plenty of time with Jordy and Michael, and when I was at Neverland, Jordy never even stayed in Michael's room with us. Not once. I had never seen anything out of line happen, and I didn't believe anything had happened, not for a single second. Furthermore, Michael had never acted in any way even approximating "inappropriate" toward Eddie or me. This story was utterly unbelievable; I simply couldn't imagine Michael as a molester. Nor could I imagine Jordy making such an accusation.

"Is Michael going to be okay?" I asked.

"Yeah, he's going to be fine," my mother replied.

As this disturbing news sank in, I couldn't help remembering some of what Jordy had said about his father during the trip we had taken to Disneyland together and later at the ranch. Jordy was an open, honest kid, and I didn't have the sense that he was hiding anything. The night we'd gone to Toys "R" Us, he told me that his father, a dentist and aspiring screenwriter named Evan, was extremely jealous of Michael. He volunteered the information that his father thought it was weird that Michael was so close to Jordy and the rest of the family, and that the relationship had become a problem for the Chandler family. Thinking back on it, I remembered how Jordy had said that Evan had a terrible temper, that when he was upset he'd scream and bang things around the house.

In retrospect, it's not hard to see that Michael was a father figure for Jordy, that Jordy's mother was attached to Michael, and that this most likely made for a problematic family dynamic. But at the time I wasn't thinking in these larger terms. All I knew was that I was certain that Michael was being falsely accused—whether it was because of Jordy or his father didn't matter.

My mother had heard about the allegations on the news. In the days that followed, my parents reached out to Michael, who was still touring abroad for the *Dangerous* album. They told him they were one hundred percent convinced of his innocence and assured him that they would be there to support him if he needed them. Being on tour was always an isolating experience for Michael, and an hour later he sent back a fax. Faxes were big in those days—a primitive form of text messaging—and our family started exchanging faxes with Michael a couple times a day, sending silly drawings and little notes.

At first Michael told my parents not to worry about him. He said it was a matter of extortion, and that they shouldn't believe what they saw and heard on the news. He didn't need to elaborate. My parents already knew the truth. They knew and trusted Michael in the face of a world that judged him with a severity that was as ignorant as it was cruel.

Meanwhile, Eddie and I started attending our new school—the good school for which my parents had moved to our new neighborhood. But only a week or two after the school year began, before I'd even had a chance to see about this Mike Piccoli and his alleged soccer skills, an unexpected phone call came from Bill Bray. He told my parents that Michael wanted to invite the whole family to join him on tour in Tel Aviv.

My mother was busy with my brother Dominic, who was six years old; my sister, Marie Nicole, who was three; and my baby brother, Aldo. There was no way she was flying to Israel.

If we left now, Eddie and I would miss school, which certainly mattered to my parents. But first and foremost, what mattered was that we had a friend in need. This was not a local news story. It was global. And given the reach of Michael Jackson's fame, the toll of the false allegations would be exponentially more damaging. My parents saw that the fallout from this scandal could have a devastating effect on Michael's career, and on Michael's entire life, and they knew that seeing Eddie and me at this time would cheer Michael up.

So, the day after we got the call from Bill Bray, my father, Eddie, and I boarded a plane. We flew first class to Israel.

Our arrival in Tel Aviv was carefully coordinated. A car picked us up and drove us through the city. Then, at some prearranged place, the driver pulled over and told us we were going to switch cars. We got out of our car and were guided through a crowd of fans to Michael's car. When I got into the vehicle, I gave my friend a big hug and said, "Don't worry, we're here for you, we're going to get through this together."

Michael smiled and just said, "Thanks." But later, my father tells me, Michael expressed his gratitude to him for our visit. Michael said he would never forget this act of support, and that his friendship with our family was for life.

Since Michael had the day off, we spent the next several hours sightseeing, driving around with a guide who was the head of Elizabeth Taylor's security team.

As well planned as the day was, though, it didn't pass without a couple of hitches. As our guide drove us up to the Wailing Wall, for example, a veritable sea of some three hundred people began following the car. They pushed their faces against the car windows, trying to see through the tinted glass, some of them waving gifts they had brought for their beloved star. Helicopters circled over our heads. It was a scene unlike anything I had ever experienced. These people were all there for Michael. Unfortunately, we happened to arrive right at prayer time, causing a major interruption, to say the least. Michael had no idea that this was a sacred time of day, but in the next day's papers, the media took him to task for his alleged lack of consideration.

Back at the hotel, Eddie and I hung out with Michael in his room, distracting him, giving him support, and watching old movies on laser disc. My dad came and went, checking in on us and spending time with his buddy Bill Bray. As we watched the Bruce Lee movie *Enter the Dragon,* Michael got up and began mimicking Bruce Lee's karate movements. He talked to us about every detail of the film—commenting on technical details about specific shots and explaining exactly what it was he worshipped about Bruce Lee. Through the years I would see Michael studying any number of great showmen: from Bruce Lee and Charlie Chaplin to James Brown, Frank Sinatra, Jackie Wilson, the Three Stooges, and Sammy Davis Jr. As he was doing now with Bruce Lee, Michael had a unique gift for incorporating the tricks of his heroes into his dancing. The hat, the glove, the walk—he got all that from Charlie Chaplin. There's one move that he used when he performed "Billie Jean," where he slid his neck forward and sideways, then bent over and did a strange walk—he got that from watching the movements of the Tyrannosaurus rex in the movie *Jurassic Park*.

As the movie ended, Michael said, "Bruce Lee was the master. There will never be anybody like him. Whatever you do, you should master your craft. Be the best at it."

Even at this difficult moment, Michael was opening my mind in ways I wasn't fully aware of at the time. He was teaching me to see things in a more complex way than I was used to. Instead of just absorbing entertainment at face value and unconsciously, I was beginning to analyze the art of it.

But being with Michael wasn't just about studying the subtleties of pop culture. The next stop of the tour was Istanbul, Turkey, where we stayed in a huge, beautiful hotel suite. Whenever Eddie and I had been with Michael, we had always been playful, tossing pillows around and stuff like that, but on this particular day Michael suddenly got an impish glimmer in his eyes and announced, almost in a whisper, "Let's trash the hotel room."

That seemed like an excellent idea, so together with Michael, before we left Istanbul, Eddie and I wreaked havoc on the hotel room. We moved couches across the room, leaving them at odd angles. We tilted the pictures so they hung crooked on the walls. We scattered rose petals all over the floor. As far as trashing hotel rooms went, we weren't what anyone would call masters of our craft. As his coup de grâce, Michael hauled back and threw a fork into a painting.

The next day, backstage at the concert, Eddie and I were sitting in the dressing room right behind Michael watching his makeup artist, Karen, getting him ready to go out onstage. Michael warned us that Bill Bray was angry.

"Bill's gonna have to talk to you guys," he told us. "We shouldn't have trashed that room. I told him it was my fault and he should take it easy on you, but he has to talk to you."

While Michael was onstage performing, Bill Bray showed up and gave us hell for what we'd done.

"I don't think you realize that we have to pay for the damage you did," Bill said, suddenly looking every inch of his not inconsiderable size. "We can't leave hotels like that. It reflects badly on Michael." Bill threatened to send us home, and Eddie and I started crying. I felt terrible, like it was the end of the world. And Eddie was equally devastated. Michael's nickname for him was "Angel" because he always tried so hard to be good and respectful. We apologized to Bill. We didn't want to cause problems. All of us, Bill included, knew that Michael had been the instigator of the trashing, but nonetheless, Bill wanted us to take responsibility for our own actions.

Whether Bill intended it to be so or not, his verbal dressing-down of Eddie and me was a turning point in my life, a moment that instilled in me an early instinct to protect Michael and his reputation, even from his own actions, if necessary. We were the kids, it was true, but when it came to Michael's impulses, sometimes we would have to be the adults. We had to think of the consequences to his image and reputation at all times, even when he didn't.

AS FAR AS WHAT WAS GOING ON WITH JORDY'S FAMILY, we only talked to Michael about it when he brought it up. When he did speak about it, it was often in a wistful tone, and I could tell that he was still trying to comprehend the fact that this horrible thing had occurred.

"I did so much for his family," he'd say.

I would almost always respond with anger, saying things like "I just don't understand how he could do such a thing."

"You don't understand," Michael would reply. "I don't blame Jordy. It's not his fault. It's his father's fault."

Michael forgave Jordy. He knew that a child wouldn't come at him and ruthlessly attack him of his own volition. He believed it all came from the father. Later, when I was older, Michael would tell me that Jordy's father had wanted Michael to invest in a film he wanted to make. Michael initially liked the idea, but his advisers were against it. They dismissed Jordy's father rather thoughtlessly, and Michael, not one for confrontation, blew him off, too. Michael thought that this, more than anything else, had set Evan Chandler off. (The movie Chandler had written, *Robin Hood: Men in Tights*, was eventually produced and directed by Mel Brooks and came out that same year.)

Michael was clearly upset about the circumstances he found himself in, but he always kept his composure when he was around us, remembering that we were kids. He was sensitive to what we would take away from this experience and to the effect it would have on our lives as well as his.

At a certain point, my father had to get back home to his restaurant and my mother. At first Michael accepted this, but when the time came for us to go, he went to my father and broke down crying.

"I know you have to get back to work," he said through his tears, "but I'm asking if Frank and Eddie can stay here with me. I would really love for them to stay. You have no idea—just having you all here for this short amount of time has helped me so much. I promise you, Dominic, I'll take care of them and watch over them as if they were my own."

We'd already missed a week of school. If we continued our stay with Michael, we would be traveling with him from country to country, finishing the European segment of the tour and then heading to North and South America. We wouldn't be home until December.

Missing school for a rock tour was a big deal, and my parents weren't cavalier about the decision. But my father saw that Michael was alone. He had no family or friends near him on tour, just the crew, and he was dealing with just about the worst kind of accusations an innocent man could imagine facing, internationally famous or not.

One thing that was not a factor in my parents' decision was the allegations that had been leveled against Michael. People might question my parents' judgment in sending two young boys off to spend time alone with a man who had been accused of molesting another boy. But to us, the suggestion that we were in any danger was completely absurd. My parents knew that Michael was innocent. They had known him well, for years, and to them he was family.

Though they were aware of how odd he seemed to the outside world, they understood Michael's idiosyncrasies from his perspective, and from this angle they came into focus and made some sense. When he wore a surgical mask, people thought he was hiding some new plastic surgery—in reality he was at first protecting himself from getting sick before performances; then he found that wearing the mask made him feel like he was in disguise (when in fact it called more attention to him); and ultimately he turned it into a one-of-a-kind fashion statement, having his silken surgical masks custom-made. When he was photographed in a hyperbaric chamber, rumors began flying that he slept in it—in reality he'd donated it to a local hospital to be used in the treatment of burn victims. Of course, sometimes Michael was just being a character, joking around, but the impetus for his behavior was never as freaky as people were always so quick to assume.

To us, Michael was the funniest, nicest, and most playful friend imaginable. With my parents, his behavior was that of a humble, kind, and mature adult, a brilliant, well-read man with interesting, thoughtful opinions. My parents spent entire evenings talking with him, learning from him. They saw him as a good influence on their sons.

Above all, my parents knew Michael's true heart. They were well aware of how responsible and loving Michael was, and they had absolute trust in him, his staff, and his security guys. My father had already spent a substantial amount of time with us on tour, so he knew the crew personally and knew what the schedule was like. He also had a very close relationship with Bill Bray, who ran security. There was a long-term, high level of trust and confidence that was already firmly in place. We would be safe.

My father is fiercely protective of his family. We mean everything to him, and he would never put us in harm's way. In my dad's book, never mind prison, pedophiles should be thrown to the wolves. (He's from Sicily, after all.) If he and my mother had had any doubts about Michael's innocence, no matter how small, believe me, my brother and I would *not* have been there, much less stayed.

I want to be precise and clear, on the record, so that everyone can read and understand: Michael's love for children was innocent, and it was profoundly misunderstood. People seemed to have trouble accepting all the good qualities of this incredible man, and were always asking how it could be that he was the greatest singer on earth, the greatest dancer on earth, and yet enjoy hanging around with children all day? How could he write and perform such explosively sexual, complex songs, and then have nothing but harmless interactions with the kids with whom he surrounded himself? How could he have so many idiosyncrasies that seemed weird to the outside observer—the plastic surgery, the bizarre purchases, the secrecy—and then not be "weird" in other, more offensive ways?

Yes, Michael had different personas. The same way I myself became a different person depending on whether I was home with my family, traveling with Michael, or back in school in New Jersey. The same way we all put on different faces for dealing with different parts of our lives. If Michael's different images seemed extreme, it was only because his life was more extreme than anyone else's.

For all the hard work he'd put in during his own childhood, for all the perfectionism that drove his music, Michael craved the simplicity and innocence of the youth he had never fully experienced. He revered it, he treasured it, and, especially through Neverland, he tried to offer it to others. People had trouble understanding all this, and many assumed the worst. This misunderstanding was the greatest sorrow of Michael's life. He carried it with him to the end. I am here to say that I knew the real Michael Jackson. I knew him throughout my childhood. In all that time, he never showed himself to be anything but a perfect friend. Never did he make a questionable advance or a sexual remark. My parents were older and wiser than my brother or I. If anything, their perspective was broader and more encompassing than ours. And they trusted Michael implicitly.

When my father talked to Bill Bray about the possibility of Eddie and me remaining on the tour, Bill said, "Yeah, Michael's been down. Those kids, they keep him going." My parents knew that we would be a great source of comfort to Michael. They checked with our school to see if we could make up our classwork with a tutor. Then, at last, my father said the magic words: "You can stay."

CHAPTER FOUR

EXTRAORDINARY WORLD

ND SO, MY BROTHER AND I WERE ON TOUR WITH Michael Jackson. My parents flew out to meet us in various cities on the itinerary, but through it all, we stayed—traveling, attending concerts, and spending time with Michael. I already knew him as a father figure and a friend. By the time it was all over, I would know him as an entertainer. I would also witness and feel deep compassion for the struggles that began for Michael on the day when he was accused of molestation and continued to haunt him for the rest of his life.

Before heading to South America, the tour took a weeklong break in Switzerland. Dad left us in Gstaad, where Michael's friend Elizabeth Taylor had offered him use of her chalet. Gstaad was a beautiful village in the mountains where you could see cows walking down the streets among the people, shaking their heavy heads and sounding their cowbells.

The first night in the chalet, we ordered cream of chicken soup from a hotel called the Palace right down the street. It was so tasty that we ordered it again every night. In the chalet, there was a sweet grandma of a woman who took care of us. She was small and a bit doddering, and we had fun responding to her warmth with exaggerated enthusiasm. We showered her with hugs and kisses until she giggled with embarrassment. Be it soup or old ladies—we thought it was funny to be over the top.

Gstaad was a perfect escape from the rigors of touring. It was such a small town, and so remote from the rest of the world, that—in the beginning at least—Michael could walk freely down the streets, undisguised, without being bothered. This was a rare joy for him. Our first day, we wandered in and out of the quaint shops together, admiring and commenting on all that Gstaad had to offer. At some point I'd decided I would start collecting pocketknives and handcrafted lighters. I guess I'd heard of Swiss Army knives, but I have no idea why I thought I needed more than one. Anyway, once I'd made this decision, the three of us were wholly committed to it, so in the course of our stay, we found (and Michael purchased for my collection) just about every pocketknife in the entire town. As for the lighters, I liked to use them to set pieces of paper on fire. (No, not a pyromaniac, just a teenage boy.) Later, when we were leaving Switzerland, Bill Bray asked me to hand over my lighters. He didn't want them to go on the plane, for security reasons, so he said he'd hold on to them for me. As it turned out, I never saw them again.

Unfortunately, Bill Bray passed away several years ago. Where my lighters went is a mystery he took to the grave with him.

One thing I'll always remember about our time in Gstaad was Michael introducing me to new music. We'd always listened to music together, and anytime we were in a record store together, I'd walk right next to Michael to see what albums caught his fancy. I'd also seen him follow the songs that were popular on the radio, keeping abreast of current hits. He had an employee whose sole job was to prepare cassette tapes of each week's top songs from around the world and ship them to Michael.

Anyway, back at the chalet, we sat rapt, listening for hours as Michael played DJ, saying, "You have to listen to this song. Now you have to hear this group." We listened to Stevie Wonder and all of the Motown stars. He had us listen to the James Brown song "Papa Don't Take No Mess"—all fourteen minutes of it. We listened to the Bee Gees song "How Deep Is Your Love?" (I still believe that it's one of the greatest songs of all time.) Michael went on about Aaron Copland, whom he considered the greatest composer of the twentieth century. He introduced me to all types of music—country, folk, classical, funk, rock. He even turned me on to Barbra Streisand. I fell in love with her song "People." Michael liked to go to sleep to classical music, especially the works of Claude Debussy.

I remember him putting on a group called Bread. I didn't pay much attention to the music—I was too busy making fun of the name. "Bread? What kind of name is that? Want some butter with your bread?" and that kind of nonsense. But when I settled down for a minute and really listened instead of making sarcastic remarks, they became one of my favorite groups. I wanted to know everything there was to know about Bread. Yes, Bread was my jam (bad pun intended).

Michael often talked about the universality of music. He wanted to write music that anyone in any country could sing, and as we traveled I would hear people who didn't speak English singing "Man in the Mirror," "Heal the World," and, later, "Stranger in Moscow." He always said that the lyrics to his songs wrote themselves. It was all about the melody. A musician, Brad Buxer, was with us on the tour, and as they composed together, Michael would tell him, "Play the piano like a five-year-old child, Brad. If you can play it like a child, it will last forever."

During our second day in Gstaad, it snowed, but that evening, around dusk, the sky cleared. Michael said, "Let's go make wishes on the stars." We went out to the backyard and lay flat on the ground, looking up at the incredible night sky. Michael said, with a hint of mysticism in his voice, "Be careful what you wish for—it'll come true."

All of a sudden there was a movement nearby. A man appeared at the side of the yard. Nobody was staying in the house with us, and this unexpected apparition was definitely not something that any of us had wished for. In a flash, Michael jumped up and started screaming to try to scare the guy away. He threw a glove at him. (If the guy had had any sense, he'd have made off with that glove and kept it for his grandchildren.)

The guy threw his arms in the air, saying, "No, no, it's okay." He turned out to be a harmless worker who'd come to check on something in the house, but in that moment we could see how, for all his love of childlike things and the childlike absorption he found in them, Michael absolutely saw himself as responsible for us. He was our protector, and in that mantle, he wasn't scared of anything or anybody.

By the next day, word had spread about the famous visitor who was staying at Elizabeth Taylor's chalet, and some fans showed up. Late that night, they gathered outside the chalet and began to sing some of Michael's songs. We went to the window and spent some time talking to them. This wasn't unusual: wherever we went, Michael struck up conversations with his fans. He wanted to know where they were from, what they liked to do. He loved them, and no matter how enormous their number, he never stopped seeing and respecting every one as an individual. The swarms of fans that found him wherever he went might have upset someone who prized his solitude as Michael did, but he always found a way to show his appreciation by giving still more of himself to his fans. He was as open to people as he was to experience, and this, too, was a lesson I learned from him.

One of the guys on Bill Bray's security team, Wayne Nagin, went to every stop on the tour a day ahead of us to coordinate transportation, hotels, and security. Security was important. *Dangerous* was a major tour for Michael. The fans always knew ahead of time that he was coming to town. We couldn't travel without a police escort. When we arrived, the route between the private jet and the hotel would be jammed with fans, as if the whole city had shut down in order to dedicate itself to welcoming Michael Jackson.

In Buenos Aires, the intensity of the fans seemed greater than ever. As we drove from the airport, hundreds of people chased the car, banging on the windows, wanting to see MJ for two seconds, trying to touch him. People on the sidewalks waved to us the whole way to the hotel, as if Michael were the pope. The car moved slowly through the throngs. Sometimes Michael would put a hand out the window and people would go wild, screaming, even fainting at the knowledge that he was so close.

I teased Michael, saying, "These people aren't fainting over you, you know. It's me. They're fainting because of me. Can't you hear them yelling, 'Fraaaank, Fraaaank!'"

He smiled and played along: "Please, don't you know who I am?"

Michael wanted to go shopping, but it was clearly impossible for him to appear in public without being mobbed. He loved his fans, but obviously he couldn't connect with them at all times. The irony was that all this love, this desire to make contact, served only to force him deeper into isolation. This had been Michael's reality for so long that he never seemed bothered by it, and I followed his lead. We had fun working around the restrictions. Often a disguise was in order, but no sunglasses on the planet would camouflage Michael's identity. On this occasion in Buenos Aires, my brother and I dressed as nerds, wearing funny hats, glasses, and backpacks. Michael, not to be outdone, decked himself out as a wheelchair-bound priest.

On our shopping expedition, he fell inexplicably in love with a statue of Napoleon riding a horse and entered into spirited negotiations with the art dealer to get the best price for it. As extravagantly as Michael spent money, he still relished a good deal. Watching him do his priest act as he purchased a massive statue for six figures . . . well, I loved that crazy shit.

Back at the hotel, Eddie and I had to do the schoolwork that we'd been sent. We were supposed to complete the assignments and return them to the school. The teachers were under the impression that we had been provided with a tutor, and we did, in fact, have one . . . but we kept his identity under wraps. We were pretty sure that the school wouldn't buy the idea of Michael Jackson as a traveling tutor. The truth was, he was genuinely committed to the job. Sure, we didn't exactly keep regular school hours—lessons happened in the middle of the night sometimes—but Michael was the one who regularly sat down with me and my brother and went through our assignments with us. When we had to read books, he would read chapters of them aloud to us, then have us recap what we had heard, asking: "So who were the main characters? What did they want? What does it mean?" In the same way that he opened our minds with the movies he had us watch, he also encouraged us to think about our homework differently than we were used to and to take it seriously.

In addition to the assignments our school gave us, Michael insisted that we keep journals of our trip.

"Document this trip," he'd keep telling us, "because one day you're going to love to look back on it." In every country he had us take pictures of what we saw, do some research about the customs, and put what we'd seen and experienced in our books. We explored the different cultures. We visited orphanages and schools. Eddie and I started to have a greater awareness of our place in the big, wide world. Only later was I wise enough to be thankful to my parents for permitting us to have this experience. They recognized that education wasn't just about reading, writing, and arithmetic. They understood that we would learn by living.

☙

MICHAEL MAY HAVE BEEN OUR TUTOR, OUR FATHER FIG-
ure, and our friend, but onstage, he became another person. We
went to every single concert in every single city. Sometimes I wore
my pajamas—I was in a phase where I liked to wear my pajamas
everywhere. As Michael warmed up his voice, which could take up
to two hours, Eddie and I played games, watched cartoons, and ate
candy in the greenroom, which was always stocked from floor to ceil-
ing with sugary distractions. When it came time for him to perform,
we usually watched from chairs on the side of the stage. Sometimes
we'd wander back to watch the show on a monitor or chat with the
makeup artist, Karen, and the wardrobe guy, Michael Bush, but for
the most part, night after night, I watched attentively.

The show never got old. I studied Michael, I watched the dancers,
who were in awe of him, and I saw the reaction of the audience, which
was always fascinating to me. In every city Michael's show generated
incredible excitement. To have that energy surrounding me was a new
experience for a good New Jersey boy. It was a sense that people could
join together, sharing thoughts and emotions without even speaking.
There was power in Michael and in his music—the power to move
people and connect strangers. During those concerts he made the
world feel like a smaller, warmer, and more harmonious place.

I loved watching the fans from the side of the stage, a sea of people
screaming, crying, fainting, hanging on their idol's every move. I'd
sit there and think, *This godlike being they're worshipping is the guy
who's helping me with my homework.* Often I wondered how it was
that I saw the same people in the front row for show after show in
city after city. How could they afford to leave their jobs and their
lives and follow an entertainer from one place to another? Those of
us who were part of the tour had the luxury of speeding around in
private jets, but how did these fans make it to each city in time for
the show? There was one fan, Justin, whom we called Waldo, after
the character from the *Where's Waldo?* books, because if we looked
hard enough we could find him in every audience.

As his last song in the show, Michael sang "Heal the World," and each time he performed it, a bunch of kids joined him onstage in costumes from countries all around the world. My brother and I would dig up robes from other cultures and slip them over whatever we were wearing, then go out onstage with the rest of the kids. We had a funny dance that we named "The House" because it was inspired by Michael's gofer, Scott Schaffer, whose nickname was "House." We loved to mess with House. We'd knock on the door of his hotel room, saying, "House, we have something for you." When he opened the door, we'd pummel him with pillows. Trust me, it was funny if you were thirteen.

After seeing House dance, we created a wholly original dance inspired by his technique. Before the show we'd say, "House, we're going to do 'The House' for you onstage tonight." And soon enough there we would be, Michael, Eddie, and I, doing "The House"— which involved, well, it was pretty much rocking from one foot to the other in a uniquely dorky manner. Seeing a couple of kids dancing awkwardly onstage was one thing, but what I loved was that Michael, the greatest dancer in the world, was putting aside all his hours of choreography and practice to perform such a silly move onstage in front of a stadium packed with tens of thousands of people. All just to make one guy laugh.

As funny and memorable as these inside jokes were, nothing in the show could compare to the moment when Michael sang "Billie Jean." Michael was my friend. He helped me with my schoolwork. We had pillow fights. But when he performed "Billie Jean," his transformation was awe-inspiring. As soon as I'd hear that kick drum come in, I'd practically go into a trance, my eyes riveted on his every move.

Part of the brilliance of his performance of "Billie Jean" was that it somehow seemed simple and effortless. But behind the simplicity, I could see the depth of Michael's understanding of composition and storytelling. For every song he performed, Michael knew exactly what he wanted the crowd to see, what he wanted to project, what he intended to give. As he performed, that ambition filtered into every aspect of his being; he *became* the song. You could see it most clearly in "Billie Jean," but it was there in "Thriller" as well. Beyond the music, the dance, the vocals, and the stadium itself, there was a feeling of energy and magic that transcended the individual elements of the performance. The sum was greater than its parts, something bigger and more unique than what anyone, myself included, could have expected. The audience felt the magnitude of the brilliance that Michael put into his performance. Every moment of creating "Billie Jean" had been leading up to this one moment, as though every time he'd sung the song before had been just a rehearsal for its unveiling on this particular night. He was one with his art.

This transformation was an art that Michael practiced and mastered. He told me, "Whatever you do or say or want the world to see, envision it and it will happen." Michael preached about channeling the power of the universe long before spiritual books like *The Secret* were published. He told me I could achieve anything if I believed in it. I try to apply that philosophy to all aspects of my life. When I know what I want, I fully envision the end result. That way all the energy I put into it along the way focuses me in the right direction: toward the end product.

"Billie Jean" was originally titled "Not My Lover." Quincy Jones, Michael's coproducer on *Thriller,* actually didn't want it on the album, but Michael insisted, and he was right. Everything Michael did was incredible, but if I had to pick one performance out of his oeuvre as the quintessence and culmination, it would be "Billie Jean." Every time I watched him perform it was a flawless, captivating moment in time. It always gave me goose bumps.

AS THE TOUR PROGRESSED, I GOT TO KNOW SOME OF MI-
chael's other friends and associates. In Santiago, Chile, Michael's dermatologist paid him a visit. Michael had a skin disease called vitiligo.
He had told me about it earlier that year, at Neverland, explaining that
it caused patches of his skin to lose their pigmentation. He showed
me some pictures of people who had advanced cases of it; those whose
skin color was dark had dramatic and disfiguring patches of white all
over their bodies. Michael told me how much he hated the disease, but
how fortunate he felt to be able to afford the treatment, which involved
lightening the rest of his skin to even out the color. Michael said that
his dermatologist, Dr. Arnold Klein, was the best in the business;
everyone went to him, even Elizabeth Taylor.

A woman named Debbie Rowe, who worked for Dr. Klein as a
nurse, accompanied him to Santiago to treat Michael's skin and to
see a couple of his shows. I liked them both right away. Klein was a
big bear of a man, a very charismatic guy. Meanwhile, Debbie was
spunky and a real straight shooter. She always spoke her mind.

On the tour I witnessed Michael working with Brad Buxer, the
musician, on the song "Stranger in Moscow." Moscow had been a
stop earlier on the tour, before Eddie and I had arrived. During his
stay in the Russian city, Michael had been feeling deeply sad and alone
because of the allegations he was facing. He had been sitting on the
closet floor in his hotel room, crying, when the song came to him.

Brad was Michael's music director and personal music producer
at the time, and there was a unique closeness to their collaboration.
Michael told Brad the idea for the song, giving him a melody. Brad,
who had set up a recording studio in his hotel room, created the song
around that melody. They worked on the song constantly, Michael
singing elements and giving beats to Brad, and Brad transforming
them into music. Watching them cowrite, I saw how a song begins
with an idea, with simple chords, and builds as time goes on. Michael
said that he liked to let a song write itself. It told him what it needed.

He'd spontaneously start singing and dancing around the hotel while the song evolved in his heart and mind.

"Stranger in Moscow" would come out on the *HIStory* album. It will always be one of my favorite songs because I watched Michael create and produce it from start to finish. I was even on the set when they shot the video about three years later. It was the song that made me fall in love with the art of making music.

Michael was introducing me to an extraordinary world. Beyond experiencing the concerts and the music, I was traveling, seeing new places, meeting fans and dignitaries. My whole world broadened dramatically and permanently. I saw that the world was a whole lot bigger than junior high school. I learned to appreciate and respect different cultures. But my biggest personal revelation was discovering the thrill of making meaningful art and having people respond to it. Michael, as my mentor, recognized that impulse and nurtured it in me.

As for Eddie, Michael saw his interests and talents and mentored him in another direction. Eddie was always a fantastic musician. As he got older, he would expand his knowledge by learning the technical aspects of record producing. Michael always said to Eddie, "Be a master at this. Your time will come. Be patient. Keep writing. Stay focused." I dimly saw that under Michael's tutelage, Eddie and I were having something like parallel experiences. Close as we were, we didn't talk much about what was happening on the tour, with Michael, and inside ourselves. We were too busy living it.

What was nearly impossible for us to comprehend was that, at the same time as Michael was giving us a life-changing experience, he was enduring one of the hardest times of his own life.

CHAPTER FIVE

THE TOLL

T HE YEAR 1993. THINK ABOUT ALL THE HORRIBLE things you heard about Michael Jackson around this time. Think about all the jokes on late-night talk shows, all the ugly rumors, all the accusations and all the names. Now think about being the person—the *innocent person*—toward whom all this hatred and ridicule and negative energy is being directed. Imagine the damage that it would cause even the strongest of men. Michael was a professional. And while his performances never suffered during this time of trial, he himself did. He'd said, "I have rhinoceros skin. I'm stronger than all of them," but Eddie and I could see the truth behind the bravado.

The accusations that Jordy's father had leveled against Michael were a source of unrelenting anxiety to him. At night he would sometimes vent: "I don't think you realize"—and we certainly didn't—"I have the whole world thinking I'm a child molester. You don't know what it feels like to be falsely accused, to be called 'Wacko Jacko.' Day in and day out, I have to get up on that stage and perform, pretending everything is perfect. I give everything I have, I give the performance that everyone wants to see. Meanwhile, my character and reputation are under constant attack. When I step off that stage, people look at me as if I were a criminal."

I think that without our knowing it, the support my brother Eddie and I gave Michael helped him continue that tour as long as he possibly could. Especially Eddie, who was only eleven. Michael was responsible for us. He couldn't fall apart in front of children. He had to be strong for us, and in some small way, this helped keep him going.

When we arrived in Mexico City, nobody, including Michael himself, knew that it was going to be the last stop on the tour. Whether from the mental anguish caused by the accusations or the sheer physical toll of performing so many concerts, Michael was in extreme pain every night. During every show, he lost a lot of water and was at risk for dehydration, and he required a doctor, sometimes two of them, to help him recover. They visited throughout the day to give him nutrients and rehydrate him by IV. He drank Ensure, a protein-and-vitamin-supplement drink, to replenish himself.

But then, at night, a doctor always came in right before he went to sleep to give him what he called "medicine." I was a kid. All I knew was that the doctor gave him this medicine to help him fall asleep. Only later would I learn that it was Demerol.

Michael was first introduced to prescription medicine, and Demerol in particular, before I met him. In 1984, his hair caught on fire while he was shooting a Pepsi commercial. He suffered second- and third-degree burns on his scalp and body. They were horribly painful, and doctors prescribed painkillers.

Now, on tour, and again in deep physical pain, Michael turned back to those drugs. Maybe he was simply following doctors' orders: his adrenaline was so high after each show that it was the only way he could sleep. For all I really know, the treatments may have been his idea. However it came about, over time Michael began to rely on Demerol to wind down after the shows, and most likely to escape from the overwhelming stress, pressure, and responsibilities of his extraordinary life.

Who can truly imagine what it was like to be Michael? Devoted fans screamed around him all day, and at night he performed for several hours as the King of Pop. Coming home, he had to shift into reverse, trying to rest in order to do it all again the next day. How impossible it must have been to dial down from the hyper mode of the show to the complete calm of sleep. It wasn't a natural way for a human being to live. Only a machine could have done it.

This was his schedule, day in and day out. And then, on top of all of it, the crushing weight of the false accusations of child molestation.

I couldn't tell that he was upset, exhausted, or overwhelmed, but when my father periodically joined us during the tour, he saw that Michael was under a lot of stress and that it was taking a physical toll on him.

As I see it now, when he became completely exhausted and overwhelmed, Michael had only two options. One was to say, "I can't do this anymore" and walk away. But Michael was a perfectionist. He didn't want to show weakness. He wanted to prove to the world that he was innocent of the charges against him and that he was strong enough to fight them. So to him, quitting wasn't an option. His only other option was to use whatever means he could to simply endure it. Michael wasn't trying to get high. He had to go on with his life despite the intolerable pressures, and he did it the only way he could.

At the time, the "medicine" that Michael used in order to fall asleep didn't really affect my experience of him. The doctor came, and then Michael went right to bed. I understood that he was taking medicine to help him go to sleep. I knew nothing about prescription pain medicine. The doctor was there to make sure he was healthy. For the young teenager that I was, the world was still a simple, black-and-white place, where doctors always prescribed medicines to cure their patients. I assumed that my friend was in good hands.

Now that I look back on that trip through adult eyes, I can discern a couple of instances when the stress Michael lived with daily, and the devastation it was causing, were evident.

One instance occurred when Eddie, Michael, and I were doing schoolwork. Michael seemed fine. Normal. Then, all of a sudden, in the middle of a conversation he said something really strange. "Mommy," he said, "I want to go to Disneyland and see Mickey Mouse."

I was taken aback, confused.

"Applehead? Are you okay?" I asked. At the sound of my voice, Michael snapped back into reality. He didn't seem to realize what he'd just said.

When I repeated his words back to him, he said, "It must be the medicine. Sometimes the medicine makes me do that." That was the first time I ever felt that he wasn't all there. I was worried, and later I asked the doctor about it. He said that Michael's lapse was a normal side effect of the medicine he was taking, that it was nothing to worry about. I was thirteen years old. Again, I trusted doctors. Why shouldn't I? Only now does it strike me that if, in a moment of psychic confusion, Michael was revealing his deepest truths, it was simply that he longed to be a kid whose parents were taking him to Disneyland.

Another time, in Santiago, there was the incident in the hotel's hot tub. Eddie, Michael, and I were soaking in the hot tub, maybe playing around and seeing how long we could hold our breath underwater. (For some reason, whenever Michael went swimming, he wore pajama pants and a T-shirt. He never wore a bathing suit.) All of a sudden Michael said, "I'm going to hold my breath," and slipped under the water. Time went by. More time went by. I looked at Eddie nervously. At first I could see the bubbles rising from his nose. Then there were no more bubbles. Finally, I couldn't take it anymore. I dove down and pulled Michael up to the surface. I said, "Applehead, are you okay?" He was conscious, but kind of out of it.

"Yeah, I don't know what happened," he replied. "I must have fallen asleep."

This may sound strange, but despite the way it may seem, I'm almost certain he wasn't on drugs. Over the many years I knew him I had a chance to develop a pretty good idea of when he was on something and when he wasn't, and in retrospect, I really think that in this instance he was sober. He had a stunned look on his face, as if he couldn't really believe what had just happened. He kept apologizing and saying he didn't want to scare us. He knew we depended on him, and he didn't want to show his vulnerability.

Nonetheless, I thought Michael was fine until, before one of the concerts in Mexico City, Elizabeth Taylor suddenly showed up. Michael adored certain screen icons, and Elizabeth was one of his favorites. He especially identified with current and former child stars, as Elizabeth had been, because he knew they shared some of the same experiences growing up.

My father was actually the man who arranged for Michael and Elizabeth Taylor to meet for the first time. It happened when one of Elizabeth's daughters was getting married and she was staying at the Helmsley Palace at the same time as Michael. Although he was leaving that day, he called my father up to his room and said, "Dominic, please give this note to Elizabeth Taylor. I'd really love to meet her." He handed my father a handwritten note. My father duly delivered it to the star when she returned to her room from the wedding. When Michael came back to the hotel, two or three months later, he kept asking my father, "Did you give the letter to Elizabeth? Are you sure she got it?" He couldn't believe she hadn't been in touch with him.

A month later Elizabeth finally called, and the next time my father saw him, Michael happily reported that he and Elizabeth had

had dinner. The rest is history. She was a warmhearted woman, and was very maternal toward Michael. They had dinners together when their paths crossed and did favors for each other: she lent him her chalet in Gstaad; he hosted her eighth, and final, wedding, to Larry Fortensky at Neverland.

By the time she visited him at the hotel in Mexico City, Michael considered her a trusted ally, so when she showed up, he was, initially, thrilled. But backstage, before the show, Elizabeth took me and Eddie aside.

"Michael has to go away for a little bit," she told us confidentially. "He's not feeling well, and we're going to get him some help. After the show, he's getting on the plane and we're taking him to a safe place."

That was it. Michael was going to rehab.

Michael, Eddie, and I had been together for almost two months when all of a sudden our Huck Finn adventure came to an abrupt end. Michael knew that Eddie and I were part of a bigger package. We came with our parents and our brothers and sister. We had all been family to him during the most difficult time that he'd experienced in his life. He had found people who supported him and loved him for who he was, no matter what others were saying about him. I often ask myself what it was that he saw in me, and I think that the answer was simple: in my eyes, he felt recognized, seen as his real self. I liked him for the same reasons he liked himself. He was simply one of my best friends.

Eddie and I watched the final show that night, but we knew that everything had changed. The rest of the tour was going to be canceled, and this made us terribly sad.

After the show, Eddie and I went with Michael to the airport, where a private jet was waiting. We said our good-byes in the car, all of us crying like babies. Michael boarded the plane, which soon took off for London, where he was to enter rehab. Nobody but us knew that Michael was gone. When we arrived at the hotel, a security guard with a dark towel over his head waved to fans and entered the hotel with us, pretending to be Michael. That night Eddie and I climbed into Michael's bed and stayed awake talking most of the night. The room felt strange and empty without him.

My parents were already en route to join us; they had been planning to visit us again in Mexico City. When they arrived, Bill Bray explained the sudden change in plans. Michael was canceling the rest of the tour and entering rehab. All my parents saw was that Michael wasn't well, that he needed a break from nonstop performing. They didn't think that he was entering rehab because he was addicted to drugs, or that they had left their children in the care of someone who was using drugs—a thought to strike horror in the veins of any parent. Michael's relationship with drugs, which would one day become much more complicated and evident, wasn't on their radar. At any rate, they were right to trust Michael—he never would have let anything interfere with the care of their children.

In later years, Michael would explain to me that the cancellation of the tour had had nothing to do with drug addiction. It was because his next tour date was in Puerto Rico, on American soil, and if he had entered the United States at this time, there was a very real chance that he would have been arrested on the allegations of child molestation. To avoid his arrest, his team of handlers had to come up with a way to get him out of the rest of the tour. The only way to guarantee that the part of the tour that was canceled would be covered by insurance would be if Michael opted out because of a medical problem. So he told the world that he had a problem with prescription medicine. It was humiliating—another serious blow to his reputation—but he had no other viable choice.

Leaving the tour under such humiliating circumstances must have been devastating to Michael. As for me, in my own, much smaller world, after flying to exotic cities around the world and being part of the concert tour of one of the most famous entertainers in the business, having to return to eighth grade in New Jersey would be its own harsh awakening.

CHAPTER SIX

TWO WORLDS

EDDIE AND I LEFT MEXICO ON NOVEMBER 13, 1993, our fantastic trip cut unexpectedly short. Going back to school and readjusting to my normal routine were difficult. Before the tour, I'd been excited about attending a new school in a new town. My mom took me shopping for new clothes and everything, but my dramatically late arrival cast a spotlight on me, and my excuse for missing school was kind of mind-blowing. I was famous among my eighth-grade classmates before I'd even met them.

Michael was being accused of child molestation, and here I was, a young boy who had been traveling with him. From the outside, I have to admit, it did look rather strange. Not everyone knew Michael well enough to trust him the way my parents did. Even the district attorney sent my father a fax expressing concern that his children were at risk spending time with Michael Jackson. My father ignored it. Perhaps not surprisingly, the press was all fired up about me and

Eddie. They set up camp outside our new house. One reporter, Diane Dimond, a correspondent for *Hard Copy,* showed up at the front door and stuck a microphone in my father's face. People followed me when I left the house. Sometimes the media arrived outside the school, asking kids questions about me. Our new neighbors, who were still strangers, later told my parents that reporters had offered hundred-dollar bills to their kids if they could procure snapshots of us. The school issued a memo telling students not to talk to the press.

Given all of this hubbub, Michael sent his head of security, Wayne Nagin, to stay with my family and help us manage until the situation died down. My parents tried not to make a big deal about what was going on. They kept it simple, saying to Eddie and me, "Be careful what you say. Go on living your life."

But my life had changed. When I walked down a hall at school, I heard other students whispering, "That's the kid who was with Michael Jackson." Some people thought I was weird, strange. Other people were intrigued. The most popular girl in the school wanted to hang out with me. That was cool. I was happy to go to parties with her, but I knew her interest didn't really have to do with me. I befriended a guy named Brad Roberts, who understood that I was being judged and was kind of protective of me: I knew he had my back. Ordinarily I didn't mind a bit of attention. A tireless prankster, I did things like covertly shining laser pointers on people and watching them try to figure out where the light was coming from. I was that kind of kid. But at this point even I wanted to shift the spotlight away from myself.

The experience of entering school that year changed me. I wasn't stupid. I knew that the attention stemmed from my association with Michael. I became very careful about whom I chose to be friends with, what I said, and to whom I said it. And I was generally reserved, keeping my mouth shut about everything I'd just experienced. If my experience might have won me some momentary status, I wasn't interested. For whatever reason—most likely my parents' example—

I was wired to be loyal. I wanted to protect Michael, and I didn't know whom I could trust. I didn't know what people's motives or agendas might be—especially after Jordy's accusations. It was hard to put my experiences with Michael aside, but discretion came with the territory.

It was during this time that I truly learned to compartmentalize my life. In one compartment were my family and social life at school, and in the other was my life with Michael. Most adults do this kind of thing to one degree or another: there is a natural divide between their work lives and their home lives. The split between the public and the private that evolved in my life was not dissimilar. I never mentioned Michael, who was very much part of my life. Trips with him, vacations, phone calls, laughs, worries, life lessons—I kept all of it to myself. I became a person who thought carefully before he spoke. That caution has never left me.

AT FIRST, MICHAEL WAS IN A REHAB HOSPITAL IN LON-don. My family and I talked to him on the phone every day for hours, passing the phone around among us to keep him company. It got to the point where we had to install what we called a "bat line" just for him. Line one was the house phone, line two was the fax, and line three was Michael's dedicated line. He complained about how the staff at the hospital was treating him. The place was almost like a psychiatric ward, he said, and he knew full well that he wasn't crazy.

One day he couldn't take it anymore and made his escape, bolting down the street. Some orderlies chased him down and brought him back. Finally Elton John stepped in and coordinated his transfer to another rehab place—a private estate outside London that was much more Michael's speed.

Soon after Michael's transfer, he asked us to come and visit him in rehab. Thanksgiving break was beginning, so my parents gave the okay and Wayne brought me and Eddie to London for four or five days.

This new rehab was located in a house in the country, a warm, comfortable, homey place, complete with fireplaces. Michael was really happy to see our familiar faces. He gave us a tour, introducing us to the friends he'd made and explaining his routine—like a child showing off his school. Come to think of it, it was probably the closest experience to going to school Michael had ever had. The patients had a daily schedule, spending time playing games, reading, watching movies, and doing arts and crafts. Michael was kind of proud of the artwork he'd been doing. He showed us a dinosaur he'd made out of paper and beamed like a little kid.

During that visit, Michael was back and forth on the phone with the lawyer Johnnie Cochran. They were talking about settling the case—paying Jordy's family a substantial amount of money to withdraw their accusations. Michael didn't want to settle. He was innocent and saw no reason to pay people to stop spreading lies about him. He wanted to fight. But things weren't quite that simple. The fact was that Michael was a money machine, and nobody wanted him to stop being one. If he took time off from his career for a two- to three-year trial, he would stop producing the billions of dollars worldwide that made him an industry. Because the legal fees of a trial would cost far more than any settlement, his insurance company, who would bear those losses, was determined to settle.

Johnnie asked him if he really wanted to go to trial, was willing to have his whole life exposed to public scrutiny. If he settled, Michael could call it a day: move on with his life and get back to doing what he did best. And so Michael agreed to settle for what I believe was something in the range of $30 million. As I would later understand it, he didn't have much of a choice in the matter. At the end of the day, the decision to fight it out in court or to settle out of court was in the insurance company's hands.

The settlement was in the works before we arrived in England,

and it was finalized while we were there. Michael was now free to return to the United States, and he was eager to come home. So, after only two days in London, Eddie and I joined Michael on a private jet to Neverland to finish our visit there.

It was hard for Michael to return to Neverland knowing it had been ransacked by police in search of evidence against him. His staff had cleaned up, of course, but personal items like books were still missing and would be returned only gradually. Michael felt his privacy had been invaded. But Neverland was still his home, and it was the safest place to be.

Michael tried his best not to put the burden of his troubles on us. There were times when I could tell that his mind was elsewhere, and he'd excuse himself to make a phone call. But he didn't want Eddie or me to have to cope with such adult issues, and we remained, for the most part, blissfully ignorant, emphasis on "blissfully." While Eddie and I were on tour with Michael, we had designed custom golf carts to use at Neverland. Michael had ordered them, and they were waiting for us. My own golf cart! It was practically as big a deal as getting my first car, and it was a sign that I had an open invitation to Neverland. Macaulay Culkin, whom I'd met a couple of times in New York because of Michael, was, along with his siblings, a frequent guest at Neverland. He and Michael had been friends ever since Mac had starred in *Home Alone*. Mac already had his own golf cart—his was purple and black. Mine was black and lime green. Eddie's was black with a picture of Peter Pan on the front. The carts were equipped with CD players with superb sound systems. We hopped in those carts and drove them everywhere, at great speeds. I was more adventurous than I am now, and I'd go as fast as I could on the steep, narrow dirt roads that stretched up from the ranch into the mountains, precipitous drops on either side.

At night, as usual, Michael, Eddie, and I made beds of blankets and pillows on the floor of Michael's bedroom. As a result of the accusations and the lawsuit, Michael's innocent childlike qualities had been warped into something pathological and creepy in the public's perception, but none of the talk had influenced our sleeping arrangements, and none of us had a moment's pause about it.

Everyone knew not to think about taking the space next to the fireplace. That was mine. We called those floor beds our "cages," and if anyone came near mine, I'd say, "Hey. That's my cage. Don't think about stealing my cage." I put on classical music and fell asleep to beautiful melodies and the cozy warmth of the fire.

However, because I frequently had trouble sleeping, when the house was dark and quiet I often went into Michael's bathroom to listen to music. That might sound odd, but the bathroom had an amazing, studio-quality sound system, with Tannoy speakers and everything. Michael had had the speakers installed because he liked to blast music while he was getting dressed and ready for the day, and he got plenty of use out of them: it took Michael a long, long time to get ready. Michael found it amusing that I rarely slept. He liked to suggest that I just move my bed right into the bathroom. But sometimes in the middle of the night he'd shuffle in and listen with me.

In that bathroom, Michael kept a lot of his own music: demos of stuff he wanted to record or songs he was working on but had yet to finish. So at night, alone, that's mostly what I played—music that Michael had never released or was still developing. I sometimes sat in that room for hours, listening to certain songs over and over again. It was like my very own private unplugged concert.

One of the unreleased songs that I loved the most was "Saturday Woman," about a girl who wants attention and goes out to party instead of spending time on her relationship. The first verse went, "I don't want to say that I don't love you. I don't want to say that I disagree . . ."—then Michael mumbled the rest of the lines because he wasn't sure of them yet. The chorus went, "She's a Saturday woman. I don't want to live my life all alone. She's a Saturday woman." I liked

"Turning Me Off," an up-tempo song that hadn't made it onto the *Dangerous* album; a song called "Chicago 1945" about a girl who went missing; a pretty song called "Michael McKellar"; and a song that eventually came out on *Blood on the Dance Floor* called "Superfly Sister." I listened to that song over and over for years before it was released.

While recording a song called "Monkey Business," Michael had squirted his chimp Bubbles with water and taped him screaming in response; you hear this at the beginning of the song. That song was only available on a special edition of the *Dangerous* album. Another song I loved was called "Scared of the Moon," which would come out in *Michael Jackson: The Ultimate Collection*. Michael told me that he wrote that track after having a dinner with Brooke Shields during which she told him that one of her half sisters was scared of the moon. He said, "Can you imagine? Being scared of the moon?"

Some of the songs that I listened to were so rough they were just chords with hints of melodies, but I'd think to myself that rough and unformed as they were, they could probably be hits.

I knew those unreleased songs so well that I started to play them on the piano. Michael would joke, "See, now you're stealing my songs. You're not allowed to listen anymore." He said this in a joking way—and really my piano playing was bad enough that it alone was capable of obscuring the value of the songs—but he made it clear that he didn't want me playing his music for anyone outside our family. He was paranoid that someone would steal his ideas, a harmless paranoia that seemed, at the time, to be about an artist's possessiveness of his vision. Eventually, though, before our very eyes, we would see this paranoia expand far beyond his music to become a dominant part of his personality.

Once, in the Beverly Hilton at Universal Studios, I was doing whatever it was I did on the piano, and I came up with some chords. I played them for a while, and before I knew it, I swear Michael was playing the same chords in the song "The Way You Love Me." I said to him, "Where's my half of the publishing?"—joking of course—but he took me seriously and insisted that the chords he was using were different. Michael and I fought all the time about who was ripping off whom.

Being in that bathroom was one of my favorite things about Neverland. I was there almost every night. I played mostly mellow music: even the music I listen to today tends toward the sad and depressing. But sitting there alone with the incredible Tannoy speakers and the unreleased Michael Jackson songs, I was happy.

AGAIN, I LIKE TO THINK THAT THE YOUTHFUL DIVERSION Eddie and I offered Michael helped him endure the stresses of his life. I kept him company, and I kept him positive. Yet there were cracks in the facade, moments when his eyes would suddenly darken and he'd seem to drift very far away. I know that the argument for settling out of court with the Chandler family made a certain amount of sense, but I have to say that as incredible a lawyer as Johnnie Cochran was, I don't think he should have settled that case. Michael was never the same after it. Not fighting for the truth took a heavy toll on him. He was the biggest star in the whole world. The unresolved accusations cast a shadow on his character. They damaged his reputation. They threatened his legacy. And they wounded his soul. From then on, people wouldn't know what to believe about Michael Jackson. Above all, they challenged his love for children—something that was central to his being—and that hurt far more than the media circus that had been stirred up by the accusations.

During the *Dangerous* tour, Michael had made a point of visiting orphanages and children's hospitals. In every city we visited, we brought toys to these children, and it was clear that Michael wished he could adopt them all. He could not stand to see a child suffer.

There were times during those visits when Michael would break down crying because he couldn't stand seeing a child in pain. He was moved and inspired by the innocence and purity of youth, and always said that of all the creatures in the world, children were closest to God.

After the purity and genuineness of Michael's love for children was called into question, he became a different man. Inevitably, his relationships with children changed forever. The days of the innocent freedom with which he'd played with kids were gone for good. In addition, he now saw what a target he had become for people who were looking to exploit his eccentricities for cruel and selfish ends. Family excluded, he stopped hanging out with kids in the same way as he'd done before. It wasn't worth the risk.

Beyond this, if I had to sum up the change I saw, I'd say that Michael lost his confidence. Not just in himself—the way he would boldly and without a second thought do whatever he felt like doing, no matter how unconventional or immature it might have seemed— but in others as well. He lost his faith in the fundamental decency of his fellow humans. Where once he had seen only the good in people, now he worried about the intentions of those around him. He questioned their motives. He thought everyone around him was trying to take advantage of him, to manipulate him. That hint of paranoia he'd expressed when it came to other people stealing his musical ideas started spreading to other areas of his life. Sometimes, even if he encountered someone whose intentions were good and sincere, he'd look for reasons to doubt that person. He created scenarios in his head that didn't exist in reality as a way of guaranteeing that he would again never be caught off guard.

My family, however, was exempt from Michael's escalating paranoia. Eddie and I were innocent kids, and his faith in our parents never wavered. As for his own family, they stood by him, with the notable exception of his sister La Toya. She had issued a statement claiming that she thought the allegations might be true. Later she said she did this under duress from her abusive husband. Michael eventually forgave her, but he really didn't want much to do with her after that. As for the rest of his family, I didn't see Michael having much real contact with them, but they were supportive in public, and he always said that he loved them and knew they were on his side. My sense was that they would have done more to show their support, but Michael kept them at a distance, as he kept so many people at a distance. He never explained why members of his family were excluded from his small sphere of intimates, but over time I saw him do everything he could to protect himself from real and imagined foes . . .

The one thing I never imagined was that one day he would add my name to that list.

EDDIE AND I RETURNED TO SCHOOL, BUT SOON ENOUGH we were back at Neverland. That Christmas, the Christmas of 1993, was the first Christmas that my family spent with Michael.

Michael was raised as a Jehovah's Witness, which meant that when he was growing up his family had never celebrated birthdays or holidays. He'd enjoyed the Christmas experience before—at least once with Elizabeth Taylor—but as a guest of someone else's family, not as a member of his own. It was one of his fantasies to have a big family with whom he could share the Christmas tradition.

So this time my whole family flew to Neverland, which was quickly becoming my home away from home. The house was beautifully decorated with white Christmas lights outside, wreaths on the door, and garlands encircling the banisters. In the entrance hall there was a Santa hat on the butler statue. A big, beautiful tree dominated the living room.

On Christmas Eve, a woman dressed up as Mother Goose showed up at the house. We all sat around the fire, even my parents, drinking tea and eating cookies as Mother Goose read us nursery rhymes and sang to us. I know. Mother Goose—not exactly a perennial Christmas fixture. But she fit in perfectly at Neverland.

The next morning was Christmas Day. It was the usual rush to open presents. Michael led the proceedings like an old pro, picking out gifts from under the tree and handing them out. Michael shared my offbeat sense of humor: as I've said, we were always playing jokes on each other. So for Christmas that year, he bought me ten presents. Ten! What could be in them? From a guy who gets you your own custom golf cart for no reason at all, what could *ten* Christmas gifts possibly be? I opened the first one. It was . . . a pocketknife. Okay, that one was a pretty good joke, since after all, in his company I had already bought all of the pocketknives in the town of Gstaad. We all had a good chuckle about it, and then Michael, who at this point was failing miserably at hiding a mischievous smile, told me to keep going. So I opened my second present: another pocketknife. And another. By the time I was done, I had ten identical pocketknives. We laughed from start to finish.

Not to be outdone, I had a very special present ready for Michael. What do you get for a guy who can buy the world? I had taken a pile of garbage—toilet paper rolls, plastic bags, and empty candy wrappers—and wrapped each item carefully and put it in a box. Yep, I gave Michael a box of garbage for Christmas. When he opened it, he said with picture-perfect mock sincerity, "Oh, thank you so much. You shouldn't have. You really shouldn't have."

From then on, Michael always spent Christmas with my family, at Neverland or in New Jersey. He always showed up in New Jersey with a giant tub of Bazooka bubble gum. Michael constantly chewed huge wads of that gum, blowing enormous bubbles. Snapping the gum as he chewed was perfectly acceptable for him, but whenever I chewed gum, he'd say, "Can you please close your mouth? You sound like a cow."

Bazooka was his favorite gum. He always said, "It's the best gum in the world, but you have to keep popping new ones in your mouth."

On Christmas Eve, there would be a huge turkey dinner. If we were at Neverland, we could expect an appearance from good old Mother Goose, or sometimes a magician, and the lousiest gag gifts you could ever imagine: a year's supply of tampons, an unappetizing bundle of food scraps from our Christmas Eve dinner, a collection of mouthwashes and toothpaste (a reference to our long-running joke about each other's bad breath).

It was hysterical. It was strange. It was tradition. In short, it was Michael.

CHAPTER SEVEN

MAKING *HISTORY*

THAT YEAR, 1993, WITH THE ACCUSATIONS BY THE Chandler family, had been the hardest of Michael's life. But now that the case was settled, he turned his attention to a new album: *HIStory*. He was working on it at the Hit Factory, a recording studio in New York, and staying in Midtown at Trump Tower.

I was, of course, still in eighth grade, an unexceptional student, but a decent soccer player. I made some friends and settled into a rather unremarkable suburban life.

But when Michael came to town, I had another life. After school, my brother Eddie and I, and sometimes our younger brother Dominic, would go to the city, spend the night with Michael, then wake up early to be driven back to New Jersey in Michael's car. On weekends we'd either visit him or he'd come to see the whole family in New Jersey. We spent as much time with him as we could. I know it's not looked upon as normal for a kid to drop everything and rush off to spend time with a world-famous adult friend, but it seemed completely normal—and fun—to me.

Michael's apartment at Trump was over the top, with dramatic views and gold fixtures in the bathrooms. On the second floor there were three bedrooms. He transformed one of them into a mini dance studio by having all the furniture removed and putting in a dance floor. He did a version of this almost everywhere he went. In the studio were the biggest speakers I've ever seen in my entire life: they must have been five feet tall. Michael also had a video camera in the dance room that he used while he was working on the choreography for his videos or stage shows. When he was dancing, he let the music guide him, and as a result, after the fact, he couldn't always remember the exact sequence of his moves. Thus he'd review the tapes to see what he liked, and wanted to remember and reuse.

On weekends in the city, we often went to the movies or comic book stores, but what I remember most fondly about those visits was that Michael introduced me to the joys of books. I was dyslexic, and reading had always been tough for me, but when I complained that I didn't like to read, he said, "Well, then you will be dumb and ignorant for the rest of your life. Frank, you can do anything you want in this world, but if you don't have knowledge, you are nothing. If I gave you a million dollars right now, would you take it? Or would you want to have the knowledge of how to make that million on your own?"

I knew the correct answer to this question. "I'll take the knowledge."

"That's right. Because with knowledge you can make the first million into two."

The first book Michael had me read was *The Power of Positive Thinking*. I saw how the ideas in that book connected to some of the things that Michael had been talking about. I was intrigued, and just like that, the barrier between me and reading was broken. So just as I followed Michael's lead in record stores, curious about what he was interested in hearing, I started reading the books he recommended and peeking into whatever he happened to be reading.

During that period I met Michael's nephews—Tito's sons, Taj, TJ, and Taryll—for the first time. 3T, as the music group they had formed was called, had yet to release its first album. But I had heard the songs and was a big fan. From the start, I loved Taj, TJ, and Taryll, who were only a few years older than I was. We used to say that I was going to become the fourth member of 3T, and the group would be called 3TF. Michael's nephews were also really into books, and in this respect they were a further inspiration to me to read. At the bookstore, Michael would say, "Get whatever you want. It's an investment."

So we'd all buy a bunch of books, then head back to Trump, where every boy would find a place to sprawl out with his books and pens and notebooks. We called this our "training." We would say to one another, "Time to train," find a comfortable spot, and read for hours at a time.

Michael told us to cherish our books. He got us into the habit of kissing every corner of a new book, as he did. When he read something incredible, he'd start clapping his hands, laughing, and kissing the book.

"What did you read?" we would all start asking. "What did you learn?"

"Don't worry," he'd say. "Just know it's over. You all better watch out. I'm going to take over the world." We'd try to grab the book out of his hands, but he'd hold it out of our reach, teasing, "No, no. You don't get to read this yet."

I'm sure that if you'd asked the average American what it was like to spend a night in a hotel room with Michael Jackson, his three musician nephews, and a few friends, they would never picture this scene.

As far as my family knew, during this period, Michael was dividing all of his time between working on his new album and hanging out with us kids. We were with him all the time. And we had no idea that he was falling in love. Or at least his version of falling in love.

Then, one spring night in 1994, when Eddie and I were the only ones spending the night with Michael, the phone woke us all up at four in the morning. It was Wayne Nagin. When Michael got off the phone with him, he told us that the next day the news was going to break that he'd gotten married to Lisa Marie Presley.

I was incredulous. "What? You got married?" I asked him. "We never even knew you were dating anyone!"

I knew Lisa's name from the stories Michael recounted. He had told us that back when the Jackson 5 were performing, Elvis would sometimes drop by at their shows, bringing Lisa with him. Even as kids, it seemed, they'd had a flirtatious relationship, and Michael always had a special place for Lisa in his heart. But I hadn't seen this coming. I don't think anyone did.

But it was true. Before Michael had arrived in New York on this most recent trip, he'd married Lisa Marie. Even my parents hadn't known about it. I suspect Michael didn't tell them, because when they asked him the inevitable question—*why?*—he wouldn't be able to answer it. He didn't know how. That was just the way Michael was. He kept the various parts of his life separate from one another, and his reasons for doing so were his own.

Now that we knew, we would have gladly accepted Michael's marriage without any explanation at all, but he told us that he had made the decision for business reasons. At the time, he was doing business with Prince Al-Waleed bin Talal, who was known as "the Arabian Warren Buffett." They were business partners in a newly formed company called Kingdom Entertainment. According to Michael, the prince and his colleagues liked to do business with family men, and so he wanted Michael, as his partner, to be married. Especially after the allegations in 1993. The prince was investing a lot of money in Kingdom Entertainment, and he believed that by marrying, Michael would restore his tarnished image. So Michael had married Lisa Marie Presley. Or so Michael's story went.

My father, who had an adult's perspective on the whole affair, saw a simpler scenario. He believed that Michael wanted to be a father and hoped that he would have children with Lisa Marie. It was an unconventional courtship, to be sure, but Michael led an unconventional life.

Did Michael love Lisa? I never really asked myself that question at the time. But thinking back, I have to say that if he was going to marry anyone, she was the one. First of all, he thought it was a great story: the King of Pop marries the King's daughter. And certainly, if anyone understood Michael's lifestyle, it was Lisa. But it was more personal than that: Michael trusted Lisa. After what he'd just been through with the Chandlers, that feeling of trust was paramount. Moreover, their relationship predated all the madness of the last decade. He adored her and her young children, Benji and Danielle. They traveled and visited orphanages together. I'm sure he opened his heart to her. What remains in question is how much Michael actually wanted to have an adult relationship, and whether he was even capable of sustaining one.

Michael told me that while growing up, he'd got a bad taste in his mouth regarding marriage. Watching his brothers endure divorces, he resolved never to be in the same position. He was always worried about going through a divorce and losing all of his money. He said, "I can't go out and date any random person. In my situation, who can I trust?" From this perspective, it was easy to understand why Lisa was a wise choice.

But the issues he had with women ran deeper than fears about the financial cost of divorce. Like me, he had youthful crushes in which he worshipped iconic women from afar, taping their pictures to his wall. But I was thirteen. Michael was thirty-five. Because of his stature in the world, some of these women—Tatum O'Neal, Brooke Shields, now Lisa Marie—were accessible to him, but I'm not sure that when push came to shove, he didn't prefer the images to the reality.

Nonetheless, Michael was giving it a go, doing it his way, and the news was about to break. On the phone, Wayne Nagin said that he would meet me and Eddie downstairs in the car. We had to leave the hotel right away, before the hordes of reporters pounced on Michael. Michael always protected me and my family from the media as best he could, as he would later protect his own children.

Half an hour later, we hurried into the car with blankets over our heads. We ducked down until Wayne told us that no one was following us and the coast was clear. Wayne took us home to New Jersey, and sure enough, in a couple of hours, the news of Michael and Lisa's marriage was being broadcast all over the world.

A month or two later, in August, he and Lisa returned to New York. Michael wanted my family to meet her. So the entire clan—my parents and all five kids—took a car service to the Trump building, and from there followed Michael's van to the Hit Factory. We gathered in a private room that the studio had set up for Michael. It was filled with candy, drinks, and toys.

"Lisa," Michael said, "meet the Cascios. This is my family from New Jersey. Everyone, meet my wife, Lisa." It was strange to hear Michael call Lisa his wife. But, to be honest, I thought she was sexy.

Lisa was very nice to us, if a bit quiet. Who could blame her for being reticent? We were a group of seven outgoing Italian Americans, and there were a lot of different personalities in the room. I imagine she was trying to find her place. Eventually, she entered the convivial conversation—she was clearly making an effort—and we all welcomed her to the family.

While Lisa was in New York with Michael, we saw them frequently, but soon she flew back to Los Angeles, and we didn't see her again until we visited Neverland for New Year's, in December 1994. That year for Christmas, Michael and Lisa got me a DAT machine and a studio mixer. A lot more useful than ten pocketknives. Maybe Lisa put the kibosh on the gag gifts: after all, it was she who handed me my amazing present. On New Year's Eve we went to the Neverland theater to watch the ball drop in Times Square. Michael loved to watch Dick Clark hosting the proceedings.

By this point, Lisa and I had gotten to know each other. She was more comfortable around all of us. Having her around shifted my relationship with Michael slightly—how could it not? I no longer stayed in his room with him at Neverland. But I was fine with that. I liked staying in the bungalows, and I was open to whatever Michael wanted. I never had the sense that I was losing him in any way. Despite his marriage, Michael's behavior didn't change much around us, and I imagine that this meant that Lisa was now seeing another side of him. It wasn't just that her new husband liked playing with water balloons. I didn't think about it that much at the time, but now that I'm an adult, it strikes me that it might seem odd to a recently married woman to find that her husband already loved and seemed to be a part of another family. Of course, Lisa Marie had to understand that in marrying Michael she was not signing on to a conventional life. But it wouldn't surprise me to learn that she had no idea of how much time he actually spent with us, or if she did know, that she had assumed his priorities would begin to shift once he was married.

Still, it wasn't hard to see the issues he'd brought to the marriage, and the trouble he had being a husband. And there was also the fact that Michael did not like confrontation. I remember the day when he began talking about staying in Lisa's L.A. apartment with her and her children.

"She likes to fight," he said. "When she complains, I start clapping my hands and smiling." There wasn't a hint of self-awareness in his tone, a sense that perhaps he could have handled the situation more maturely. If anything, he sounded pleased with his reaction.

"Does that work?" I asked.

"Well, it makes her stop, and then I ask her if she's done arguing."

Not exactly dialogue a couples' counselor would condone. I had a sense that things weren't going very well. They had married on a whim, without developing any ability to communicate about the issues that might crop up in their life together, and they had widely different expectations for the relationship. For all his study of people, their likes and dislikes, his deep recognition of the words and rhythms that touch people's hearts . . . well, Michael didn't seem to bring any of that depth to his marriage.

Michael was also a star, one who was very much set in his ways. He was accustomed to being alone and doing whatever he wanted to do whenever he wanted to do it. In her past relationships, I imagine, men had pampered Lisa, as they should have. It was something she and Michael had in common—their worlds revolved around them—but that dynamic made it hard for them to take care of each other. Lisa tried to understand and accommodate herself to Michael's personality, but I think the burden of making the relationship work fell entirely on her. As far as I could tell, Michael was never emotionally there for Lisa. She definitely tried to make the marriage work, but it must have been hard for her to figure out what her role was in Michael's complicated life.

The *HIStory* album was released in June 1995. Michael didn't want to release a two-disc album. That added to the price and Michael wanted to keep his music affordable for his fans. But Sony wanted to do one disc of greatest hits and another of all new songs, and so the album came out. It was well received by critics and nominated for five Grammys. It remains the best-selling multidisc release by a solo artist of all time.

Michael had a break between the release of the album and the beginning of a major concert tour, and it was during this period that his marriage to Lisa fizzled.

In the end, the union had lasted about a year and a half. When they split up at the end of 1995, Michael claimed that one of the main reasons was that Lisa was jealous of us (she called us the "Jersey family") and the relationship he had with us. He preferred spending time with us to spending it with her. Personally, I had seen no evidence of this, and I don't believe my family had very much to do with the failure of the marriage, but I'm sure Lisa had been hoping to build a life with Michael. And I can certainly imagine that this

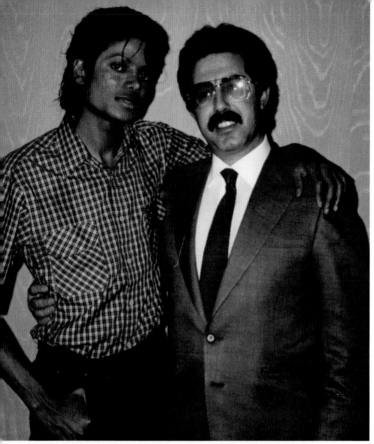

When my father, Dominic Cascio, and Michael first met, my father was working at the Helmsley Palace Hotel in New York City.

This shot of Michael and my father was taken at the Helmsley Palace shortly after Michael's infamous commercial shoot for Pepsi, during which he suffered second-degree burns. (That's why he has a bandage on his head.)

This photo of Michael and me was taken during my first visit with him at the Helmsley Palace in 1984.

Emmanuel Lewis was also at the Palace when I first met Michael.

Emmanuel Lewis, my father, and me (with my toy limousine in hand).

Saying good-bye to Michael at the end of that first visit.

This picture is very special to me. It is the first picture I personally took of Michael, which is why I chose it for the cover of this book.

One of our early visits to see Michael at the Helmsley Palace. This time my father brought me and my brother Eddie, who's sitting on my father's lap, as well as my mother, Connie, who's seated on the far right.

During the time when my father worked at the Helmsley Palace, he also opened up a restaurant with his brother Aldo. This picture was taken at the restaurant, Aldo's, in Wyckoff, New Jersey. From left to right: my father, Dominic; Bonnie; Michael's former manager Bill Bray; and Frank DiLeo.

After I first met Michael at the Helmsley Palace, he began to drop by our house in Hawthorne, New Jersey, in the middle of the night. No one in my family knew when he was coming, which is why my brother Eddie (*left*) and I usually had our pj's on.

Another one of Michael's late night visits to our house in Hawthorne. From left to right: my mother, Connie; me; Michael; Eddie, my brother Dominic; and my father, Dominic.

Michael was not the only member of the Jackson family with whom my father came into contact at the Helmsley Palace. In this photo he's with Tito (*left*), Jackie (*center*), and Marlon (*right*).

Periodically Michael and members of his family would stop by Aldo's for a bite in the private upstairs dining area where this photo was taken. From left to right: my father, Dominic; Latoya Jackson, Rene Elizondo; Janet Jackson; Jack Gordon; and my mother, Connie.

At the Helmsley Palace after a New York concert during the *Bad* tour. That night, we gave Michael the POP watch that we are all wearing on our shirts. From left to right: me, Eddie, Michael, and my cousin Danielle.

Eddie and me with Whoopi Goldberg waiting to watch Michael perform in New York.

Michael visiting my father at Brioni clothing store in New York.

Backstage before a concert on the *Bad* tour in New York/New Jersey. From left to right: my "Aunt Roro" (as Michael called her); my mother, Connie; Michael; our family friend Christine; my father, Dominic; me; and Eddie.

My father and Michael with Sophia Loren backstage during a concert on the *Bad* tour.

From the start my father made a strong impression on Michael. He would tell me, "You have such a wonderful father." People are always comfortable around my father, and once Michael realized that he was no exception, their friendship was born.

Me (*left*), Eddie (*right*), and Michael backstage on the *Dangerous* tour in London in 1992. Even Michael liked to help support our family restaurant by wearing "I love Aldo's" T-shirts.

I traveled all over the world with Michael, but no place we visited was as special or as magical as Neverland. This sign greets you when you get past the first set of gates at Neverland.

Michael often hosted families at Neverland so that others could enjoy the rides and the animals in the zoo.

Michael's Sea Dragon ride at Neverland, the site of many candy wars.

Michael's Bentley parked in the back of his house. To the right was Michael's office (with Peter Pan outside the window).

The Sky Gazebo at Neverland. We used to have breakfast and lunch up there, and at night we would go up to look at the stars. There were binoculars built into the ground that you could use to view the stars and the property. The vista from up there was absolutely amazing, especially at night when the Neverland lights were on. Words cannot describe how beautiful Neverland was at night.

Neverland landscaping at its finest. These bushes shaped like giraffes were behind the pool.

My golf cart at Neverland, which I designed while on the *Dangerous* tour. My golf cart was the fastest one on the property, and it had a built-in CD player and speakers.

The bridge you crossed on the approach to the main house. We all Jet Skied in the lake to the right of the bridge.

Michael spent years perfecting Neverland, paying attention to every detail. He would walk the grounds and point out flaws or things he wanted changed. He was as meticulous about that ranch as he was about his music. Everything had to be perfect.

This sign was in front of the train station on the road to the amusement park, the zoo, and the movie theater.

The main entrance to Michael's house. When guests arrived, the Neverland staff would line up along the stairs to greet them.

My brother Aldo and my sister, Marie Nicole, playing with Michael's orangutan Brandy at the Neverland Zoo.

Marie Nicole on the Neverland Valley Train heading to the theater/ amusement park.

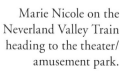

Inside the main train station at Neverland. The station was always filled with candy and fresh pastries.

Backstage with Michael on the *Dangerous* tour. From left to right: my father, Dominic; Eddie; Michael; and me.

On the *Dangerous* tour in Tel-Aviv, Israel, with my brother Eddie (*left*), Michael, and Bill Bray (*behind me*). My father is in the background on the left.

One of Michael's idols was Bruce Lee, and Michael was definitely responsible for getting me into him—so much so that I dressed as Bruce Lee for Halloween one year in New Jersey. Michael went trick-or-treating with us disguised as a doctor. Also pictured: my brother Dominic; Marie Nicole; and Eddie.

life didn't include a family from New Jersey. Michael shifted some of the responsibility onto my family—perhaps as a way of telling us how important we were, or maybe to convince himself that Lisa was asking him to make impossible sacrifices—but I believe we were only part of the greater routine of his life that he was unwilling to change.

There was also the issue of children. Ambivalent as he may have been about having a serious relationship with a woman, there was one thing Michael was sure about: he longed to be a father. At one point he had wanted to adopt a child from Romania with Lisa, but she didn't like the idea. Then he wanted to have a child with her, but she was not ready.

Overall, although they did love and have a tremendous amount of respect for each other, I don't think they were ever emotionally connected enough to sustain a long-term marriage. Michael inhabited his own world and had little desire to leave or adjust it. He didn't know how to be in a relationship, and he wasn't willing to learn. He only knew what he knew. Marriage, with its sharing, conflicts, and compromises, just didn't work for him. When he and Lisa split, he seemed to me to be a little sad, but not entirely heartbroken. That, more than anything else, told me they were better off without each other.

From my perspective, Lisa Marie disappeared as abruptly as she had arrived. Apparently she and Michael stayed close, but I rarely saw her anymore. Though I was never jealous of Lisa, when Michael told me they were parting ways, I have to admit to feeling a little relieved. I mean, I was a teenager and he was my friend. In most ways, it was as if we were high school peers, playing together, having fun, talking about girls. When you're high school buddies and one of the guys gets a girl, things inevitably change. I knew that his having a wife meant that I would see less of Michael, but I accepted Lisa and loved her. That's what buddies do. After all, I hoped to have a girl of my own one day, and when that day came, I would want Michael to do the same for me as I had done for him. When he and Lisa broke up, all it meant to me was that I had my friend back.

CHAPTER EIGHT

MIND MAPS

SIX MONTHS AFTER MICHAEL'S DIVORCE FROM LISA Marie, he and I embarked on that classic of buddy adventures: a road trip. During the summer of 1996, after my sophomore year of high school, and just before he began what would be two years of touring for the *HIStory* album, Michael and I went to Europe together. Because my siblings had school conflicts, it was just the two of us.

Michael came to visit my family in New Jersey before we left for Europe. One afternoon we were playing video games when he suddenly said, "Frank, I have to tell you something, but please don't mention it to anyone."

"Of course. What is it?" I asked.

"I am going to be a father."

"What? How?" I was surprised to say the least.

"Debbie is giving me the greatest gift in the world."

The Debbie he was referring to was Debbie Rowe. Over the years, Michael had confided in Dr. Klein and Debbie about how much he wanted to be a father, and how difficult it was because he couldn't trust anyone. Then, according to Michael, one day Debbie told him, "You deserve to be a father, and I want to make your wish come true. I will carry your baby and make you a father."

As he told me this, he was the happiest I'd ever seen him, and I was thrilled for him. I wasn't shocked. I knew Michael could make anything happen. As he was explaining how all this had come to pass with Debbie, he said, "Hold on. I want to play something for you."

He played me a tape on which I heard Debbie's voice. She said something like "Michael, I want to make you a father. This is my present to you. I do not want anything from you. In fact, if the kids ask where their mother is, tell them I died in a car accident." Michael trusted Debbie, and I saw why. Debbie worked around celebrities every day. She wasn't starstruck. Nor was she flighty or impulsive. Rather, she was a thoughtful, measured person with a degree in psychology. If she'd made this offer, she went into it knowingly and was doing it because she truly believed Michael would be a great father. Debbie's intentions were true. She meant what she said.

Michael was going to be a father. It made perfect sense. As my father would later say, Michael had had plenty of practice running around after us Cascios.

Our first stop was London, where Michael had some meetings. After his obligations there were done, he had some free time before he was scheduled to record two songs at a studio in Switzerland, and he decided to take advantage of it. In the hotel he came to me with the following suggestion:

"Hey, let's drive through the countryside to Scotland." He always flew in, performed, and then flew out of cities, and so he rarely had a chance to spend any time exploring. And with him preparing to be a father, he figured this might be our last chance for a while to embark on a solo trip.

"Absolutely," I said. "Let's do it."

Cue the Steppenwolf.

Before we got in the bus Michael had chartered for the trip (what, you thought we were gonna be doing this in a VW bug?), he and I went shopping for supplies. He said, "We're going to make a mind map." Now, growing up in Michael's sphere meant absorbing his one-of-a-kind philosophy. I may not have been a straight-A student, but we all learn in different ways, and I had a rare and inspired teacher. A mind map, as I learned that day, was a book in which we would paste pictures of things that inspired us—places, people, images of what we liked and what we hoped to achieve. Materials required: piles of magazines full of photos, blank notebooks, glue, and scissors. Purchases made, we boarded a big luxury tour bus outfitted with comfortable couches and beds, and soon we were departing London en route to Loch Lomond.

A driver and two security guards accompanied us. Michael and I had the bedroom at the back of the bus. When we weren't taking in the scenery, we were in that back room, making our mind maps. Making mind maps was new to me, but it wasn't the first exercise Michael had given me that had to do with how I conceived of and planned my future. Michael had already given me some of his favorite books about success: *The Greatest Salesman in the World, The Power of Your Subconscious Mind, Creative Visualization,* and many, many others along these lines. Now, while we worked on our mind maps, he helped me see that the opportunities were endless. There was no limit to what one could achieve. He talked about how his album *Off the Wall* had sold extremely well, and that afterward nobody thought he could top its success. Hearing this only made him all the more determined that his next album, *Thriller,* would be the biggest-selling album of all time. In fact, his goal with *Thriller* was to sell one hundred million copies worldwide. That was his goal, and he achieved it. God-given talent only gets you so far in this world, he told me. He'd achieved success because he believed he would do so.

As the gorgeous landscape rolled by, Michael lay on the bed, and I sat on the floor of the bus, both of us paging through magazines, ripping out images, snipping around thought-provoking words and phrases, talking about which castles Michael wanted to own, which girls he wanted to date (Princess Diana was top of his list), which hotels and resorts I fantasized about owning, the Academy Awards and Grammy Awards I hoped to win. I was about to turn sixteen, and the world seemed limitless. It was easy for me to hear Michael say he wanted a castle and to reply, "Yeah! I want a castle, too!" It was the perfect time and the perfect place to entertain outsized fantasies and ponder the meaning of life.

Michael had also recently introduced me to meditation. The spring break before our trip to Europe, I had spent two weeks of my vacation staying with Michael in a bungalow at the Beverly Hills Hotel. I knew that he often meditated, and on that trip I told him I wanted to try it, too. He encouraged me from the start.

"You should definitely do this. It's a time to think for yourself, clear your head, and manifest what you like. When you meditate, it's like planting a seed. You plant a seed in your mind, and your mind will manifest the reality."

When we were staying at the Beverly Hills Hotel, Michael's driver, Gary, became my meditation guide. Now, Gary wasn't exactly the most obvious candidate to be a spiritual guru, especially considering how much time Michael and I spent making him the target of our silly jokes. I'd known Gary for a while: he was the guy who had picked me and Eddie up at the airport the very first time we went to Neverland. Gary was from Texas, and he loved to write music. He was very sincere about his songs, which were so bad that they were great. Once he said, "Mr. Jackson, I'd like you to listen to this song I wrote last night. It's about a red hawk."

"What inspired this song?" Michael asked.

Gary told us that he'd been standing by his window and a bird (not a hawk) flew by and made a noise that sounded to Gary like the words "red hawk." The story of his inspiration caused Michael and me to crack up. He had another hit song called "Powder Blue." We knew every single word.

"Gary, you should go on tour," Michael would say. "The girls will be fighting over you."

"Gee, Mr. Jackson, I don't think so," Gary would respond.

In 1996, Michael had done a concert for the sultan of Brunei's fiftieth birthday. He brought me, Eddie, and Dominic to Brunei with him. We were staying in one of the sultan's guest houses. (He had about twenty guest houses, all staffed with housekeepers and cooks, which would have been considered luxury homes in the States.) Before we'd left for Brunei, Gary had given us a cassette tape of his greatest hits. I'll never forget when the four of us got in a golf cart to drive around the sultan's property. We were already five minutes away from the house when Michael realized something.

"Oh no!" he exclaimed. "We forgot Gary's Greatest Hits!" We turned the golf cart around and drove back to get the tape. As we drove around that foreign land, we blasted Gary's music, the four of us singing at the top of our lungs. We knew every word to every song. We were his biggest (and possibly only) fans. We teased Gary, but it was only because we loved him. He'd been with Michael for a long time and was completely loyal.

And yet, when it came to meditation, friendly, naive Gary proved himself to be a natural instructor. He taught me the technique in the Beverly Hills Hotel. In his hotel room he had made a little shrine of sorts out of candles and a handkerchief spread out on the floor. He told me to close my eyes and take deep breaths. Gary took what we were doing very seriously, and so did I. After several days of this, he gave me my mantra, a sound that I still use to bring myself into a meditative state, one in which I'm not thinking but am at the same time in control of my thoughts.

Now, during our bus ride through Scotland, Michael and I started meditating together. Michael would time us, and we'd meditate for twenty-five minutes, with a five-minute rest at the end. From then on, whenever we were together, we made it a ritual to meditate at least once a day. We kept each other focused. It was like having a gym buddy. After this trip, meditating was something we would continue to do together for years.

And so we made our mind maps, meditated, and thought about how our minds worked and what our places were in the universe. I still have the mind map I made back then, and looking back on it, I see that the fantasies I had then have evolved into the goals I have today. I wanted apartments in Los Angeles, New York, and Italy—all of which I ended up having at one point or another in my life. I wanted to own a hotel and a soccer team, and both of these dreams have nearly come true. I wanted to produce films and music, which I am working on now. And I wanted to model. (I was sixteen. Cut a kid some slack.)

Without realizing it at the time, one of the earliest lessons I absorbed from Michael had to do with understanding the opportunities that came with empowerment, ambition, and self-awareness. Thinking in those terms is enough to make a kid want to grow up to change the world.

Every so often we would ask the driver to stop the bus. We'd get out and look around, and Michael would talk about where we were, what we were seeing, and why it was important. I remember stopping the bus to watch a particular sunset. There was an expanse of green grass, and tall, beautiful trees framed our view.

"Look at that," he said. "You know that there's a God when you see a landscape like that. We're so fortunate to have the opportunity to travel like this. If people saw this every day, they'd probably take better care of this earth." Michael taught me to see nature. If I hadn't had him as a guide, I might never have learned to pause at the side of the road and let the landscape have its effect on me. I don't care how cheesy it sounds. Michael was open about loving our earth with great passion. He wanted to help preserve it forever. I'd heard him say so before, both in person and in his music, but now, as we took time to appreciate God's handiwork, I felt it in a new way.

One of the books Michael told me to read on that trip was *Jonathan Livingston Seagull.* Jonathan, out of all the seagulls, saw that there was more to life than just being a seagull—more than what was right in front of him. Michael wanted to live that way—to fly beyond all expectations, to live an extraordinary life. He instilled that ambition in me, often asking me, "Do you want to be Jonathan, or one of the other birds?"

That bus ride was one of the most memorable times I spent with Michael. We never got bored. We never fought or argued. We rode through Scotland, talking about life, bonding, and as the miles clicked off on the odometer, our exchange became less that of a teacher and his student and more that of peers. It didn't matter that I was more than twenty years younger. For the first time, Michael and I started having a real dialogue.

"All you have to do," he'd say, "is study these pictures and these words. Look in the mirror and tell yourself what you want to happen. Do that every day, and it *will* happen."

"That's it?" I asked. "That's all you have to do?"

"It's not just about thoughts and words. It's an emotion that drives through your blood. You have to feel and live it every day until you believe it."

"Wow," I said. I was blown away. "That makes a lot of sense. So that's what you do with your music."

"Yeah, Frank, that's exactly right. And soon I want to take the same formula and do it with movies." Our exchanges were heartfelt and meaningful to both of us. I was still young, of course, but Michael saw that I was curious and ambitious, and, as my life teacher, he embraced the opportunity.

ON THAT TRIP, THE JOURNEY WAS MORE IMPORTANT than the destination. But eventually our big bus rolled up a gravel road to a castlelike hotel on Loch Lomond.

It was already dark when we arrived. We were met by a receptionist with round glasses. I think his name was Herron. He seemed calm and businesslike, but as he walked us to our room he said, "By the way, there is a ghost in your room."

Michael and I looked at each other.

"Great, a ghost. What's its name?" Michael asked.

"Her name is Katherine," Herron responded. Michael's mother's name. Spooky.

We got to the room and settled in. It was after midnight. The security guys went to bed, but Michael and I were night owls. And it felt like we'd been cooped up in that bus forever. And there was a ghost in our room. No way were we about to go to sleep. Without missing a beat, Michael said, "Let's go explore."

We walked through the empty halls: it was a big hotel. Where were all the other guests? we wondered. Were they all sleeping? We headed out to the lake to see if we could summon the Loch Ness Monster. So what if this was the wrong loch. Nessie was a monster of mystery. Who knew where she might appear? Besides, it was very pretty out by the lake. The air was fresh and chilly, though there was no sign of Nessie. Michael said, "This place is weird. Why aren't there any cars in the parking lot?"

All of a sudden Herron, dressed in black, appeared right there next to us. A reflection of the moon glimmered in his round glasses. He scared the shit out of us.

"Can I help you?" he asked in an eerie monotone. "I don't want you to go too far and get lost."

The haunted castle, the lake, the creepy receptionist. It was straight out of a *Scooby-Doo* episode. I was sure that if we ever saw the ghost Katherine, I'd be able to pull her mask off to reveal that she was really none other than Herron, dressing up as part of some evil scheme he had concocted in order to get rich.

"Oh, I'm so sorry," Michael said, trying his best to disguise how strange everything seemed to us. "I just wanted to see the property. It's so beautiful." Michael loved to go overboard with people, being effusive and flattering them, so he started laying it on about how enchanted we were with the hotel, how unique it was, and how Herron was doing such a wonderful job taking care of it. I joined in. Then we asked him all about the Loch Ness Monster and if he'd ever seen her.

"I've never seen her," Herron said, probably restraining himself from saying, "You dumb tourists. This is Loch *Lomond*."

There was an awkward silence. Then Michael said, "It's cold out here. We're going to go get some rest." Our host walked us back to the hotel. The place was quiet as a tomb, and by now we had realized that we were definitely the only guests. After Herron escorted us back to the room, we thanked him, bade him good night, and closed the door behind us. But we still weren't remotely tired. There was nothing to do besides continue our investigation of this big, empty hotel.

We stepped out into the hall. There, walking down the corridor, was a young woman in a beautiful white wedding dress. Her hair was puffed up on top and cascaded over her shoulders in long curls. She glanced at us without slowing down. Then she was gone. Michael and I stood in stunned silence. If that wasn't our ghost, Katherine, then who the hell was it?

That vision should have scared us off, but instead we continued—in the opposite direction from the spook, of course—peeking around corners and testing locked doors. Then we saw a sign for an indoor pool. We opened the door, and there he was again: Herron. It was after midnight, but there he was, in his little round glasses, cleaning the pool. This guy was everywhere. We apologized again, saying we just wanted to see the beautiful hotel, and headed back to our room for real.

We sat on the bed, talking about this strange place. Why would they tell us there was a ghost in our room? How were we supposed to sleep? All of a sudden the curtains moved. I started to leap to my feet, but Michael stayed me with his hand. "Wait a second," he said. "You don't ever have to be scared of a ghost. If you don't challenge them, they won't do anything to you. Just say a little prayer and they'll go away."

He wasn't afraid. And because he wasn't, I wasn't either.

Ghosts or no ghosts, now we were hungry. Was there any food in this place? The menu said that there was twenty-four-hour room service, so we ordered egg whites and Tabasco. Michael and I loved egg whites and Tabasco. We ordered about four or five egg-white-and-Tabasco omelets. When the food arrived and we opened the door, there was Herron standing there holding the tray. (At least it wasn't Katherine the ghost.) It was impossible to be spooked out when enjoying egg whites and Tabasco. We ate until five in the morning.

Our next stop on the scenic route to Switzerland was Paris, where Michael would introduce me to someone who would become a familiar figure in our lives.

I had come down with a cold. Michael was due to record a couple of songs in Switzerland, and whenever he had to record or perform, he became especially worried about germs and getting sick. Every time I coughed, Michael would use a fan or a towel to push the germs away from himself. He really couldn't stand it if anyone sneezed around him: he'd walk out of the room.

So in Paris I stayed in my own room and didn't see Michael for a whole day. The next day he called me to his room.

"I'd like to introduce you to someone," Michael said. "You can call him 'Little Michael.'"

In came a thirteen-year-old kid with long hair, dressed exactly like Michael. He wore black pants, penny loafers, a fedora, a red shirt, and eyeliner. He really was a miniature Michael, which I thought was kind of cute . . . albeit in a creepy sort of way. We had dinner together. Little Michael (whose real name, I would later find out, was Omer Bhatti) didn't really speak English. He was quiet, and when he did speak, he talked so fast I couldn't understand a word he said. But I was polite, as I always was.

At some point during the night, Michael pulled me aside and revealed that Little Michael was his son.

Huh? His *son*? I'd never heard of this child, never seen him, didn't recall a single reference to him in the ten years I'd known Michael. But in Michael's world I knew to expect the unexpected. This was just another unpredictable turn. I started laughing, saying, "Are you serious?"

Michael told me that once, on an earlier tour, he'd met a blond Norwegian girl and that he'd had an affair with a fan for the first time. This girl had gotten pregnant, but when she had the baby, she literally went mad, overwhelmed by the notion that she was having Michael Jackson's baby. (I know what you're thinking. Believe me, I had my doubts, too.) Now, his story went, the mother was in a mental institution. The baby supposedly was adopted by a Norwegian woman named Pia, who was a nurse in the psychiatric hospital, or something like that. He'd been raised by Pia and her husband, Riz Bhatti.

Then, as Michael told it, he was in Tunisia on the *HIStory* tour. When Michael was on tour, fans often gathered outside the hotel, singing and dancing for him. I'd seen him invite random fans up to the hotel room to meet him and take some pictures. Sometimes the fans would try to dance like Michael. It was so funny to behold that I'd have to cover my face and run out of the room to keep from making a spectacle of myself.

So Michael was in Tunisia, and he heard about a kid who had won some kind of Michael Jackson look-alike dance competition—possibly one of the kids in the crowd outside the hotel. Michael wanted to meet him, so the winner, Omer, was brought up to the hotel room. When Michael saw him, he noticed the similarities in their appearance and wondered if this could be his child from the affair in 1984. Indeed, as fate would have it, he was that very child, or at least, so Michael said.

How was I supposed to respond to this?

It was a great story, however implausible, and Michael really tried to convince me that it was true. He was absolutely certain that he'd finally found his long-lost son. He'd always known about him and now he was bringing him into the fold. Michael expected me to believe his story, and he kept pushing me to believe it, even though we both knew there wasn't an iota of truth in the whole thing. Finally, after we spent a few minutes going back and forth on the subject, I didn't see any harm in it, so I relented and said, "Okay, that's your son."

Ultimately, it was harmless, but it was also indicative of something that wasn't. Omer was the beginning of a trend that was developing in Michael's life. He had started to surround himself with people who put him on a pedestal, who said what he wanted to hear and did what he wanted them to do. Such people made his life easier, and maybe being surrounded by yes-people gave him the sense of safety he needed, but I always felt that being truthful was more important than currying favor. Even going along with Michael's benign story about Omer was hard for me. Being a real friend meant being truthful, and I wanted to stand by that principle, no matter what it cost me.

AFTER PARIS, OMER RETURNED TO HIS SO-CALLED adoptive family in Norway while Michael and I continued on to Switzerland, where he was slated to record two songs: "Blood on the

Dance Floor" and "Elizabeth, I Love You." The latter was a tribute to Elizabeth Taylor, which he would present to her at a celebration of her sixty-fifth birthday almost a year later, in February 1997.

In Switzerland, we stopped at Charlie Chaplin's house near Vevey and visited his grave so that Michael could pay his respects. We had dinner with his family, including his beautiful granddaughter, on whom I had a big crush. (Yes, I had a lot of crushes.) Charlie Chaplin had long been one of Michael's heroes, one of the people he thought of as great entertainers, innovators, and/or visionaries, whose lives and accomplishments he studied in depth: Walt Disney, Bruce Lee, Fred Astaire, James Brown, and Charlie Chaplin. From Disney he learned that he could create a world out of his fantasies. From Charlie Chaplin, Bruce Lee, and Fred Astaire, he learned attitudes, positions, postures—ways of moving that he incorporated into the choreographed stories he wanted to tell and made his own.

Most of the time we were in Switzerland Michael spent working in the studio, but we still found a few spare hours to visit a museum in Zurich. At an early age, Michael had introduced me to art, and we tried to go to museums whenever we traveled. As soon as we entered this particular museum, we met the director, who was a very nice middle-aged woman with glasses and bobbed hair. When it came to humor, Michael and I had always had a unique connection, and he seemed to intuitively understand the random, crazy ideas that always popped up in my mind. Now, as soon as the museum director came up to greet us, I saw a familiar glint in Michael's eye and thought, *This is going to be fun.*

Michael and I had a favorite shtick. We loved to act as if we were deeply serious about a completely made-up or trivial topic, just to see what reactions we could get from people. One time we'd rented a house in Isleworth, Florida—Michael was always interested in real estate in the area—and a real estate agent was taking us to the house of Shaquille O'Neal, who at the time was playing for the Orlando

Magic. Shaq was a big fan of Michael's, so the agent had arranged a meeting.

As we drove to our appointment, Michael said, "Wow, what beautiful thesasis trees. They are amazing." There is no such thing as a thesasis tree, of course, but who was going to question Michael Jackson?

"Yes, they are gorgeous, aren't they?" said the agent. Michael went on to have a long conversation with him about thesasis trees. It was hilarious.

Thinking of that moment and others like it, I said to the museum director, "What perfume are you wearing? It's delicious. Michael, you have to smell her perfume—it's incredible."

I sniffed one wrist while Michael sniffed the other. He said, "You smell so good."

She said, "Oh, I'll get you the name. I'll write it down for you."

Now we had her. I moved on to the hair. "Your hair. It's beautiful. What do you do to it?"

She said, "Nothing special, I just shower." And then she said, "Actually, I do use a spray—it gives it volume." I made her write down the name of the spray along with her perfume.

Now, while Michael was truly passionate about art, this museum was nothing short of horrible. But this didn't matter to us. We were on a roll. Michael went up to what had to be the most hideous painting in the room and exclaimed, "Oh my God, we have to stop here." He pretended to be overcome by the beauty of the canvas. "I'm so sorry, but do you by any chance have a tissue?"

"Is everything okay?" I asked him.

He just shook his head. "Feel it," he said, as if deeply moved. "This work of art is special."

"Yes, I feel its beauty, too," I said, keeping as straight a face as Michael had.

The director was clearly impressed. She said, "You both have such an incredible connection to art." Now Michael was pretending to cry. The director turned to me and said, "Wow, he's very sensitive."

"Yes, very sensitive," I replied. "He's taught me everything I know about aesthetics. I feel what he's feeling, but I'm just a little better at containing my feelings."

"You guys," she said, pausing dramatically for a moment, "are so special."

We continued this journey, entertaining ourselves by alternating between asking her random questions about the crappy art and raving about her dress, exclaiming, "What's this material? You've got to feel this material."

The security guys with Michael were shaking their heads in mock disapproval at us the whole time. Our behavior was obnoxious, sure, but it was a lot of fun.

Sometimes our pranks weren't so elaborate. There was that time in the south of France, for example, when we went to see Prince Al-Waleed bin Talal and played Ping-Pong on a gold table. We were staying in a fancy hotel. Down there, the nightlife never stops. One night Michael and I were standing on the balcony of his hotel room, watching people eating dinner at three in the morning, when Michael said, "We should do a prank." We filled a bucket with water and . . . *splash!* . . . dumped it off the balcony onto the unsuspecting diners below. We ducked our heads and scrambled back into the room before anyone could see us. Nobody ever figured out that we were the culprits.

BY THE TIME MICHAEL WAS DONE IN THE SWISS RE-cording studio, I had to get back to high school. When I flew home by myself on the Concorde, I was seated next to a man in a suit. As we shot through the air at supersonic speed, my seat mate and I got into a conversation about spirituality, business, and life in general. After a few minutes, the man asked, "What line of business are you in?"

Surprised by the question given my age, I answered, "Sir, how old do you think I am?"

He said, "Twenty? Thirty?"

I replied, "Sir, I'm sixteen."

A look of astonishment on his face, he said, "Sixteen? How do you know all these things at sixteen?"

I was flattered and partly insulted that he would think I was so much older than I was. I liked the idea of being wise beyond my years, but I didn't want to look like an old man. And yet, I realize that over the course of that trip, I had grown up in many ways. The friendship that had begun on the *Dangerous* tour had now evolved into something quite different. For the first time, I felt quite clearly that I was growing up, that I had become more attuned to the world, that the experiences I was having with Michael had pretty much equipped me to hold my own in a conversation with just about anyone, anywhere. Michael had noticed the change in me as well and had begun speaking to me in a different way than before. Although he'd never really treated me like a child even when I was one, he now discussed everything that was going on in his world with me. He made it clear that he valued my perspective, young and inexperienced as it was.

Yet, despite this change in his attitude, and despite my newfound maturity, I don't think either one of us had the slightest inkling of what was in store for us, or where our friendship would eventually take us.

CHAPTER NINE

A NEW FATHER

W HILE MY FRIENDSHIP WITH MICHAEL WAS
evolving, Michael was undergoing changes of his own;
he was getting ready to be a father, a role that he took
very seriously.

Michael as a father made much more sense to me than Michael as
a husband. Maybe being with Lisa, loving her children, and wanting
to have a child with her had made him see that he was now ready to
raise his own children. Much as Michael acted like a child at times,
the truth was that he was a grown man, and he always cared for the
children in his life the way a responsible father would do. For years
he'd had hands-on experience with me, my brothers, and my sister,
and over the course of our long friendship I'd watched him part-time
parent all of my younger siblings. His instincts were excellent: he
knew how to listen to kids and his patience with them was infinite.
In addition, he researched parenting the way he did his other pas-

sions—through books. In our many trips to bookstores, Michael always stocked up on titles about parenting and child-rearing. He was determined to be the best father he could possibly be and sought to understand the psychology of children and the meaning of their interactions with their parents.

Michael's care for every element of his baby's experience began the moment his son was conceived. He knew, before the baby was born, that he was going to name him Prince. He said that the name had run in his family for generations. Michael taped himself saying, "Prince, I am your father. I love you, Prince. I love you, Prince. You are wonderful. I love you." He also recorded himself reading children's books and classic novels, like *Moby-Dick* and *A Tale of Two Cities*. At night, Debbie would put earphones to her belly or play the tapes aloud so that when the baby was born, Michael's voice would be familiar to him.

I was excited for Michael, in no small part because I had every confidence that fatherhood would only strengthen our friendship. In the past, I had worried about how our relationship would change if Michael fulfilled his dream of having his own family. Once, he had come close to adopting. At the time I asked him, "If you have a family, are you going to forget about us?"

"You *are* my family," he told me. "You never have to worry about that." But he also seized the moment to remind me how lucky I was to be healthy, to have a wonderful mother, father, and siblings, and to have the kind of loving childhood that I'd had.

When he said this, I realized how much Michael was a part of all the things that I should appreciate and feel lucky for having. He had been a third parent to me. As I grew older and made more and more of my own decisions, his words of advice stayed with me as much as or more than those of my parents. That's why I say with confidence that Michael Jackson was meant to be a father.

After that conversation, my insecurities about the impact that Michael's starting a family of his own would have on our relationship disappeared. That he should be having a baby felt like the most natural thing in the world. But I was still a little shocked in November 1996, a few months before Prince was born, when Debbie and Michael got married.

"Why get married?" I asked Michael. After the whole experience with Lisa Marie, it was hard to understand why Michael would want to take this step again.

Once again he told me that the powerful Saudi prince Al-Waleed bin Talal had influenced his decision. When the prince found out that Michael was going to have a child, he wanted him to be married. Michael didn't want to jeopardize his working relationship with bin Talal, so he married Debbie. Or so his story went.

And just as he had done with Lisa, Michael downplayed the importance of the marriage, insisting that it was merely a formality.

"Debbie does not want anything from me," he insisted. "All she cares about are her horses. Besides, she's Prince's mother." I guess it made sense by his logic. Debbie was pleasant to be around; their dynamic was friendly; she seemed to have his best interests at heart; and maybe the semblance of a traditional family structure would be good for the baby.

Prince was born on February 13, 1997. I was in New Jersey when the phone rang. Michael was calling from the car as he brought Prince from the hospital to Neverland. He spoke to my mother first; then we passed the phone around, taking turns congratulating him. Michael said that holding the baby was the most amazing feeling in the world, that this was what life was all about. I thought back to all the images of babies Michael had taped to the walls of various hotel rooms around the world. For all his talent, all that he had to give the world, he longed for this more than anything else: a baby to nurture and love. His joy was almost palpable. As we were speaking, I noticed that the TV that was on in the room was showing the news cameras that were following Michael's van all the way to the ranch.

"I can see you on TV," I told him. It felt funny to know that the image I was seeing on the TV screen was synced with the words we were speaking on the telephone, sort of like a primitive video chat.

For most of the first year of Prince's life, Michael was still on the eighty-two-concert, fifty-eight-city *HIStory* tour. But the baby was aptly named: he was Michael's little prince. All of Michael's plans at this time revolved around his child: he didn't believe a baby should be dragged from city to city, so he set Prince up in Paris, a central location in terms of the tour's itinerary, with two nannies to care for him day and night. Each night after he finished his concert, Michael flew back to his apartment on the Champs-Élysées by private jet. Whenever he wasn't performing, he was with Prince. It was a tough schedule, but Michael was trying to be both a father and a mother to his son. My mother, my brothers Aldo and Dominic, and my sister, Marie Nicole, accompanied Michael for the majority of the *HIStory* tour, along with Prince and the nannies. Eddie and I couldn't leave high school, but we escaped for long enough to meet the baby at Disneyland Paris.

In the hotel, as he would wherever they traveled, Michael made sure to create a stress-free, stimulating environment for the baby. My mother remembers that there was always beautiful harp music playing and that she, Michael, and the nannies read to Prince from the day he was born. I was happy to hold the new bundle. He slept in my arms, as babies always do.

The nannies were named Pia and Grace, and I would come to know both of them well. Pia, who was the primary nanny at first, happened to be the mother of Omer Bhatti, Michael's "son."

Not long after Michael had introduced me to Omer, he'd told me the truth—that Omer wasn't really his son. His parents were Pia and Riz—the couple who, in Michael's original story, were his adoptive parents. I didn't even pretend to be surprised. Omer looked just like Pia and Riz. By way of an explanation, Michael gave me the same reason he'd given for his marriages to Lisa Marie and Debbie Rowe. He needed to show the Saudi prince and the rest of the Arab business world that he had a family. I wasn't sure how discovering a long-lost illegitimate son boosted Michael's image with bin Talal, but that was his story. Questionable as it was, I bought it for Lisa Marie and for Debbie, and now I was buying it for Omer. At least he was consistent in his explanations.

Omer and his family began to celebrate holidays with us, which made sense given that Pia was working as Prince's nanny. Riz, Omer's father, ran errands and took care of the cars in California. Omer was the first kid to spend a lot of time with Michael since the 1993 allegations, but Michael had taken a liking to the whole family, and he mentored Omer and treated him like a son. I liked having Omer around. He was a nice kid: my only complaint was that he still spoke so fast that I was constantly asking him to slow down. My nickname for him was "Little Monkey."

Meanwhile, Michael and Debbie seemed to be getting along very well. They spoke on the phone every once in a while. There was no romance or intimacy between them, but Michael truly loved Debbie as a friend. He was endlessly grateful to her for making him a father. And she believed in him as a father. As I'd discovered at the age of five, Michael had no trouble connecting with children. He had an innate ability to see the world through a child's eyes, and he didn't have to change at all to become the kind of father he wanted to be. His heart and mind had long been committed to the challenge. Once Prince was born, Michael wanted another child almost immediately, so the two of them could grow up together. Five months after Prince was born, he and Debbie arranged another pregnancy.

IN THE FALL OF 1997, I BEGAN MY SENIOR YEAR OF HIGH school. I was something of a phantom at school—not a hotshot student, not a partyer—but I had very good friends. I played soccer, and for fun I did the same thing I'd been doing since I was fourteen:

I called up Mike Piccoli and maybe a few other people. My former rival had become one of the few people I could really talk to. We'd get dressed up, and we'd go to my father's restaurant for dinner. The waiters might sneak us glasses of wine, and we'd have good conversation. That was my ideal night out.

Sometimes Mike and I would cut school, go to the restaurant for lunch, and return to school. One time we were in the middle of eating huge plates of pasta when our varsity soccer coach walked into the restaurant. We were busted.

"I know we're supposed to be in school," I told the coach, "but we wanted to make sure we had a lot of protein before the game."

"Are you crazy?" he said. "You can't be eating pasta with pink sauce." That was about as much trouble as I ever got in. That year, I drove Eddie to school every day, and every day we were both late. Eddie's teacher started giving him Saturday detentions as punishment, but somehow I talked my way out of it. I never had a single detention.

I didn't worry much about what life after high school might bring. I knew how to cook and was good with people, so I always had the option of working at my father's restaurant; he was planning to open another one, Il Michelangelo, and my parents would have loved for me to help out in the place. Or, I thought, I might go into the entertainment business, as an actor or otherwise.

That Christmas, my entire family flew out to the ranch. Michael was in great spirits when we arrived. The *HIStory* tour had finished in October, and he was glad to be recuperating at Neverland with Prince. I remember that we were all in the dining room just talking— my family, Omer, and his family—when Debbie showed up to say hello and wish everyone a happy holiday. Michael and Debbie may have been married, but it was obvious to all that the marriage was not real, or traditional, in any sense of the words. By that point, Debbie was visibly pregnant, and Michael told everyone that the name of the new baby was going to be Paris. He said that the reason for her name was that she'd been conceived there. He let people believe that he had been intimate with Debbie, although he had told me that this wasn't the case. Much as the public seemed to care about such matters, it was an insignificant detail to Michael. Debbie had given him the greatest gift in the world and was about to do so again. That was all that mattered to him.

Before Paris was born, Michael asked my mother to fly out to Neverland. I guess he wanted to have family with him: he didn't want his kids to always be with the nannies, and he knew how much my mother loves children. On Paris's birth date, April 3, 1998, my mother was at Neverland with Prince, waiting for Michael and the newborn baby to come home from the hospital.

Michael was a great father. People can say what they will about his life and his choices, but nobody will ever take that away from him. He loved his children deeply. He fed them, changed their diapers, held them, spoke to them. Michael didn't believe in baby talk.

"Speak to children as if they're adults," he said. "Trust me, they understand. And it's better to train them to speak properly from the start."

Michael raised his children the way every parent should raise a child, but from the outside, his approach seemed strange. His children never went out in public without wearing masks or blankets to shield their faces. People didn't know what to make of this bizarre practice, and some thought it was eccentric at best, cruel at worst: why would a father force his children to hide from the world? But Michael's world was a different place from the world the rest of us live in. He felt he had to protect his children from the media, from the public, from the circus he had known his whole life. He knew what it was like to grow up in the public eye, and he wanted something different for his children. Besides wanting to shield them from photographs, Michael was also afraid that if the world knew them as his children, they would be vulnerable to kidnapping for ransom.

All parents have some fear of kidnapping—a parent's worst nightmare—and those fears were multiplied in Michael, given his unique blend of wealth, fame, and paranoia.

Aside from the extreme measures he felt he had to take, Michael was a thoughtful, attentive, loving parent, and his children grew to be the most intelligent and well-behaved children I have ever met. In *Peter Pan*, it is thinking happy thoughts that allows the children to fly. His children were the happiest part of Michael's being.

Seeing Michael's sincere joy with his children made me realize that he hadn't been happy in a long time. I don't know when exactly—to my mind it started with the accusations in 1993—but it was dawning on me that Michael lived in a constant state of depression. If he was alone, he often forgot to eat. Sometimes he slept through the afternoon. He kept his room dimly lit at all times. Of course, he and I still had plenty of fun, but in the quieter moments it was clear to me that something was wrong.

Michael had been born with a rare talent that drove an intense showbiz childhood. That kind of life takes a harsh toll on most children, and the world watches—as much in judgment as with fascination—as, one after another, they crash and burn. Michael fought his darkness in his own way. He didn't party recklessly. He didn't turn to recreational drugs. He didn't act out his pain in the public arena. But that didn't mean that he wasn't suffering.

All of this, however, seemed to change when he became a father. There was a renewed vibrancy to him, an energy that had been missing for years. An enthusiasm appeared, one that my whole family could see. For all his attempts at meditation, turning Neverland into a sanctuary of happiness, and freeing himself from his own demons, the best remedy turned out to be his children. They made him the happiest person in the world, and knowing Michael was building his family gave me the reassurance that he would keep fighting the darkness that hid below the surface of his day-to-day existence.

☙

IN SPRING OF 1998, SOON AFTER PARIS WAS BORN, I graduated from high school. I was as untethered and ambivalent as any seventeen-year-old. My soccer coach thought he could help me get an offer to play soccer for Penn State, but I hadn't decided whether I wanted to pursue it. I looked at a college in Santa Barbara, privately fantasizing that I could live at Neverland and commute to school.

Then, unbeknownst to me, some TV scouts saw me playing a soccer game in New Jersey. I was a showy player—always dribbling between my opponent's legs or doing a rainbow over someone's head. Sometimes I got in trouble with the coach for never giving up the ball. I thought I could take on a whole team by myself. I definitely wasn't the greatest player in the world, but I scored goals and hammed it up for the audience.

When I was done with this particular game, a couple of scouts came up to me and asked me to audition for a Powerade commercial. My father brought me to the audition, which was in Manhattan, and for some reason I can no longer recall we were late. I was one of the last candidates to audition. There were tons of people there—maybe three or four hundred; I guess it was an open-call audition. But soon after, I got a call telling me they wanted me for the commercial.

Immediately after the shoot for the Powerade commercial, I was in New York getting my hair cut at Tony Rossi's hair salon. Sitting in the next chair was Danny Aiello III, the son of the actor Danny Aiello, who was a family friend of ours. He told me that he was directing a film starring his father called *18 Shades of Dust*.

"Actually, you'd be perfect for my movie. Want to be in it?" Danny said.

Coming on the heels of the Powerade ad, it seemed easy enough to give this a try. I read some lines and ended up getting the part. It was a bit part, playing Danny Aiello's character as a child. My little brother Aldo, who looked a lot like me, got a role, too.

These were only small roles, of course, but they had fallen effortlessly into my lap. I was two-for-two in landing parts without trying. What would happen if I actually made an effort? I'd always been interested in films but hadn't done anything to try to start a career. Now I figured, *Okay, I must have something.* I got head shots done and found an agent-manager in New York who started sending me out on auditions. I was ready to take the time and effort to pursue an acting career . . . but as things turned out, I never really even had a chance.

One night—about a year after I graduated from high school—I was playing beer pong with my friends Mike Piccoli, Frank Barbagallo, and Vinnie Amen in the backyard of our house when the phone rang. It was Michael. He asked what I was doing.

"I'm playing beer pong and I'm three-for-three," I replied.

"Listen, I need you to come to Korea tomorrow," he said. "I could use some help out here."

I didn't hesitate. Michael didn't specify what the job entailed, but that didn't matter to me. I didn't think of it as a job. I thought of it as an opportunity. I had seen Michael's world and I was fascinated by it. After all the books, the meditation, the mind maps—it was as if Michael had been grooming me for this role, whatever it might be. Of all the people in the world he could have called, he had chosen me to help him.

"Of course. I'd love to come," I said.

I took my parents aside and had a private conversation with them. I told them that Michael had invited me to travel across the world, and that it was what I wanted to do. They gave me their blessing.

I went back to playing beer pong and, it should be said, continued to win. But my mind was on the next day. I was leaving for Seoul. I had no idea how long I would be gone, but I was almost nineteen years old and I was ready to seize the day.

The next morning I packed one suitcase and left.

It was a fifteen-hour flight direct from JFK to Seoul. The whole first-class cabin was empty except for me and another gentleman, but the flight attendants were pretty. I had learned to flirt with flight attendants from Michael: they always had interesting stories to tell. Michael and I always asked them about their favorite travel destinations, whether they were married or had boyfriends, and so on. On this trip a pretty young attendant asked me why I was going to Korea. I told her I was involved in an entertainment-related project. I had been keeping my relationship with Michael confidential for years—by now it was a habit—but just saying those words made me realize that this time, my visit to Michael was no longer solely about friendship: this time it was business, too.

One of Michael's security guards picked me up at the airport. It was around nine P.M., and we drove through the city. Seoul was magical—with lights everywhere, it felt like a futuristic version of New York. I was thrilled to be on the other side of the world.

I went directly to my hotel room, and before I'd finished unpacking, Michael called. He said, "Oh good, you're here. How was your flight?"

"It was great. I'm excited to be here. What an amazing country."

"Yeah, it's wonderful. Did you eat?"

"No, did you?"

"Come to my room, we'll order something. Make sure you wash your black ass and brush your teeth. Don't come in here smelling all funky." That was how we talked to each other.

I went to his room and knocked our secret rhythm on the door. He opened it and said, "Frankfrankfrankfrank," his odd, familiar nickname for me.

Michael was wearing his pajama bottoms, a white V-neck T-shirt, his fedora, and black penny loafers. Classic Michael loungewear. He wore pajamas everywhere, even, eventually, to court. And he had those fedoras custom-made by the boxful. When he was on tour or traveling, he liked to throw his hat out of hotel windows to the fans. They would fight over it, so he'd throw another. And another. He went through a whole lot of hats that way.

I gave him a big hug, and he showed me around the beautiful hotel suite. While he was doing this, I thanked him for the opportunity he was giving me and told him how honored I was to be there with him.

"Frank," he said, "I could give this job to anyone, but I chose you because I trust you and I love you like a son. Remember, I raised you. I know what buttons to push to get you going. You have a lot of potential, and I want to see you grow."

Over kimchi and bibimbap, we caught up. He asked about my family, and explained that he was doing two benefit concerts—one there in Korea and another immediately afterward in Germany. The show was called *Michael Jackson & Friends*. It featured Mariah Carey, Andrea Bocelli, and other musical luminaries and would benefit a group of children's charities.

By way of explaining what my role would be, Michael said, "Frank, I can't go out all the time. There are things I need you to get for me." I knew this was true. Because the fans made it tough for Michael to go out in public, in the past he'd had an assistant who would pick up T-shirts, movies, whatever Michael needed or wanted. Now I was going to be that assistant, although at that point we didn't name the job or put a salary on it. Initially, I refused to be paid. I just wanted to be part of it. But Michael was having none of that.

"This is a job," he told me. "One day you'll have a family. You need to start somewhere." He told me I'd have a driver and my own security. I didn't know what to expect, but I was thoroughly optimistic.

That was the start of my professional relationship with Michael, and once it was launched, I never looked back. I didn't regret not going to college: I already knew that what I would learn from Michael would surpass any mainstream education. It would be a one-of-a-kind experience, and to me that was priceless.

PART TWO

FRANK TYSON AND MR. JACKSON

CHAPTER TEN

STEPPING UP

O N THE NIGHT AFTER MY ARRIVAL IN SEOUL, THE first of two *Michael Jackson & Friends* concerts to benefit the children of Kosovo took place, with performers including Slash, Boyz II Men, Andrea Bocelli, and Luciano Pavarotti. I sat on the side of the stage to watch Michael perform, as I had done so many times in the past. Although I knew my role was going to be different now that I wasn't a schoolkid, the change would come more suddenly than I expected.

After the concert, I was standing backstage with Michael when Mariah Carey, who had just performed, appeared with her boyfriend at the time—the Mexican singer Luis Miguel. Luis and I chatted about soccer—he initially thought I was from Spain because at the time my orange hair matched their team colors (I can't explain the hair. I have no idea what I was thinking)—while Michael and Mariah talked. They were debating who-sang-it-better: the song was

"I'll Be There" and both the 1970 Jackson 5 version and the version Mariah did twenty-two years later with Trey Lorenz had been No. 1 hit singles.

"Michael," insisted Mariah, smiling from ear to ear, "no one could ever sing that song better than you." A blush swept over Michael's cheeks.

"No, no," he blurted out. "Really, you did a better job."

Mariah seemed honored to be in Michael's presence—she was acting like a dazzled fan—and as the two stars chatted, I noticed the smile leave Luis Miguel's face, and I got the impression that he was slightly annoyed at the attention Mariah was giving Michael. I myself was a little surprised to see Mariah, who was such a successful singer in her own right, appear so awed by Michael, but in the years to come I would see many stars behave that way in his presence.

Turning toward me, Mariah asked Michael, "Who's your friend? He's so cute." She started rubbing my (inexplicably) orange hair.

"Please don't stop," I said, leaning into her like a puppy.

"Frank, stop," interrupted Michael. "Mariah doesn't want to rub your head. God knows what you've got in there."

Luis Miguel looked a little awkward and perplexed, standing there waiting in his skintight suit. I couldn't help it. I pulled out my favorite old routine. "I love your suit," I told him.

Michael mumbled, "Stop," but I was under the sway of an irresistible impulse.

"What brand is it?" I asked. Out of the corner of my eye, I saw that Michael was trying not to laugh.

Luis Miguel mumbled a designer brand, but he wasn't smiling. He definitely didn't like the head rubbing or the friendly flirting between Mariah and Michael.

As they said good-bye, Michael seized the moment to exact a bit of revenge. He said to Mariah, "Frank's a big fan of yours and has a massive crush on you." I turned red. Did I have a crush on her? I ask myself now. I really don't know, but I do recall thinking she was sexy.

After Mariah and Luis left, Michael and I teased each other about Mariah. Michael told me I wouldn't know what to do with her if she were in my bed, and I retorted that if he was given a chance with her, he'd probably ask her to play video games or watch cartoons. He said, "Shut up, Frank," in a funny way, and we both started laughing. That's the way Michael and I acted when it came to girls, like adolescents, fighting over the same hypothetically available girls. I was still young, and it was something I would outgrow soon enough (well, for the most part, anyway), but Michael remained most comfortable in that fantasy world.

For the second charity show, we flew from Seoul to Munich, Germany, in a chartered plane that could hold the entire crew. Michael and I sat next to each other in the front of the plane along with a few other stars and security.

As the plane took off, Michael said, "Listen, when you're flying with me, you don't have to worry about the plane going down. I'm not going to die in a plane crash. No, that's not going to happen. I'm going to die from a shot." I remembered these words—and this was not the only occasion when he uttered them—because for all our deep conversations, Michael didn't really talk much about death. He was too excited about raising his family.

We arrived in Munich in the early evening and headed straight to the hotel—the Bayerischer Hof. As we approached the building, I saw hundreds of fans, among them a handful that I recognized: we'd just seen them in Korea.

Outside every hotel in every city where he performed, fans awaited Michael's arrival like this, most of them clutching poster-size collages covered with images and inspirational quotations. His fans knew exactly what he liked, and they put a great deal of time and effort into the gifts they made for him. Michael loved pictures of Mickey Mouse, Peter Pan, Charlie Chaplin, the Three Stooges, babies—any of the many subjects or performers that he found inspirational or just plain funny. Babies, for instance, he saw as pure and innocent, and when he was feeling blue, pictures of them never failed to cheer him up. In their collages, the fans juxtaposed the images they'd collected in interesting and creative ways, placing a photo of Michael dressed as Peter Pan standing right next to one of Charlie Chaplin, for example. Or they would cut out cute baby pictures and use them to frame a poster of Michael. Of course, not all the signs were so elaborate—some simply stated, "I love you, Michael."

And Michael loved them back. Many times when we were trying to move through a mob of people, he would take notice of a particular fan and stop in his tracks to reach out to that person, say hello, ask a question, and make a momentary, but real, connection with him or her. This happened everywhere we went. In every city and in every country, fans would show up at the hotel bearing personal gifts, and on his way into the hotel, or later from the window, Michael would point out the gifts he wanted. A member of his staff would bring his favorites up to his hotel room, which he would then decorate with these souvenirs. After each stop on his journey, he had the fans' gifts shipped back to Neverland, envisioning that one day he would make a museum of all he had collected.

In Munich, after I was settled in my room, I got a call from Michael to join him in his room. When I arrived, he was ready to put me to work.

"Frank, see those posters down there . . . ," he began, and then proceeded to point out the ones he wanted me to bring up to his room. Escorted by security, I went to the front of the hotel and started collecting. Having seen me with Michael over the years, all the fans knew my name. As I made my way through the crowd, people said things like "Frank, please tell Michael we love him," and "Frank, please ask Michael to say hello from the window."

I had seen this happen all the time, everywhere we went, ever since I was a child. But now I was the one representing him.

I had no grand plan for Munich or what would follow. In those first days I was just trying to take everything in. I wanted to observe as an adult the business of being Michael, to understand how it all worked. After his Munich performance, Michael's focus would shift to the studio and I would work alongside him.

He was poised to plunge deep into the making of his next album. By the time he had finished touring for the *HIStory* album in October 1997, Prince was eight months old and Debbie was pregnant with Paris. That year Michael had also released *Blood on the Dance Floor*, a remix album with five new songs. He had taken most of 1998 off to spend time with his children. His next album was widely anticipated, not least by his label, Sony.

The night of the second benefit concert we got into a black van and headed to the stadium with a police escort. This was something I had done many times before, but I still liked watching the crowd part to make a path for us as we left the hotel.

When we arrived backstage at Olympic Stadium, the show had already been going on for a while. There were over sixty thousand people in the audience, and artists performing from all over the world. As we watched the other performers on a screen, I greeted some familiar faces. There was Karen Faye, Michael's hair and makeup stylist. I had met Karen on the *Dangerous* tour, at video shoots, and before public appearances and had had a secret crush on her as a kid. I called her by the nickname Michael had given her—Turkle. Michael loved Turkle and messed with her all the time. If she was wearing a zippered jacket, he'd try to unzip it. If she was wearing a skirt, he'd lift it up. When we saw each other, I gave Turkle a big hug and a kiss.

Turkle did Michael's makeup while Michael Bush, who designed clothes for Michael, was getting him dressed.

I had already seen the benefit show in Korea. I knew what was—and wasn't—supposed to happen. Michael would do a thirty-minute performance at the end of the show, after all the other performers were done. After his makeup and wardrobe were completed, Michael sat on the side of the stage, enjoying the show. Everything was going smoothly. Then he went out to perform "Earth Song," a song that was dear to his heart. It is a song about the beauty of the world and how we are destroying what we were given through war and selfishness. His live performances of it always evoked wartime suffering. During the Munich performance, he stepped onto a big bridge that spanned the front of the stage. It was raised up, lifting him fifty feet in the air, just as it had in Korea. It was supposed to descend gradually during the song. But this time, instead of coming down slowly, the bridge fell. It plummeted to the stage with a loud crash. This had not happened in Korea. *What the fuck?*

Ever the showman, Michael never stopped singing, even as he fell. When the bridge landed, he was still standing. He later told us that he had jumped at the moment of impact, which may have saved him from more serious injury, but even so, he wasn't in great shape.

Instantly, without thinking, I ran onto the stage along with the security team. At the end of the song, the lights went out, and Michael collapsed into our arms. With security, I helped him off the bridge. The audience, who at first must have assumed the falling bridge was part of the show, saw us rush in and realized what they had witnessed. A worried murmur went through the crowd.

A full-size tank rolled onstage, and a soldier emerged from it holding a gun. Offered a flower by a child, the soldier sank to his knees and wept. Michael finished the performance, at times bending over in pain. Afterward, backstage, he was clearly in a lot of pain, but continued the show.

"My father told me no matter what, the show must go on," he said.

So he went back out, sat down on the edge of the stage, and sang his last song, "You Are Not Alone." Security helped him off the stage.

For some reason—I can only think it had to do with the press—we didn't take an ambulance to a hospital. Instead we got into the black van we'd arrived in and started driving around, trying to find a clinic that was open at that hour of night. It took the driver forty-five minutes to find one. As we drove in circles around a city that was strange to me, I grew increasingly frustrated. I couldn't believe this was happening. Our driver was German, but he kept getting lost. Why hadn't we taken an ambulance? Ordinarily I'm a pretty patient and respectful person, but when people aren't on top of things, it drives me crazy. I lost it and started yelling at the driver. Meanwhile, Michael was in the backseat, barely conscious. The tour's doctor was taking his pulse, and I was telling him that everything was going to be fine. Moments earlier, I had been casually absorbing the rhythms of Michael's world. Now my instincts kicked in. Michael's welfare became my responsibility.

At last we reached a clinic, and I filled out the paperwork to check Michael in. A short time later, when I went back to see him, he was lying in a hospital bed. Miraculously, or because of his instinctive jump at impact, he hadn't broken anything, but his lower back hurt so much that he could barely breathe. Speaking very softly, he told me to find out who had been responsible for the accident. He wanted someone fired. I hesitated when he asked me to call Kenny Ortega, the producer of the show, to get to the bottom of it, because it was three o'clock in the morning and Kenny Ortega was a big deal, but if Michael wanted it done, I was his man. I found the number and woke up Kenny. Michael was in too much pain to speak to him, so I spoke for him. Kenny apologized and told us he would figure out what had gone wrong and why.

By the time we finally made it back to the hotel, it was five in the morning. Michael and I were alone in his suite for only a few minutes before a doctor, who had traveled with Michael from New York, came into the room with two other people. They started to set up some medical equipment next to Michael's bed.

"Who are these people?" I asked the doctor.

"They're doctors," he responded. "They're going to help Michael fall asleep." He paused for a moment, then added, "They need to concentrate on what they're doing. It would be best if you went back to your room. Michael's going to be just fine."

"Yeah." Michael's voice suddenly came up from the background. "I'm going to be fine. They're just giving me some medicine to take away the pain and help me sleep." Satisfied with this answer, I left him with the doctors, and returned to my room.

Only later would I fully understand what I had witnessed that night. It was the first time I saw Michael about to receive the drug propofol, which is a powerful anesthetic. Only an anesthesiologist can administer propofol, and there were two doctors present because, given the strength of the medication, anyone receiving it requires careful monitoring. At the time I didn't know this, having had no experience with such things. As far as I was concerned, Michael was under the care of a doctor whom he presumably knew and trusted. It seemed safe and appropriate to the circumstances. What else was I supposed to think? The dangers that those drugs represented to Michael were foreign and utterly invisible to me.

In the aftermath of the Munich fiasco, Michael, the kids and their nanny Grace, and I took a plane first to Paris, which had been their home base during the *HIStory* tour, and then to Sun City in South Africa. My parents met us in Johannesburg, where Michael was treated like a king. We went on an amazing safari and were guests at Nelson Mandela's birthday party at his house. We stayed at a hotel called the Michelangelo, which, along with Michael, inspired the name of the restaurant my parents would one day open in New Jersey: Il Michelangelo.

Between aiding Michael's recovery from his injury and assisting him on these early travels, my job began to take a clearer shape. Initially my role was simple—helping him decorate his rooms and going out into the world to pick up T-shirts, food, books, magazines, and such. I was thrilled to be traveling with Michael, and glad to help however I could. I was in an odd, but fortunate position. Michael would sometimes say, "You have no idea how lucky you are. So many people would love to be in your position, but I picked you for a reason."

"Trust me, I know how fortunate I am, and thank you again for everything," I always responded.

Being around the biggest entertainer in the world *was* special to me—I knew that and appreciated the adventure of it—but it was also all I had known for as long as I could remember. My friends didn't know much about my experiences, but from time to time they saw my face pop up on the TV news, or in magazine photos, next to Michael. When they were intrigued, I got it, of course. But, as always, it was still *my* normal. So while I felt grateful and excited to be living in that world, I didn't dwell on my good fortune. Not in the way I might have if I hadn't grown up with Michael. I loved the adventure, but what I took for granted was simply my time with Michael himself. I didn't realize how special that was.

No matter what was going on, good or bad, being with Michael made me feel like I had a purpose in the world. From the moment I started working for him, we had talks about the shape my future was going to take, both short and long term. In one of those early conversations about my new role, Michael said something important to me, something that would resonate in the years to come.

"Frank, you're in a position of power," he said. "People are going to be jealous of you. People will try to pit us against each other. But I promise you I will never let that happen."

For some reason, those words seared themselves into my memory. I never forgot them. But I had no idea what truth, and what heartbreak, they foretold.

BY AUGUST WE WERE BACK AT NEVERLAND. FROM THE time we left Munich, Michael's back, still painful, became a chronic problem. Nonetheless, he had business to attend to. He put me to work organizing his massive video library, and though this seemed like a pretty straightforward exercise, as always, Michael had a master plan.

"Frank," he said, pulling me aside, "I know this is not rocket science, but I need you to do something else at the same time. I want help figuring out how to restructure the ranch." The reorganization of the video library, he explained, was just a decoy. For some time Michael had been unhappy with the way Neverland was being run, and what he really wanted me to do was to be his eyes and ears—to figure out what went on while he was away.

Michael was rarely at Neverland, but it cost him $6 million a year to maintain that ranch and to pay the fifty or so people who worked there full-time. Yet despite the expense and the size of the staff, when he'd come home from a tour or a trip, things were not in tip-top shape. A ride wouldn't function properly. There would be patches of yellow in the grass or the seasonal flowers would have yet to be planted. Although everyone would start scrambling like mad to bring the place up to Michael's standards as soon as he showed up, the situation was extremely frustrating.

"What do they do all day?" he asked me, exasperated. "All they have to do is maintain the property. It's the easiest job in the world!" Did anybody work when he was gone? He wanted me to find out. I had never looked at Neverland—or Michael's life, for that matter—in terms of who did what and whether they did it well, but this evaluation made sense to me. Michael was a manager in absentia, and he wanted to assess his employees' performances, especially now that he had two small children who were spending time at Neverland. He wanted to make sure Prince and Paris were surrounded by staff he liked and trusted. But I would come to see that Michael had a general distrust of those around him, doubt that bordered on paranoia.

With this task delegated to me, he left to return to Sun City, where he was accepting an award, and I stayed home to observe what I could about the situation at Neverland and figure out how to resolve the problems. Everyone at the ranch had known me since I was a kid, so Michael figured if I hung around, allegedly working on the video library, I'd eventually get an idea of which mice were doing what while the cat was away. So I went about my work, and I spent time with the staff, all of whom I liked. As soon as Michael left, I noticed that the energy of Neverland changed. He embodied the spirit of the place, and without him the magic faded a little.

I also quickly realized that with the boss away, the rhythm of the place slowed down. The staff was very relaxed, to say the least. Although people understood that I was close to Michael, not all of them avoided me. In fact, just as Michael had hoped, some of them started talking. And talking. Turned out they had a lot to say about some of their colleagues. I took it all in.

Eventually it became clear that there was a problem with the ranch manager. She had been working for Michael for years. She was a very nice person, but she wasn't as on top of things as she'd once been. Maybe she was getting complacent or burned out. And she had the gardeners from Neverland doing maintenance at her house, on Michael's dime. The ranch manager was part of the problem.

When Michael returned, we let the ranch manager go and appointed someone else. And that was just the beginning of the Neverland reorganization. In each department—security, maintenance, grounds, fire department, housekeeping, train station, zoo, amusement park, and movie theater—I identified people who could assess what needed to change. I was nineteen, so I was very careful about my approach. The last thing I wanted to be or sound like was some obnoxious, know-it-all kid. I listened, tried to make it work for everyone, and ultimately set up systems to make the employees accountable.

In the end, it was the perfect first task for me, one that served the dual purpose of getting the staff at Neverland comfortable with my

CHAPTER ELEVEN

NEW SHOES

MICHAEL HAD ALWAYS RELIED UPON A STAFF member who was also a trusted ally—a kind of buffer between him and the rest of the world. It felt perfectly natural to step into the place he had created for me; though it took some time, I became not only his ally on the staff but his protector as well.

At first, our professional relationship experienced some growing pains. Building my character had long been a project of sorts for him, and his efforts to mold me continued with my change in status. When it came to work, Michael enforced firm rules. For starters, he told me we had to keep our friendship separate from our working relationship. He didn't want the staff to see us hanging out as we once had, not while I was on the job, and even asked me to call him Mr. Jackson when I was arranging a meeting for him. This seemed like a reasonable request, and I understood his rationale, but still, it felt strange for someone who was so used to calling him "Applehead," or whatever name came to mind in the moment. I had so many nicknames for him, but now I had to impose an artificial distance between us. As much as Michael fancied himself a Peter Pan figure, his ongoing influence on my intellectual, spiritual, and now professional development showed that he had always expected me to grow up eventually. Especially now that he needed my help.

There were moments when Michael was strict with me. It wasn't a radical shift—he'd always been strict in certain areas: educating oneself, respecting one's parents, not doing drugs, and so on. But now the terrain had changed.

That fall, my entire family met up with Michael and me at Disneyland Paris, one of Michael's favorite escapes. Just a year or so before I'd begun working for him, I'd been there with Michael and Eddie and we'd had one of our amazing midnight adventures. After hours, we sneaked from the hotel into the park—something we did frequently over the years (knowing, of course, that if we got busted, Michael had something akin to diplomatic immunity). We loved the thrill of getting away with something we knew we weren't supposed to be doing.

All the rides were closed, of course, but during the night many of them were put through routine maintenance runs. We saw that "Pirates of the Caribbean" was moving, so we slipped past the maintenance workers and hopped on one of the boats that floated in a line through the animatronic-pirate-infested lagoon. We jumped from boat to boat, then leaped onto the exhibit to steal some treasure.

The pack of boats started floating away. We hurried to jump back in, and Eddie and I made it onto the last boat. Michael, who was behind us, leaped toward the boat and . . . didn't quite make it. For a moment he clung to the stern of the boat, his legs dangling into the lagoon; then he lost his grip and slid into the waist-deep water. When he emerged, his pajama pants were soaking wet. He was holding his fedora, which had fallen into the lagoon. He slowly dumped a gallon of water out of it. I had never seen anything so funny.

Only a year had passed since then, but during this trip to Disneyland Paris, I was working for Michael. For the first time in our travels, I had my own hotel room. It made sense that Michael and I would no longer share a suite: not only was it more professional, but I was older and wanted my independence and privacy. But that wasn't the only shift that came with my new position.

On the first night, my family had gathered in Michael's room. I called Michael and asked, "Can I come over?"

"No, not now," he said. "You're working."

"But everyone's here!" I protested. Michael had never before denied me access, and I was mystified. Work could wait. It seemed obvious that I belonged with him and my family, and I couldn't understand why he didn't want me there.

"What would you think if security waltzed in and started hanging out?" Michael said. "Trust me. I'm doing this for a reason. It's for your own good."

It took me a while to see his point, but eventually it sank in. This was his way of demonstrating that it was time for me to step out of childhood and assume responsibility. Work involves discipline. It doesn't stop just because something fun comes up. This is something that most people absorb at their first jobs, and Michael wanted me to learn the normal lessons of the working world. He took responsibility for helping me transition to adulthood, something I appreciate now much more than I did back then.

I wasn't the only one who had to get used to my new position. Wayne Nagin, the personal security guard who had met me at airports and supervised me in various ways throughout my childhood, was now Michael's business manager. I loved Wayne. He was practically family to me, too. But now that I had become Michael's mouthpiece, there were times when I had to call Wayne to follow up on his work. Michael would want to know whether his financial manager, Myung-Ho Lee, had finalized a deal, or why it was taking so long to get the contract signed. This might not have been such a big deal, but if it was three in the morning and he had a question for Wayne, Michael wanted an answer right away. So now this kid was hassling Wayne at all hours. I was polite, of course, but Wayne was not thrilled. In fact, he called Michael and told him that he didn't want his orders to come from me. He wanted Michael to call him directly. But Michael didn't go for that.

"I don't always have time to get on a call with you," he told Wayne. "Speaking with Frank is like speaking to me." Michael defended me and my position, but for a while there was some tension between me and Wayne, whom I really liked and respected.

Though there was never an official job description, Michael liked having me represent him. Because he'd helped to raise me, my interactions with people echoed the courtesy he always showed his employees and associates, and he knew that I would persist until I saw that his requests had been fulfilled. Above all, I had demonstrated my discretion and loyalty through all the years of our friendship, and he knew it was at the core of who I was.

I was young for my position, and too many people knew it. The fans and media recognized me as Frank Cascio, a kid who was Michael's friend. Now that I was working with him, I didn't want to be seen as that kid anymore. Plus, I wanted to emphasize the line that I had already drawn between my life with Michael and my life with my friends and family. One night, as Michael and I were watching TV at Neverland, I had an idea for how to delineate my new role. Ever since I was a kid, Michael and I had introduced ourselves to different people with made-up names, partly because it was always easier for him to be incognito, and partly for the fun of it. Now I said, "Do you think I should change my name to differentiate family and work?"

Michael turned to look at me, nodded his head slowly, and said,

"Do what you want. It's a good idea." Just then a commercial came on for Tyson chicken.

I said, "Frank Tyson. Perfect." From then on, I introduced myself as Frank Tyson, or just Tyson. It was my professional alias. I had entered a new world. I was no longer a kid from New Jersey whose family happened to be friends with a world-famous star. Now I was an adult with responsibility. I worked for Michael Jackson. I was a trusted ally, positioned to help him personally run the day-to-day business of his life. Nobody called me Frank Cascio anymore. My name, plucked (no pun intended) from a chicken commercial, was Frank Tyson.

With my new identity, representing Michael out in the world grew into my primary responsibility. Some people were surprised when they met me for the first time. One of my early assignments was to work on a deal with Mercedes to do a special line of Michael Jackson SLRs. I was handling all the negotiations with Ferdinand Froning, head of Mercedes' entertainment liaison office, and I was assertive on the phone. Then I met Ferdinand in person at the Four Seasons Hotel in New York. He came up to the suite, and we all got down to business. Suddenly Ferdinand interrupted me while I was speaking: "Hold on," he exclaimed. "Wait a second. *You're* Frank Tyson?"

"Yes," I said.

He said, "So *you're* the one who's been giving me such a hard time on the phone?" We all started laughing, and Michael told him not to let my appearance fool him.

At the same time, my new position of power was readily apparent to those who wanted Michael as a partner. After another meeting at the Four Seasons, a businessman who was eager to make a deal with Michael handed me a briefcase full of money. He said, "This is for you. We really need Michael to be part of this company."

"Listen," I said, "I don't want your money. If a deal happens, it happens, but I can't be a part of this."

Later I told Michael what had happened.

"We can't do business with these people," I said without hesitation. "They just offered me cash. I turned it down, of course."

"Thank you," Michael said. "If it was anyone else, they would have taken the money. You see what I deal with? This has been happening forever. Everyone takes kickbacks. I appreciate your honesty."

He said that it happened all the time, and named a few of his closest employees who had been taking kickbacks for years. I was shocked that this actually went on. It was criminal.

Despite our transparency and professionalism, Michael and I still shared the same jokey rapport we'd always had. I quickly developed a sense of when it was appropriate to be serious and when it was okay to have some fun. I had a great propensity for milking random jokes or pranks for all they were worth. We went through one phase when I always greeted Michael with a weird handshake that wasn't actually a handshake, and is pretty hard to explain. It involved elbows. Then Michael had a thing where while I was talking to someone he'd stand behind the person, pretending he was kicking his ass. At Disneyland, we'd pretend to kick Mickey Mouse's ass.

Of course, Michael and I still loved to mess with strangers. One time we were antiques shopping in New York. I was wearing a suit and tie. In a broken, generically foreign accent I said to a vendor, "I must go—for my religion—I have to throw the chicken from the roof. It's very good luck. I have to do it at seven-thirty or else it's very bad luck."

As always, Michael was right there with me. He joined in, saying, "Yes, he's very spiritual. It's very important for his culture. I must support him in throwing the chicken off the roof." People believed us, and we loved having that shared, secret understanding that we were the only ones in on the joke.

Every so often, fans were allowed to visit Michael in his hotel room. We called the girls fish—because there were lots of fish in the sea—and we called the most aggressive ones barracudas. We'd fight over them, joking about which girl was for him and who was for me. I'd say, "Let's be realistic, you're just the decoy." That's why on the *Invincible* album notes when he thanked me he wrote, "Stop fishing." Over the years, Michael grew close to some fans and occasionally had casual girlfriends, but he was a married man, so nothing untoward happened.

We always tried to embarrass each other in front of women. I was shy—in many ways I still am—and knowing this, Michael would put me on the spot with women, saying, "Frank thinks you're beautiful. He wants to kiss you." Or we'd be standing in the back of an elevator car behind an attractive hotel maid, and I'd feel Michael subtly nudging my hand toward the girl's butt. I'd shake him off before the girl noticed. It was juvenile—maintaining this private exchange that kept the girls at a distance.

It was silly, pointless, fun stuff, but when he wasn't teaching me the boundaries of my new position, Michael still just wanted to be a ten-year-old kid. To be himself. My role was to be beside him as a sounding board, a helper, an adviser, and, last but not least, a friend.

IN AUGUST 1999, MICHAEL STARTED WORK ON HIS NEW album, which would become *Invincible*, in New York City. He rented a town house on the Upper East Side, on Seventy-fourth Street. As Michael had done with his Hideaway in Culver City, we transformed that Upper East Side town house into a mini-Neverland. Michael wanted to create an environment where he felt comfortable, and he felt most comfortable when he was being a kid. So up on the fifth floor was a game room, with video games, a pool table, a movie projector, a popcorn machine, and a fully stocked candy counter. Michael asked for some mannequins, which I picked out at showrooms. They were delivered, assembled, and dressed in sportswear.

We posed them around the first floor. To keep them company, there was a life-size Batman from Sharper Image standing in the middle of the room.

The mannequins were odd company, especially on first sight, but Michael talked to them and joked with them as if they could understand him, the same way people talk to their dogs. I teased him, saying, "She has something to tell you. She wants me to tell you that your breath stinks and you should take a shower." The mannequin concept may sound unusual. It's not like everyone has mannequins in their living rooms. But I have to say that once they were set up, the effect was artsy and kind of cool.

This town house wasn't just about toys, though. Another whole floor was full of elegant art and china. Michael liked the paintings of William Bouguereau, a nineteenth-century French realist, so he had an art dealer go out and bid on some canvases that Sylvester Stallone had put up for auction. He purchased two—one for $6 million, and one for $13 million. The first depicted an angel and a fairy with a baby between them. The second showed a beautiful woman surrounded by angels. The canvas must have been ten feet tall.

The kids and their nanny, Grace, came everywhere with us. (Pia, the second nanny, had worked for only the first year or so. When Grace needed a break, Michael generally turned to the Neverland staff.) If he was traveling, his children were with him, and his time was split between business meetings and taking the kids on excursions. At night, depending on Michael's schedule, they slept in his room or with the nanny if he had to wake up too early.

When it came to his children, Michael was much stricter than one would expect, given his own extravagances. There was Neverland. There were the games and toys that he loved. There was the omnipresent candy counter no matter where he was lodging. There was a "train room" back at Neverland with two sets of electronic trains. (Prince loved those trains.) Nonetheless, Michael wanted to make sure that his children weren't spoiled. At Neverland, their use of the amusement park was limited to special excursions two or three times a week, and they knew they had to behave themselves if they wanted to go on the rides. Whether at home or traveling, they weren't allowed to watch TV. Michael spent time reading books with them. He loved books with Disney characters like Mickey Mouse and Snow White, but he also bought them children's encyclopedias. He wanted his children to be well educated. Michael saw a learning opportunity for his children in every situation. If something broke, he explained how it worked. If it was raining, he talked about the water cycle. He loved to give them little lectures.

There were plenty of toys, of course, but Prince and Paris were expected to treat them with respect. The luxuries were there for the taking, but the children had to behave themselves to earn them. They were taught to be appreciative and thankful.

Michael wanted them to understand the value of working hard.

"If it wasn't for my father," he often said, "I wouldn't be here. He used to wake us up at five in the morning to rehearse. First thing when we got home from school, we'd rehearse more. He pushed my family to be the best they could be."

He didn't want his children to follow his fast and complicated footsteps in entertainment, but he often gave Prince daily assignments, like suggesting that he walk around with a video camera, observing his world. When Michael returned home at the end of the day, he'd say, "Did you work today, Prince? Did you make me a movie?" As much as Michael indulged his own desire to play, he was thoughtful and aware of developing every aspect of his children's experience.

As much as Michael wanted to be there for his kids, there were simply times when it wasn't possible. Grace, Prince and Paris's live-in nanny, did a wonderful job of caring for them. When Prince was born, she was working as an assistant for the Jackson family organization, and it was Katherine, Michael's mother, who'd suggested her as a nanny.

"She'd be great with the baby—she's such a wonderful person."

It was true. Grace was (and is) trustworthy, sweet, and loving. Those were the qualities Michael was looking for. Grace stepped into the role effortlessly. She raised the children, loved them like a mother, and would do anything for them. Most of the time Michael and Grace were very close. Nothing was more important to him than his children, and they were in her hands.

But it was hard for Michael—as it is for many parents—to see how maternal the nanny was with his children. He didn't want them to grow up thinking of Grace as their mother.

"She works for you," he would sometimes tell them when Grace wasn't around. They were too young to understand, and he didn't expect them to, but that was his way of venting his discomfort with the situation. Whenever he subconsciously felt that the relationship was getting too close, he seemed to put distance between the children and Grace. The unpredictable paranoia that increasingly overshadowed many of his interpersonal relationships came into play, and not even Grace was immune.

At a certain point, when we were living on Seventy-fourth Street, Michael finally decided he didn't want a nanny watching his children. Obviously, he was too busy to take care of his children full-time. Among other things, he had to finish *Invincible*. Without the sales revenue he expected from the album, he stood to lose control of his music catalog to Sony. But he longed to be with his kids. Wasn't that the most important thing in the world? He was torn, but in the end, his desire to feel like the sole parent won out. And so, Michael decided to try doing it all: caring for the kids while working on the album. He sent Grace away, and it was just us and the kids in the town house.

In addition to my other responsibilities, I was now helping Michael take care of the kids, day and night. It may seem like a radical shift—and it was—but I was never a prima donna. I mean, I never aspired to be a nanny, but if Michael needed me to help him, how could I say no? A few months earlier, when he'd had to go out of town, I had taken care of Prince for two nights at Neverland. I read him books—at bedtime he wanted me to read *Goodnight Moon*. Every time I finished it he kept saying, "One more time." Finally, I said, "It's time to say 'good night, Prince.'" As the oldest of five, I'd been around kids my whole life and knew my way around a diaper. The familial bond I felt for Michael naturally extended to Prince and Paris as well. I was used to being a big brother, and from the moment Prince and Paris were born, I thought of them as younger siblings.

This time, in New York, I was mainly responsible for Paris, who was two, and Michael took Prince, who was three. During the day, if Michael wasn't in the studio, we'd take them on excursions to a toy store or a bookstore. Michael and I wore dark glasses and hats, and the kids always wore something over their faces—see-through scarves or masks. By the time we were living in New York, the kids were used to their head covers: they had always been a part of their lives.

"Can we take the masks off when we get in the car?" they would ask, the same way other kids might beg to take off their winter boots.

"Yes, you can take them off in the car," Michael would say. What seemed eccentric to the outside world was ordinary and harmless in their household, and it was normal to me, too. Michael had his reasons, and inconvenient as they may have been at times, neither the kids nor I was going to question them.

There was some *Three Men and a Baby* comedy to it—the two of us, ignoring the ever-ringing phones, changing diapers, tossing ointments back and forth, throwing diapers at each other to make Prince laugh. Sometimes when I was changing one of the kids, I'd take the dirty diaper and put it in Michael's face.

"Smell this," I'd taunt. "This is what your children do." He'd run away, shielding his face, and I'd follow, diaper extended toward him.

When Michael was at the studio, I was often on the phone, exhausted after a night of baby tending, trying to change Paris's diaper while conducting a business call. It wasn't easy, but it was fun.

At dinnertime, we'd all gather around the kitchen table with Paris in her high chair. We'd cut up the kids' food, feed them, bathe them, comb their hair, change their diapers, and get them into their pajamas. Before bed, Michael would sit on the floor doing puzzles with Prince while Paris climbed all over him.

Prince slept in Michael's bed and Paris slept in a crib next to mine. Paris, like her brother before her, liked to sleep in my arms. I mean, all babies sleep eventually, but I'd hold Paris, walking and singing to her, and she always fell asleep. As soon as I put her down, she'd start crying again. Believe me, Paris was not an easy baby, especially not at night. She was tough. Sweet, of course, but when she woke up in the middle of the night for a diaper change, she did not necessarily see any reason to go back to sleep. There were times when I didn't get much sleep. Luckily, I was used to that.

The kids were adorable, Paris following Prince around like a little shadow, and they were happy with us. I treasure the memory. That said, it was time for Grace to come back. Yeah, we lasted about a month. Two days after I called her, Grace returned, and I, for one, was relieved.

The night Grace returned, Michael and I went alone to a kosher Chinese restaurant to decompress.

"Those kids can be a handful, huh?" Michael said. I nodded and ordered us some wine. We had just ordered our food when Michael suddenly grabbed my arm.

"We gotta go," he said urgently.

"What?" I said. "We just got here!"

"Look to your left," he whispered. I glanced over, expecting to see an unhinged fan or a window full of paparazzi. Instead, there on the wall near my head was a cockroach.

"Check!" I said. I muttered an excuse and paid the waitress. As we left we saw her grab the cockroach with her bare hand.

"Did you see that?" Michael said when we were back out on the street. "Did you see her grab it with her hand? That can't possibly be kosher."

Though he was technically married to Debbie, Michael saw himself as father and mother to the kids. This dual role of his solidified in October 1999, when, after three years of marriage, Debbie Rowe filed for divorce. Being married to Michael had taken a toll on her private life. She couldn't even ride her horses without being assaulted by the paparazzi. She hoped getting a divorce would pull the spotlight from her, and it did. Otherwise, the divorce didn't change anything. Though she and Michael were still on friendly terms, Debbie rarely came to Neverland. The kids were not in the habit of seeing her, so there was no disruption to their lives.

All in all, there was nothing shocking about her decision: it simply felt like the inevitable conclusion to an arrangement that, according to Michael, had been based on his business with Prince Al-Waleed bin Talal from the beginning. Since Michael wasn't bothered by it, neither was I.

AS THE FALL OF 1999 WOUND DOWN, IT WAS INCREASINGLY clear to me that my whole life revolved around Michael. It may seem like a tough position—being in the shadow of such a megastar and perpetually on call—but I never thought of it that way. I could never be Michael, nor did I want to be. I didn't want the spotlight. I wasn't and will never be a spotlight guy. I felt the same sense of direction he'd always inspired in me. Every day I knew what I had to do, and I believed in what I was doing. I learned from him and absorbed how he saw the world, taking in his kind, respectful, and thoughtful demeanor.

I also became attuned to Michael's more difficult traits. He could be paranoid and overly sensitive, prone to extreme emotions and jumping to conclusions. To counter that, I was careful to listen. To observe everything. To think before I spoke. He didn't like to be told what to do, so if I had an opinion, I drew him toward it, so he might think (or pretend) that he had come up with it on his own. The better I understood him, the stronger and more stable the dynamic between us became.

I had been interested in the entertainment business for a long time. Now I was living it, and all the complexities that came with it. Though Michael was starting to work on *Invincible,* his business and creative ambitions stretched far beyond music. He was always evaluating new opportunities—casinos, real estate, start-ups, film-making, and humanitarian work. On top of those projects, which were usually in various states from inception to execution, there was the ongoing business of running Neverland and managing his music business and partnership with Sony. And then, of course, there was scheduling travel for his appearances, honors, and commitments. It sounds like a lot, and it was. Michael had a whole team of advisers and support staff to handle these ventures and responsibilities.

When I was a kid, the people I'd met in Michael's organization were mostly the ones who helped him on a daily basis: security, drivers, makeup and wardrobe people, and so on. How the business of Michael Jackson was run was pretty much invisible to me. Now I started to see how complex the management was. Though I didn't have formal business training, I came face-to-face with the infrastructure of Michael's organization.

There were lawyers, managers, accountants, and publicists. And it wasn't just one lawyer or one manager. It was a team of lawyers and a team of managers. They were all involved in every deal, and at times they had different agendas. For example, if Michael wanted to invest in a company, the managers wanted to make sure the deal wouldn't take away from his music commitments, the PR people wanted it to serve his public image, and the lawyers wanted to make sure the deal didn't conflict with his other legal obligations.

And yet, for all these other interests, Michael did want to focus his energy on his next album, so he asked me to represent him when his musical obligations got in the way.

"These people work for you," he told me.

Technically, when I spoke for Michael, I was their boss, but being extremely aware of my new-kid-on-the-block status, I tried to be as polite and cautious as possible.

All the politeness in the world wouldn't have gotten me through the first few months, though, if it hadn't been for Karen Smith. Working out of an office in L.A., Karen was Michael's executive assistant, but she was much more than that. Karen had worked for Michael ever since I could remember. She knew everything that was going on in Michael's life and kept it all organized. If I didn't know who to call, I'd call Karen.

Michael had no regard for time or other people's schedules. He would call anyone—me, my parents, Karen—at any hour of the night. Nor did he have a sense of priority. He might call Karen at three in the morning and say, "Karen, can you believe one of the flamingos died? An animal came in and killed it. Can you call and say I want another flamingo? And make sure no animals can get to their island." Day or night, Karen always had pen and paper at the ready and handled his requests without complaint. She could coordinate anything. Karen's superwoman mystique was compounded by the fact that nobody ever saw her in person. She was always only a voice on the phone.

That voice was at once sympathetic and professional. Sometimes, at the end of a hard day, if I needed to vent, I would call Karen. It wasn't like I could call my best friend to complain about my boss or ask for advice. Every element of my job was confidential. But Karen was the most loyal person in Michael's organization. She had seen and been through everything before. She was the only person in the world whom I could truly confide in when it came to work.

From Karen and from acting on my own instincts, I learned that the best way to help Michael make decisions was to gather all the facts about a given situation and present them to him. From there, Michael made decisions, and I executed them. Presenting him with all the facts seemed like an obvious approach, but as time passed, I realized not everyone had his best interests in mind. Michael wasn't always given the complete picture. This was a problem of his own making: he only wanted to hear what he wanted to hear. His accountants and lawyers seemed dedicated. But some of his business associates, eager to profit, talked up the benefits and played down the risks.

I wasn't experienced, but at least I had an objective perspective. I had no hidden agenda, and my sole intention was to help Michael. As I gained confidence, I became more than Michael's surrogate voice, simply relaying his wishes; for better or worse, I started to weigh in with my own opinions.

During my childhood and adolescence, Michael had bred in me the notion that I could not trust anyone. At first I dismissed this as paranoia, but by the end of 1999, I came to see his lack of trust as an essential survival mechanism. The more time I spent with him, the more I saw that in his world, skepticism was a necessary defense. The problems went far beyond the negligence I'd seen in his Neverland staff. He lived in a world where everyone wanted something from him. They reacted to his fame and success with envy and greed. This was true even among his closest associates. It was a viper's nest.

My transformation was sort of like that of Michael Corleone in *The Godfather*. Before Michael is involved in the family business, he is nice and naive. A pushover. But when his father gets shot, he does what has to be done. He transforms overnight into a killer. I had been Frank the friend, Frank the confidant, Frank the assistant. Now Michael wanted everything run past me, and I stepped into place as gatekeeper, fiercely determined to use my powers for good. I knew there were risks involved: Michael had warned me that people wouldn't like taking orders from me, and I suspected that if I got in the way of someone's agenda, they might react aggressively, but I didn't care.

There were times when Michael didn't want to see or hear all of what I had to tell him about the corruption I suspected in members of his organization. He would say, "Frank, you just started here. You don't know what you're talking about. This is a different world," but I always told it like I saw it. That was my job—to provide an impartial perspective that Michael could take or leave as he saw fit.

Challenging as the days sometimes were, I never stopped feeling and expressing gratitude to Michael. There was not a day that passed when I didn't say, "Thank you for everything. I love you." I said that every single evening, and we'd give each other a hug. I acknowledged and appreciated him. But life in the coming year would get more complicated, and as it did, Michael's behavior would pull my loyalty in two directions, and the sanctity of our lifelong relationship would be threatened for the first, but not the last, time.

CHAPTER TWELVE

LIFE AT NEVERLAND

THE MILLENNIUM HAD AN INAUSPICIOUS START. We were supposed to go to Australia, where Michael would do a New Year's show, then immediately fly straight to Hawaii to ring in the new year at another show, maximizing the twenty-hour time difference in order to do two shows in one night. The two-show concert was brokered by Marcel Avram, a concert promoter, along with Myung-Ho Lee and Wayne Nagin, Michael's business advisers.

I was in Michael's room at Neverland when Myung-Ho Lee called to tell Michael that the shows had been canceled. I never knew whether it was Michael or Avram who called them off—later, in court, each would contend that it was the other—but when Michael took the call, he seemed both happy that he would now be able to spend Christmas with his kids and the family and a bit regretful to be letting down his fans. Avram had been involved with the *Dangerous* tour, the end of which had been canceled when Michael left

Mexico City to enter rehab, and part of the settlement agreement between Avram and Michael at that time was that the two of them would partner on the millennium concerts. But Avram was out of pocket again, and so, not surprisingly, he sued Michael for millions of dollars, blaming him for the millennium concert cancellations, as well as for the resulting damages. When the news was released, I saw it as another legal headache in the making, but I had no idea how many more legal issues would arise in the immediate future.

While the lawsuit festered in the hands of lawyers, Michael decided he wanted to move production on his new album to L.A. We gave up the town house in Manhattan and settled into Neverland for the long haul. Michael began working in an L.A. studio. As an adolescent, I'd been in the studio with Michael, when he was working on *HIStory*. I'd even seen him record parts of *Blood on the Dance Floor*. But now I viewed the production process from a new perspective as I realized how much pressure Michael was putting on himself in crafting this album. He saw himself as his own greatest competition: each album had to be as groundbreaking and unique as the last. Michael wanted *Invincible* to be a "potpourri of songs"—that was the phrase he used—each of which was a smash and a single.

His studio schedule varied. Sometimes he would go in late in the afternoon and work into the early morning, and other times he would start in the early morning so he could be home to spend the evening with the kids. But most days the kids and Grace accompanied us into the city. We set up a playroom in the studio with books and toys so that whenever Michael took a break he could spend time with them. They were happy, settled kids: they had been traveling ever since they were born, so they grew up knowing that home was wherever they were with their dad. They played contentedly, knowing he was nearby.

In addition to his work in the studio, Michael developed songs in the dance room at Neverland. He worked with Brad Buxer, the musician I'd known ever since the *Dangerous* tour, who had also been the musical director for *HIStory*. When they'd first met, Brad was the only white guy in Stevie Wonder's band, so Michael figured he had to be something special, and he in effect stole him from Stevie. Brad had an almost uncanny instinct for knowing what Michael wanted, and they developed a really good working relationship. When Michael came up with an idea for a song, Brad was the one who knew exactly how to bring it to life. Michael would call him, tell him almost every single note he wanted him to play, and then listen to Brad play the melody back over the phone. They created entire songs in this collaborative fashion.

When Michael wrote "Speechless," which would appear on *Invincible*, I first heard him humming the melody around the house. He told *Vibe* magazine that it had come to him after a water balloon fight with some kids in Germany, but I remember him telling me that the moment of inspiration occurred during a walk in the mountains of that country, when he was with some friends of ours and was deeply moved by the natural beauty of his surroundings. Knowing Michael, there was probably an element of truth in both versions of the song's origins—the beauty of nature and the thrill of a water balloon fight. Either way, he started recording it in early 2000 in the dance room at Neverland. I remember standing outside the door, listening to him sing, and thinking it was the most beautiful song I'd heard in a very long time.

Whether we were at the ranch or in the studio, there were plenty of breaks from recording. The ranch always had the newest large-scale games: a basketball game, a boxing game, and a skiing game. Michael crashed constantly on that skiing game, which usually made him break out in laughter.

Similarly, there were frequent breaks for one of Michael's favorite activities: water balloon fights. There were always enough people around for a good old-fashioned balloon fight, and we had many of them in his high-tech water balloon fort. Even though Michael had his own kids now, he still loved gathering children to enjoy the magical place that he had created. Whoever was at Neverland—Michael, the kids, the staff, local families—split up into teams of three or four while staff members stocked the fort with "ammunition." The goal of the game was to avoid being drenched while attempting to hit a button on the opposition's side of the fort. When one team managed to hit that button three times, a flag went up, sirens blared, and automatic sprinklers soaked everyone. One time, Michael's team lost, which meant that the captain had to seat himself on a perch in a dunk tank filled with cold water. Michael dutifully climbed into the dunk tank, and when the opposing team threw a well-aimed beanbag, into the cold water he plunged.

Neverland was a paradise for kids. Whether he was home or not, Michael welcomed thousands of children to the ranch—local families, patients at children's hospitals, schoolchildren, inner-city kids, and kids at orphanages. Creating a place of joy for children was a major reason why he built the ranch. Whenever he was on the road or on tour, he made a point of visiting children's hospitals and orphanages, bringing gifts and talking to the children, listening to their stories. You don't see many superstars doing this without any PR motive. Michael did it out of love. His connection with the kids he helped was often, though not always, personal. He took them into his heart. Many individual kids who suffered in one way or another came to Michael's attention. He tried to help them as best he could, often spending time with ill children who asked to meet him. The story of his philanthropic efforts would fill a book of its own.

But ever since the molestation allegations in 1993, he had tempered his genuine love for children with caution. His young visitors were always accompanied by an adult, and Michael was careful never to be alone with the kids: he always made sure another adult was around. It was easy for him to make this adjustment: spending time alone with children had never been particularly important to him. There is a widespread misconception that Michael rounded up small children to participate in sleepovers in his bedroom at Neverland. This was simply not the case. Families came to visit Neverland. Sometimes, depending on how far they had traveled, those families spent the night. These were close, intimate friends and families who'd known Michael for years. They stayed in the guest units.

Michael's suite, along with the kitchen at Neverland, was a natural gathering place for groups. The whole house was warm, but any house has places where people tend to congregate and there were two of those places at Neverland. On the first floor of Michael's suite was a living room with a big fireplace, a piano, two bathrooms, and walk-in closets. Upstairs there was a small bedroom. Everyone hung out downstairs, treating the space like a family room. People— kids—often didn't want the fun to end. So sometimes they slept over, as I did as a child, putting out blankets on the carpet around the fireplace of that family room. Michael himself slept there nine out of ten times. He always offered his bed to his guests.

Sometimes Michael invited members of his fan clubs to Neverland, and he occasionally formed a special relationship with one of the women. One time I was driving Michael into town. Someone was next to me in the passenger seat of the Bentley, and Michael was in the backseat, kissing one of his fans.

"Easy back there," I said. "Relax, calm down."

"Just keep driving," Michael said, in a joking way. "Don't worry about it, just keep driving."

Michael's dalliances with fans were infrequent, and discreet, but they were hardly unheard of. He tended to like tall, slender women whom I'd describe as nerdy in a sexy way. Once, in London, I was in his suite when he brought a friend he'd known for years into his bedroom. They were in there for about an hour, and when he emerged, his pants were unbuttoned. I smirked at him.

"Shut up, Frank," he said, smiling sheepishly. The woman, equally sheepish, said good-bye and left.

Around this time, Michael had another friend—I'll call her Emily—who visited the ranch regularly. She was a nice, cute girl, slender, with brown hair, in her early to midthirties. Emily didn't want or need anything from Michael. They just liked spending time together—talking, walking around, hanging out in his bedroom. It was a romantic relationship, but as far as I know, he didn't tell anyone about Emily but me. Michael kept her a secret—she didn't stay in his room because he didn't want her to be seen coming out in the morning—and even I didn't see real evidence of the romance. That's how I knew he was telling the truth. He wouldn't have been so secretive if he hadn't had something he wanted to hide. That was the longest relationship I saw Michael have: Emily was at the ranch frequently over the course of about a year.

The question as to whether Michael was intimate with Debbie Rowe came up often. People seemed to think that they could make sense of Michael if they could only unravel the mystery of his relationships with women, but Michael was his own man. There were no simple answers. I know he was sexually intimate with Lisa Marie when they were together—he told me so. With Emily, to be honest, I'm not sure, but I know in her he found a companion, a friend.

At night, when all the visitors had left, Michael would take his kids on twilight walks around Neverland. It was touching to see Prince and Paris walking on either side of him, their little hands in his. Michael would point out a bird or a duck while Prince occasionally scrambled ahead like a puppy and Paris stayed next to her dad, a demure little lady. Michael seized any opportunity that arose to teach the children life lessons. If they saw a deer, or another animal, he would tell them about its life and its habits while they stood watching it. The sky, the grass, a tree: Michael saw the value of every detail of his surroundings and introduced each to his children. He wanted them to love what was around them and not take the wonders of creation for granted. It never ceased to amaze me how easily he could change from a water balloon fighter to a pop music star to a caring, attentive father. It was a transition that, even now, I find hard to explain, but it was one that he did every day with ease.

On a daily basis, I was in and out of the studio with Michael, but much of the time I was out—taking meetings on his behalf. The closer I got to the workings of the vast Michael Jackson empire, the more I saw reason to worry. I had noticed the power plays from the start, but now it became clear to me that the problems were escalating. There were many firms and employees involved, and nobody was steering the ship. His talent managers would be doing one deal while his business managers were negotiating a conflicting deal elsewhere. One manager was making grandiose promises to him about the deals he was making, but then he would go MIA for up to a month at a time. Michael's organization was in a state of chaos.

The result of all this chaos was that Michael's finances were a mess. People were taking advantage of him. His organization had umpteen offices with ridiculous expenses. People on his payroll were crisscrossing the world, flying first class, and we had no idea who was flying where or why their trip was even necessary. Michael was paying five hundred cell-phone bills every month! He was hemorrhaging money. It was unsustainable, and something had to change, but when I called his attention to the issues, he asked me to fix them on a case-by-case basis. I knew we needed a more systematic approach.

Then, in early 2000, a team of entrepreneurs, Court Coursey and Derek Rundell, visited Neverland. Court and Derek had been introduced to Michael a few months earlier by one of Michael's attorneys in Atlanta. Although the two had already met with him on a number of occasions, that winter day was their first time at Neverland. They were there to pitch an opportunity similar to *American Idol* (which wouldn't premiere in the United States until 2002), called *Hollywood Ticket*. The idea was that Michael was going to find the next big superstar—with an Internet voting component. After the meeting, which went very well (Michael decided to invest in the company), Michael was unexpectedly called out of town. For the rest of their visit, I served as Court and Derek's host, little knowing that this would be the beginning of a long friendship among the three of us.

As with many ventures in Michael's life, *Hollywood Ticket* did not work out; Michael's interest waned, and without his involvement, there was no deal. Court and Derek were disappointed, but we stayed in touch. The job of handling the everyday details of Michael's business had fallen to me, but when I wanted to straighten up his organization in a more serious way, I knew that my new friends Court and Derek had the right experience to evaluate the situation.

I asked them to meet with Michael again. In advance of the meeting, with Michael's permission, I collected the financial documents they would need in order to objectively assess his situation. At this meeting, Court and Derek were extremely blunt, which was a rarity in Michael's world. They addressed the dysfunction they saw in Michael's organization. Significant sums of money were disappearing into questionable projects. It is likely that no one had ever given Michael such a candid assessment up to that point in his life. Court and Derek showed compassion for him and respect for his talents, but they made it clear that things needed to change. If he continued spending at his current rate, he would be in deep financial trouble in five years.

After that meeting, Michael gradually gave me more and more responsibility for overseeing the organization. When the task grew to be too large for me to handle alone, I told him that I needed help, and we agreed that I should bring in Court and Derek to straighten up the operations. Now we would have the manpower and the experience to solve some of the problems that so disturbed me.

The four of us happened to be in a hotel in Miami when we reached this agreement. At two in the morning we'd finished our work for the night, and were scheduled to leave the city the next day, when I suddenly got the crazy idea that we should play beer pong in our hotel room. I'd never experienced college life, but I'd been introduced to beer pong while I was in high school just before I started working for Michael.

"Let's call the concierge and ask for a Ping-Pong table," I suggested.

"You're out of your mind," Court said.

"What's the big deal?" I asked. I was so accustomed to Michael's whimsical requests, I thought it was perfectly normal to summon a Ping-Pong table to a hotel room.

"Nothing," Court said. "You go right ahead."

The Ping-Pong table arrived, and we set up six large plastic cups on either side. They were supposed to be full of beer, but we substituted Asti Spumante. If you successfully threw a Ping-Pong ball into a cup, your opponent had to chug it. The wine was definitely not a good idea. It wasn't the alcohol that killed us. It was the sugar that did us in. The next morning found the four of us sprawled around the suite, one on each couch, one on each bed. We missed our flight. It was a good night, but we had real work ahead of us.

Upon our return to Neverland, Court, Derek, and I audited the entire organization and started to streamline operations. As we reorganized, we also oversaw daily operations. Along the way, new issues cropped up at the ranch. From the new black swans that had to be rushed in after a coyote decimated the flock—we knew that Michael would be distraught should he come home and discover the damage—to discovering the duplicate billings for the alpacas, there was always something that demanded attention. We worked with his accountants to figure out who hadn't been paid. We signed off on everyone's plane tickets. Nothing got past us. We worked 24/7 for Michael, and it was hard work.

At first, I ran everything past Michael, keeping him in the loop, but the deeper he got into working on *Invincible,* the less he wanted to deal with what I was doing on the business end. When he'd made *Thriller, Bad,* and *Dangerous,* everything in his life had been running smoothly, and this lack of complication was evident in the quality of his work. But since 1993, things had been more complex, with Jordy's accusations feeding into the other mounting financial and legal troubles that had arisen. Further confusing things now was the fact that Michael hadn't recorded a full album since the birth of his kids. He wanted to spend time raising them, but he also needed to spend unwavering attention on his music.

For Michael, recording an album demanded intense focus. Five years had passed since the release of *HIStory,* which was a long time in the music industry. *Invincible* was considered a comeback album. That alone was pressure enough, but for Michael, more of the stress came from his being a perfectionist. He was never satisfied. The work was never good enough for him. His studio work was all-consuming, and there came a point when he simply didn't want to hear my reports about what was going on in his organization. He said, "I need to be creative. That's why I have you. Just deal with it. I don't want to know." Simply put, he was stretched too thin. Something had to give, and that something was his involvement with his businesses. His kids and his music always came first. So every problem that arose became ours to solve.

COURT, DEREK, AND I SPENT THE SUMMER OF 2000 AT Neverland, and in that time we worked incredibly hard to get things in order. But it wasn't all work. During those months, when the weather was perfect and the mountains were alive with color, I also managed to get my Neverland parties down to a science. My parties were always tasteful and under control. It was a rule I made early, without having to think too hard about it: no idiots at Neverland. These weren't big gatherings—never more than ten people—just some friends from L.A., even New York, who would come for the weekend. Michael encouraged me to have friends over—he built Neverland for others to enjoy—but he preferred it to happen when he was away. He didn't often want to be around people in a casual, social way, so most of my friends never even met Michael.

My guests usually arrived at the ranch in the early evening, as the sun was going down. I set them up in the guest bungalows. Once they were settled, our first stop was always the wine cellar. Ah, the wine cellar. It was hands down my favorite part of Neverland. It was a simple stone-and-wood room with some of Michael's tour jackets on display in tall cases. The walls were filled with bottles of wine. I had my own key.

We mixed ourselves drinks or opened some wine. One habit I had picked up from Michael was decanting our concoctions into soda cans or juice bottles. As a Jehovah's Witness, Michael had grown up in a culture where there was no Christmas, no birthday celebrations, and definitely no wine. He was a devoted child, proselytizing from door to door, even donning disguises in order to preach after he became a child star. But right before the release of *Thriller,* the church condemned the album as the devil's work. Michael considered canceling the whole project, but his mother said, "Baby, you go do what you need to do. Don't worry about what the church says. I love you. You leave. Go."

Although Katherine herself was deeply religious, she encouraged her son to follow his own art. And so, when the church denounced his music, he felt he had no choice but to leave it.

Once Michael had broken away from the Jehovah's Witnesses, he was free to enjoy his wine, and he referred to it as "Jesus juice" as a way of justifying its consumption: if Jesus drank wine, so could we. But he didn't drink often. He had residual reservations about partaking of the beverage—he didn't want to promote drinking wine to those around him, and the stereotypical image of superstars partying to excess was repellent to him. He wasn't that kind of rock star, and he didn't ever want to be seen as such. And so, on the infrequent occasions when he did drink, he hid his wine in juice bottles. It was a practice that became a habit. He even transferred his wine to juice containers or soda cans on private airlines when nobody was around to see.

Although I'd grown up with a very different (read: Italian) attitude toward wine and drinking in general, I had my own reasons for taking up Michael's habit. First of all, the juice bottles were bigger than wineglasses, so one could pour oneself a more generous drink. But also, like Michael, I wanted to be discreet, albeit for different reasons. When I was at the ranch, I was technically there to do work, yet Michael told me to treat the place like my home. When I had friends over, I imposed on the staff at Neverland. I asked them to keep the amusement park open for me, or to play movies for me, or to cook for my friends, or to straighten their rooms after they'd left. Although I was younger than most of the staff, they were obliged to follow my instructions. I was aware of how this might ruffle some feathers, and I didn't want to seem like I was exploiting my position or power.

Of course, the Neverland employees knew that my friends and I were drinking. I wasn't really trying to hide anything. But it seemed obnoxious to breeze around Neverland with bottles or glasses of Michael's wine. I didn't want to flaunt the freedom and access that Michael had given me. Key to the wine cellar notwithstanding, I never wanted to give off an entitled vibe.

So, juice bottles in hand, my friends and I usually spent some time in the game room, blasting the jukebox, while dinner was prepared. After dinner, and another visit to the wine cellar for refills, we drove golf carts over to the amusement park. The train also ran from the main house to the park or the theater, but I didn't usually take it.

(Once, around this time, Michael had some neighborhood friends over. Prince, who was about three, was playing host, giving them a tour of the place, and he pointed at the train station and said, "Over there, that's my train." It cracked me up. What little kid has his own train? Michael teased his son, saying, "That's not your train, that's *my* train." And it occurred to me that grown men don't usually have their own trains either.)

People always loved the amusement park. There were bumper cars, a Ferris wheel, the Sea Dragon, the Zipper, and the Spider. The Sea Dragon was a massive swing for a group of people, who were seated in the tail. When the head of the dragon swung to the top, you looked straight down at the people on the other side. Before boarding the ride, we loaded our pockets with candy. When we swung to the top, we threw candy down at our friends. It was excellent. Friends, business associates, family—Neverland brought out the kid in all of us. High-powered businessmen would come to Neverland, and the next thing you knew, they'd be riding the Sea Dragon, eating cotton candy, throwing pies, or acting crazy in a water fort. (And yet, hours after a water balloon fight, they would be making deals with Michael. He always said that bringing someone to Neverland was a surefire way to close a deal.)

After the amusement park, we'd either go watch a movie—Neverland stocked all the new releases—or if it was late at night, I would drive down to the zoo to wake up the animals. I'd grown up doing that with Michael, and I had a special fondness for the bear and the chimps. They felt like old friends. We'd feed them boxes of Hi-C, and my guests were always impressed. It wasn't like *Here's my cute doggie.* It was more like *Meet the bear!*

After the zoo, it was—you guessed it—back to the wine cellar. By this point it was usually getting late and everyone was in the groove. Sometimes we went to the movie theater—the projectionist was on call—but often we'd just stay in the game room, listening to music, dancing a little, feeling happy and free. It was always good, clean fun. Everyone was on their best behavior. No matter how wild and crazy a time people might have fantasized about having at Neverland, when they arrived and saw the place, they were inevitably humbled by its beauty and respectful of its owner.

Living at Neverland was always great—and I hosted some unforgettable parties there—but as summer came to an end, I decided it was time I had my own apartment. I picked a place on the beach in Santa Barbara—about forty-five minutes from the ranch, a pleasant drive down a beautiful mountain road. I loved the beach, and when Michael was out of town, I could do my work from there. I went out and bought furniture, and though I knew I'd be traveling frequently, for the first time in my life I had my own home.

By the time fall rolled around, Court, Derek, and I had made some progress on our work, but there was still plenty to do. I'd been in my new apartment in Santa Barbara for about a month, when Michael sent me to New York to take care of some business. It was just a day trip. I didn't even bring luggage. But that night, just before I went down to get a taxi from the Four Seasons to the airport, my phone rang. It was Michael. He told me that *Invincible* was moving back to New York.

Back to New York, and so soon after we'd moved the whole operation to L.A., where I had gotten settled. But Michael's label, Sony, wanted him to be in New York, where they could keep an eye on things and make sure the album was moving forward. Court and Derek would continue to work on straightening out Michael's finances and I would stay in touch with them from Manhattan. The kids, Grace, and I would all move with Michael to the Four Seasons.

Okay, so we would be gone for a while, I told myself. That didn't mean I had to give up my apartment in Santa Barbara, did it? We'd be back eventually, I was certain. So I held on to my new apartment.

Turned out that that was a mistake. Because we would end up being on the East Coast for a very long time.

CHAPTER THIRTEEN

100 SONGS

IN NOVEMBER 2000, MICHAEL JOINED ME IN NEW York. We rented an entire floor of the Four Seasons. Michael had a suite, as usual, Grace had a room, and I had a room. The kids usually stayed with Michael in his quarters, unless he was going to wake up very early to go to the studio, in which case they stayed with Grace.

Michael had a recording studio set up in another room on our floor and brought in Brad Buxer to work right out of the hotel. One of the songs that he and Brad worked on here was "Lost Children," in which Michael expresses the wish that the missing children of the world could be home with their fathers and mothers. If anyone thought Michael had a full-fledged Peter Pan complex, here was the proof that unlike James Barrie's character, he didn't long to inhabit a world where "lost boys" lived in an underground fort. Michael wanted children to be safe at home. At the end of the song, my brother Aldo, who was seven, and Prince, still three, carry on a little dialogue. Michael fed them the words and Brad recorded them.

"It's so quiet in the forest, look at all the trees," Aldo says.

"And all the lovely flowers," says Prince.

"It's getting dark. I think we'd better go home now," says Aldo.

The source from which "Lost Children" sprang was Michael's emotional life as a parent. He felt firsthand how important it was for his children to be with him. But Michael had possessed the instinct to protect children long before he became a father. He had always been concerned about their well-being. Fatherhood didn't transform him: it fulfilled him. And when it came to his art, fatherhood only reinforced the beliefs that were already core to who he was.

He often said that the music wrote itself, but I saw a lot of effort going into it. As always, Michael listened to the latest songs, following the top ten lists religiously. He had favorite songs that he played over and over. At this time he was into Shaggy's "It Wasn't Me" and Whitney Houston's "My Love Is Your Love." The process of creation was different for every song, but he usually started with a bit of the melody, then brought lyrics into it.

Brad and Michael worked privately, but their work was only a part of the *Invincible* production. Michael had two extremely well-known producers also working on songs with him. Rodney Jerkins, one of the hottest in the business, was based in the Hit Factory studio. Another producer, Teddy Riley, who was an artist in his own right—as part of a group called Guy and one of the original members of the group Blackstreet—was working out of a studio that was built in a bus, conveniently parked right outside the Hit Factory. So Michael had essentially three studios to work in virtually simultaneously, with everyone working around the clock. Whenever anyone's ego got bent out of shape, they called me to vent.

I loved to watch Michael Jackson make music. He was a natural-born director. He would walk into the studio, give everyone hugs, and listen to what each person had been working on since the day before. He heard every note in a song. And if something was wrong, he knew how to say so in an inspiring rather than a derogatory way. Occasionally he'd get frustrated and walk out of the studio. He was never loud or freaked out: he was respectful, but assertive.

Teddy Riley and Michael had a history: they had collaborated on the *Dangerous* album. And Rodney Jerkins had worked for Teddy Riley as a kid, so the two producers had their own shared past. Michael managed to spark a healthy competition between them. Sometimes he would have both Rodney and Teddy work on a song at the same time. He would wait for each producer's take on it, then pick which he liked better. Teddy brought some great songs to the table: "Heaven Can Wait," "Don't Walk Away," "Whatever Happens" (a duet with Carlos Santana), and a song called "Shout," which didn't make the album, but was a great song to start a concert.

At the beginning of their collaboration, Rodney presented twenty songs to Michael. Another artist would have recognized any one of them as a smash hit, but they weren't good enough for Michael. He told Rodney to scrap them all. All twenty songs! Now, Rodney Jerkins, at this time, had just come off hit after hit—"Say My Name" for Destiny's Child, "If You Had My Love" for Jennifer Lopez, "Angel of Mine" for Monica—all of which had reached No. 1 on the pop charts, and he was considered the hottest music producer around. Being told to can twenty new songs was hardly a reaction he was accustomed to hearing.

"You have to go out and find new sounds," Michael told him. "Hit on random rocks or toys. Put a bunch of glass in a bag, add a mic to it, and throw it around."

I had seen Michael play around with this kind of sound creation himself. He would record the *boing* of a doorstop's spring, and then play with the noise, mixing it with a snare to create a completely unique and original sound. Once we put a mic in a bag with rocks, toys, and some small pieces of metal, taped it to the outside of a DAT machine cushioned in bubble wrap, and threw the whole contraption down the stairs. Michael then proceeded to take all the sounds from inside that bag, put them across a keyboard, mix them, and tune them. On *Invincible,* you can hear those one-of-a-kind sounds on "Invincible," "Heartbreaker," "Unbreakable," and "Threatened."

Rodney must have been nonplussed, to say the least, when Michael sent him back to the drawing board. The songs he had presented to Michael were the kind he was famous for producing. But working for Michael Jackson, he knew that he'd have to develop something new. Michael expected it. He drove his producers crazy, but he knew how to get the most out of everyone he worked with.

So Rodney went back to work. Ultimately, he produced "Unbreakable," "Invincible," "Heartbreaker," and "Rock My World" for the album.

The time that Michael and his collaborators spent in the studios wasn't entirely devoted to work. Michael kept some of his beloved video games and other games around. He didn't just like to play himself: he liked to watch other people play them, too—especially the Knockout Kings boxing games. But despite all the hours he spent playing those games, he was never any good at them. Much like his inability to play sports, it was pretty baffling that someone as magically coordinated as Michael would be unable to dominate video games, but he just couldn't get the knack of handling the buttons. That said, he always knew how to have a good laugh about his lackluster skills, which made it fun for everyone.

Even back at the hotel Michael wasn't focused solely on work and his children. When my brother Dominic and cousin Aldo came to visit, they complained that their soccer coach, who had been my soccer coach, too, wasn't playing them enough. Michael picked up the phone at three in the morning and prank-called the guy.

"Hey, buddy," Michael said in a weird voice, "you'd better play my son, buddy."

"Who is this?" the coach asked.

"Don't worry about it, buddy. You better play my son, buddy."

Michael hung up. The four of us died laughing. The coach used *69 to figure out who was calling him, and realized that the call was coming from the Four Seasons. He put two and two together and called my parents to let them know what had happened, but I'm guessing he was a little amused to discover that his prank caller was none other than Michael Jackson.

MICHAEL WAS NEVER AVERSE TO TAKING A LITTLE downtime while at work on *Invincible,* but his commitment to the album was extraordinary. Rodney told me that whenever he was in the studio, he was focused, his voice was excellent, and he was always professional. By the time he was done, he would have one hundred songs to choose from. Sixteen of them would eventually make the album.

Because Michael wanted to keep working through the holidays, we decided to stay in town for Christmas of 2000, spending it at my parents' house in New Jersey. Given that his children were his top priority, Michael took Christmas seriously. This year he was determined to find a special present for my mother.

"What can we get your mother?" he asked me. "Something she'll absolutely love."

My father had never been especially fond of pets, so I knew an opportunity when I saw one. "A dog," I said. "If anyone can get her a dog without my father nixing it, it's you."

"Okay, great," he said. I arranged to have candidate dogs brought to the hotel, but ultimately I found a cute little golden retriever puppy at American Kennels, a boutique pet store that obtained animals from top breeders. I picked out accessories—a bed, a jacket, and enough food to get the puppy through Christmas.

We only had two pets when I was a kid. One was a mynah bird. She could say "Thank you!" and "Dominic!" but when one of my younger brothers started imitating the bird (instead of vice versa), my dad said it had to go. Then my uncle gave us a fish, but my little brother Dom or my sister Marie Nicole banged on the fish tank, and the whole thing collapsed.

"From now on the only animals in this house will be stuffed," my father declared. But when Michael gave my mother the puppy, he made sure to lay it on thick with my dad.

"Dominic, I examined lots of animals," Michael said. (Actually I was the one who did all the examining, but why split hairs when we both knew my father couldn't say no to Michael?) "When I saw this puppy," he continued, "I looked into her eyes and knew she was the one. I spoke to her and told her to be the best-behaved dog your family could ever own." As I predicted, my father allowed my mother to accept the dog from Michael. She was thrilled. They named her Versace and have had her for eleven years as of this writing.

CHAPTER FOURTEEN

HELPLESS

CHRISTMAS WAS NO MORE THAN A BRIEF RESPITE from the arduous process of making *Invincible*. Some of the difficulty stemmed from Michael's perfectionism, and some from his passionate wish to be ever present in his kids' lives. But a lot of it was the result of a steadily growing problem in Michael's life: his reliance on prescription drugs. And as the year 2000 drew to a close, I was increasingly worried.

It hadn't always been this way. When I'd first started working for him, I had called for doctors to attend to Michael because he was in physical pain. I had witnessed his treacherous fall on the bridge in Munich in 1999, and his chronic back problems had begun after that. It was evident that he was suffering. Various doctors prescribed a menu of pain medications: Vicodin, Percocet, Xanax, and so on. During this time, Michael also continued to be treated by his dermatologist, Dr. Klein, for his vitiligo. This treatment was itself intensely painful: it required that Michael endure having fifty needles stuck into his face, and for years—as far back as I could remember—the doctor had prescribed Demerol to sedate him during the procedure. Demerol was also the drug Michael had been given after the accident that had occurred during the filming of the Pepsi commercial, and it was the drug I had unwittingly seen doctors use to help him sleep during the *Dangerous* tour. It had all been a practical, reasonable plan for dealing with short-term pain. Or so it had seemed.

When we'd arrived at the town house on the Upper East Side during the summer of 1999, it had become clear to me that Michael's drug use was escalating. There were times when he would ask me to bring in one doctor, and then, hours later, a second doctor, to give him more of the same medication the first one had administered. Michael had always warned me away from cocaine, heroin, pot—a warning that he himself followed. But he didn't view conventional, FDA-approved drugs the same way he viewed illegal ones. He was searching for relief from chronic conditions. He was trying to get *better*. Different rules applied.

This situation became even more confusing at the town house when an anesthesiologist started showing up two or three times a week, some weeks, to help Michael sleep. I paid the man in cash, because all of Michael's medical issues had to be kept from the public and their cost off the books. The doctor was perfectly straightforward with me.

"What I do," he said, "is put Michael to sleep for a couple of hours. Then I ease him out of sleep." It was the same treatment I had witnessed after Michael's accident in Munich. The doctor would set up equipment and an IV in Michael's room, and would stay with him, the door closed, for about four hours. He said that the treatment was risky, but he assured me that he knew what he was doing. He promised that he would never endanger Michael's life. His candor and his expertise with the procedure made me trust him.

Whatever the doctor was doing seemed to be okay: after the

sessions, Michael was clearheaded and seemed well rested. Again, I witnessed but did not understand that Michael was being given propofol, a powerful anesthetic that is used in hospitals to knock patients out for surgery. This was a measure of the depth of Michael's pain, and the sleep problems that went along with it. When his schedule called for him to begin work early in the morning, without the option of sleeping in, he found it hard to fall asleep early enough to get the rest he needed in order to perform. On those nights, he couldn't sleep unless this dangerous drug—the drug that would eventually kill him—was administered. For a long time I thought it was okay and normal. I didn't think he had a drug problem. Over the years, I had grown accustomed to seeing doctors coming and going, particularly during tours, when Michael was under great stress and needed help falling asleep. I thought he was simply someone who had serious medical problems and used drugs to treat them.

However, as work on *Invincible* proceeded, I was becoming more and more concerned. I knew Michael needed drugs to cope with the pain of his skin treatments: that made sense. But the necessity for some of the other drugs seemed questionable—the drugs for his chronic pain, the drugs to sleep. Obviously I didn't want Michael to suffer needlessly, and I didn't want him to be an insomniac, yet it was clear that the continual use of the drugs was taking a toll. Michael's physical conditions were leading him down a dangerous path.

Even the doctor who administered the propofol had told me, "I can't keep doing this," which I took to be a clear indication that it was starting to be too much.

Michael wasn't a junkie. He never acted crazy or chased a high. However, I was wary of all the medications, particularly Demerol, the seduction of which Michael had sung about in his song "Morphine" on *Blood on the Dance Floor*. I did not like the effect the drug had on him. It made him dull. In a fog, he'd look at magazines and watch movies, and then when he came down from it, his mood was mad, bitter, and grumpy. This was not the Michael I knew and loved. Furthermore, the drug seemed to exacerbate his paranoia.

In addition to the effects of the drug that I witnessed on Michael, I had my own firsthand experience with Demerol. In early 2000, when we were working on *Invincible* in L.A., Michael and I were at Universal CityWalk with three-year-old Prince, two-year-old Paris, and Grace. Michael was disguised as a sheikh, and I was wearing a suit. The place was crowded that day, and it was drizzling as we strolled in and out of stores, shopping. Then, all of a sudden we looked around and Prince was gone.

He'd been missing for only a moment, and I had an idea about the direction in which he might have wandered—toward some toy or character that I'd seen catch his fancy. I sprinted that way, but the sidewalks were slippery, and I fell, twisting my left leg badly. My adrenaline was up, so I was able to stand up without noticing the pain in my leg.

A second later I saw a woman approaching, leading Prince by the hand. She said, "I saw you with this child in the store . . ." and in an instant we all surrounded him. Everything was okay again. Prince hadn't gone far or been in any real danger, but it was a scary moment.

Now that Prince was safe, it dawned on me that I was in a lot of pain. I could barely walk back to the car. By the time we arrived back at our hotel, my entire leg had swelled up. Michael got me to bed, propping pillows under my leg, and called a doctor. It was a strange reversal—*him* calling a doctor for *me*. Actually, it was strange just seeing him pick up a phone and dial it. Usually I set up calls for him. But Michael was always a good nurse. Whenever I—or anyone else—had a cold or a fever, he made sure to send out for tissues, medicine, tea, vitamins, whatever one might need. He would check in every hour to see if anything else was needed. One Christmas at Neverland, a chimp bit my little brother Dominic's finger. Even though the fire department medics had cleaned and dressed the wound, Michael convinced his doctor—who was on holiday with his family—to drive two hours to Neverland to examine my brother.

This time back in New York, the doctor came to examine my leg and declared it a bad sprain. He gave me Demerol for the pain. That was the first and only time that I experienced the drug. When Michael heard what the doctor had prescribed, he gathered magazines for me to read, put a glass of water on the bedside table, and made sure there was a vase of flowers nearby, because, he said, "You should have the energy and color of the flowers." Then he told me how I would feel when the Demerol kicked in.

"Everything's going to be beautiful to you," he said. "There will be a tingling feeling that starts in your toes and creeps up on you." It all happened just as he described. He was right. Demerol took away the pain. It also made me feel calm, relaxed, and happy.

I don't live with chronic pain, but as I dealt with my leg, which took a month to heal, I had a taste of what it was like to be hurting all the time. It was hard to sleep. All I wanted was for the pain to go away, and I could see how someone in this situation might become increasingly desperate for relief. I also saw that relief from physical pain came with a seductive side effect. If you were unhappy with your life, the drug had the power to make you forget your unhappiness. I started to believe that Michael might be confusing physical pain with emotional pain in his desperation to dull both of them.

Then, during those weeks of my recovery, Michael said something that gave me a further glimpse into his relationship with drugs. With an odd look on his face, as if he wasn't sure how much he was revealing, he said, "One thing doctors can't measure and diagnose is pain. If you tell them you're in pain, they have to treat you based on what you feel."

It was almost as if he was letting me in on a dark little secret, the excuse that legitimized the abuse of medicine. Nobody could quantify the extent of his suffering, so nobody could question the necessity for the drugs he relied on to alleviate it.

When we moved back to the Four Seasons in November 2000, the visits from the anesthesiologist stopped. But I came home one night to find that Michael had called the hotel doctor. He was going about his business—talking to Karen and making other business calls—but I could see that he was slightly disoriented. The next morning, I put my foot down.

"You don't want to end up like Elvis. Think about your children. Look at Lisa Marie and what she went through."

He didn't brush off my concern. That would have convinced me that I was right. Instead, he looked straight into my eyes. "Frank," he said with great sincerity, "I don't have a problem. You don't believe me? You don't know what you're talking about."

"It's not that I don't believe you—" I began, but then, before my very eyes, he dialed his dermatologist, Dr. Klein. He put the doctor on speaker and asked him to verify that the quantity of Demerol he was taking was safe and appropriate. Who was I to argue with the doctor who had been treating him for over fifteen years? Michael was right: I didn't really know what I was talking about. Everyone's body was different. Maybe he was so mentally strong that not even a drug could knock him out. And it was true that days went by without any visits from doctors. If he were a true addict, I asked myself, wouldn't he need to take drugs every day? I was worried, but because I truly didn't know how to judge the situation, there was no way for me to choose the right course of action.

The above conversation may have ended our discussion for the moment, but it did little to remove my concern. I was worried about Michael, but I also began to worry about the role I was playing in his medical drama. When we stayed at a hotel, he often called the hotel doctor to his room, and inevitably the doctor gave him a prescription. I would be the one who had to explain to the doctor that the quantities he was prescribing were not sufficient for Michael. He needed much larger doses. In order to maintain secrecy, some of the prescriptions were written out in my name. At first, I did such things because I thought Michael had a handle on his problem. I was used to his living outside the rules. Toys "R" Us opened for him in the middle of the night. Streets shut down to let him pass. It made sense that doctors were paid under the table. It made sense that prescriptions couldn't be in his name. It made sense that he needed far stronger doses than anyone else. He was Michael Jackson. As much as these bits of evidence were disturbing, they were just line items in a long list of the ways in which Michael lived differently from everyone else. Maybe he did need these drugs, and maybe they did affect him differently from other people. Otherwise why would the doctors be so willing to prescribe them?

Still, while being Michael Jackson may have exempted him from the rules, it couldn't spare him from the effects of the drugs. There were times when he would see a doctor and then go into a meeting. His eyes would be droopy. He would be lethargic, slurring his words. That was the worst of it: it was never more extreme. Still, if I happened to be around, I would cancel the meetings because I didn't want anyone to see Michael in such a state. But if I was off attending to other business, he would usually proceed with the meeting. After one meeting, Rabbi Shmuley, a friend and associate of Michael's, told me he was concerned about Michael and had asked him if everything was okay.

"Yeah," Michael had told him, "I had to take my medicine. It makes me a little out of it."

A few of these dicey meetings convinced me that I had to take action. But I had never stopped Michael from doing anything he wanted to do. That wasn't our dynamic. I told him honestly when he *shouldn't* do things, but I didn't tell him he *couldn't*.

My first approach was plain and straightforward.

"You're taking too much Demerol," I told him.

"You think I have a problem," Michael said, "but I don't. You saw what happened to me in Munich. I can't breathe. I can't sleep. You have no idea what it's like to be in this much pain. I have to work tomorrow. If I don't sleep, how am I going to go to the studio?"

As he himself had told me, it was hard to argue with someone's evaluation of his own pain, and frustrating as it is in hindsight, I deferred to this seeming wisdom. I accepted his answer partially because there were doctors standing behind it and partially because Michael was an exception to every rule, but mostly I accepted it because it was uttered by a man who had guided me throughout my life, and guided me well, a man who had always told me not to abuse drugs, not to become an addict. To think that he could be steering me wrong at this point was simply an impossibility.

My parents obviously weren't with Michael round the clock as I was and didn't have the same exposure to his behavior. There was one time when my mother was staying with Michael in South Africa and a doctor showed up.

"I gave him some medicine to help him sleep," the doctor told her. "Check on him every hour or so." This was news to my mother. Michael had never shown this side of his life to my family since he didn't want to make a bad impression on my parents or the younger kids. In a way that recalls his putting wine in soda cans, he didn't think what he was doing was wrong in and of itself, but he didn't want people to get the wrong impression. So my mother had limited exposure to Michael's interactions with doctors—that evening is the only one I can think of—and wasn't aware that they were part of a larger pattern. When the doctor arrived, my mother, like me, must have figured that both he and Michael knew what they were doing.

When Michael came to our house for the Christmas of 2000, he may have brought a dog, but he also brought his habits. No doctors ever came to our house, but one night my father arrived home from work and noticed that Michael was on some kind of medicine. He sat down with him and said, "Michael, this is not good for you."

"No, Dominic, it's okay," Michael stammered out. "I'm fine. I have to take it to sleep, but I'm fine." But my father was hearing none of it.

"I'm not going to tell you what to do, but please be careful. Please, please be careful. I love you, but maybe you took a little too much this time."

There was a moment of awkward silence between them before Michael finally said, "You're right, Dominic. You're right. Maybe it was too much."

After that night, Michael never took medicine in New Jersey again—proof that at the very least he knew that what he was doing was not okay with my parents. Although my parents were always able to ground Michael in reality, even they couldn't affect what he did when he was beyond the range of their influence.

Their insulation meant that they didn't see and experience the worst of Michael's reliance on drugs, and though I considered it often, I was not eager to share the information with them. In short, I didn't want to worry them more than they were already worried. Sadly, they were probably the only people with whom I could have trusted my fears. I couldn't seek out the help of experts. I couldn't talk to my friends about how to diagnose or handle a problem that seemed out of my league. I wanted to fix it, but I didn't want to risk having the news become known. One part of me felt responsible, while another felt incredibly disappointed in Michael for allowing such a thing to happen to him.

The only person I could talk to about Michael's "medicine" was Karen, his executive assistant. She had a sense of what was going on, and had been setting up his dermatologist appointments for years. Sometimes I called her, crying, saying, "Karen, I don't know what to do." Karen didn't have any more answers than I did, but she was a sympathetic, trustworthy confidante, and her behavior was always that of a consummate professional. Ultimately, Michael was his own man. Nobody told him what to do. Karen may have felt as powerless as I did, but the support she gave me during these times helped me get through them.

Michael's use of "medicine" wasn't a secret within the organization, but the people who might have noticed were business advisers; they were yes-men whose top priority was staying in Michael's good graces—not friends who'd risk incurring his wrath in the name of the truth. Their focus was generally on protecting his public image, not changing his behavior behind the scenes. That said, even if some of them *had* tried to talk to Michael—whether out of genuine concern or mere self-interest—they would probably have had the same experience as I had: Michael's justifications were extremely convincing.

During the first few months of 2001, I refused to call Michael's doctors. His response was "Okay, then I'll just do it myself," a threat that made me anxious because I was reluctant to lose track of how often he was calling. If I stopped enabling him, there would no longer be an intermediary between him and the doctors, and I was scared of what he would do if he didn't know I was watching his intake like a hawk.

I began keeping the drugs—Xanax, Percocet, or Valium—in my room so that Michael didn't have ready access to them. I didn't want him waking up in the middle of the night and automatically reaching for a pill. If I had to give him something, I would do so, but at least in this case I'd know what the hell he was ingesting. How could I attempt to reason with him if I wasn't armed with facts about the frequency of his drug usage and the quantities of the drugs he took? Would he bring in more doctors and more medicine? I worried that if I took myself out of the loop, I'd lose him entirely. Michael didn't love the idea of my monitoring his drug use, but he agreed to let me do so because he knew it would make me more comfortable with the situation. It was a compromise. I fluctuated between trying to intervene more forcefully and being afraid of losing my connection with Michael and my ability to help him if I did so.

One night, as we prepared to leave for a trip to Oxford University, we were drinking wine in his hotel suite and he seemed to be in the right kind of mood for me to initiate a conversation I'd been wanting to have with him for some time.

"I'm sorry I've been such a pain about your medicine," I said. "It's just that I love you. I don't want anything to happen to you."

Michael took a sip of wine.

"You don't know what it's like," he said. "I try to fall asleep, knowing everyone expects me to be creative in the morning, but I'm in agony. This is the worst feeling in the world."

"I guess I don't understand that you're in so much pain."

"Trust me," he said quietly. "This is not what I want to be doing. But I have been dancing and performing since the age of five. It's caught up with my body."

As unhappy as I was, I didn't have a response to this statement. How could I—how could anyone—know what it was like to have lived the life of Michael Jackson?

CHAPTER FIFTEEN

THE UNEXPECTED

BACK IN 1993, MICHAEL HAD LEARNED THE HARD way that his individual relationships with kids and their families could be a liability, but this didn't dampen his desire to help people, especially children, and it didn't compromise his sincerity in putting that desire into action. Just listen to "Heal the World," "Keep the Faith," "Man in the Mirror," "Lost Children," "Will You Be There," "Gone Too Soon," and "Earth Song" and you'll know how he used his music to give people hope, and understand the depth of his desire to do good in the world.

Then, while he was working on *Invincible*, he befriended Rabbi Shmuley Boteach. Rabbi Shmuley was a short man, with blue eyes, a beard, a yarmulke, glasses, a big belly, and an extremely long tie, with whom Michael decided to create a foundation for children in need. They wanted to bring families together. The mission of the "Heal the Kids" foundation was to inspire parents to set aside a day when they made sure to have dinner at home with their children so that the current generation of parents wouldn't take their kids for granted. Part of the "family dinners initiative" involved imparting to parents the skills they needed to initiate and engage in conversations with their children. It was simple: we wanted to remind them to communicate with their children, to listen to them, and to tell them they were loved.

In March 2001, for the launch of Heal the Kids, Rabbi Shmuley obtained an invitation for Michael to speak at Oxford University about the foundation's initiative to help children around the world and bring families together. By giving a meaningful talk, Michael wanted to demonstrate the seriousness of his commitment to the cause. It was something he took to heart and thought about deeply, not a public-relations ploy of a big star and his big ego.

At Oxford, Rabbi Shmuley introduced Michael, who hobbled onto the stage. He was on crutches, recovering from a broken foot he'd suffered at Neverland a few months earlier. I was with him when it happened, and my first reaction was to start laughing.

"Moonwalking motherfucker, you can't even walk down the stairs."

"Shut up, I'm in pain," he said, motioning for help. I managed to get him up and brought him a chair. He said something about Prince leaving his toys in the middle of the steps, then tried to walk. After a few moments he said he was fine, and I figured the whole episode was over. But as we went on with our mission—to raid the kitchen—he kept testing out the bad foot, and eventually he said, "Fuck. I don't think I'm okay."

Now, as he began his speech, Michael made a joke about walking like an eighty-year-old. But then he quickly got down to business.

"All of us are products of our childhood," he said. "But I am the product of a lack of a childhood, an absence of that precious and wondrous age when we frolic playfully, without a care in the world, basking in the adoration of parents and relatives, where our biggest concern is studying for that big spelling test come Monday morning."

He spoke about the great loss that went hand in hand with his success, talking about how important it was to him to ensure that children, all children, not be forced to grow up too soon. As much as he expressed regret for what he'd missed as a child, he also spoke about the need for forgiveness—forgiveness, in his case, of his father. He didn't want to be judged harshly by his own children, and he looked into his past and into his heart to find the love he knew his father had for him. It was a phenomenal speech, and Michael was given a standing ovation. It was a special moment for him: he was clearly moved by the experience of opening up, sharing painful memories in public, and it made him feel more connected with people—recognized and understood for who he truly was. Furthermore, he saw that connection in a larger context, as a way of bringing hope to all children.

We all saw that day as one of great possibility. Michael wanted to help children, and he had always tried to do this on an individual basis—visiting hospitals, befriending ill children, and so on—but here was a chance for him to have a wider-ranging and more powerful impact. Through a foundation, reaching out to children he would never have time to meet, he could accomplish much more than he could ever dream of accomplishing as a single, very busy individual.

As important as Heal the Kids was, however, we had other business to attend to in Europe. The day before the speech, while we were still in London, I'd gotten a call from Michael's business adviser, Myung-Ho Lee, who wanted us to meet with a European media magnate named Dr. Jürgen Todenhoefer. In the Italian Alps. Prince and Paris weren't with us on this trip and all Michael wanted was to rejoin them in New York. But apparently this was a very important meeting, so instead of heading home, we found ourselves driving higher and higher into the mountains, where spring turned back into winter and the increasingly remote villages seemed to be frozen in time.

The night before, I had, uncharacteristically, been at a nightclub with the magician David Blaine until five in the morning. I was tired and a bit hungover, and the drive was long and winding, but at last we pulled up in front of a house.

As we gathered ourselves, a few people emerged from the front door, among them a strikingly beautiful young woman.

"Look, there is some fish for you," Michael said. We hadn't grown out of calling attractive women "fish." It was unclear if we ever would.

"No, no, that's your fish," I said.

We went back and forth like that until finally Michael said, "She is perfect for you. There are plenty of fish in the sea for me."

Her name was Valerie. She was Dr. Todenhoefer's daughter.

Michael's foot was still in a cast, and the altitude was causing it to swell. As soon as we entered the house, a warm chalet, I started trying to get him a doctor. Valerie and her mother, Françoise, explained that there was only one medical doctor in Sulden, Italy, population four hundred. Her name was Maria.

Françoise called this woman and told her she really needed to come to the house. Like any busy doctor in a small ski village would have done, Maria said, "Bring the patient in, but he'll have to wait for me to attend to some other patients first."

Françoise explained that this person could not just wait in the waiting room. She would not reveal the patient's name, but she emphasized that he could not come to the clinic. It took a bit of doing, but finally Maria was persuaded to come to the house without knowing who this mysterious patient was. When she arrived, Michael was sprawled out on the couch, looking like nothing so much as a caricature of himself. The look on Maria's face when she recognized him was priceless.

After the doctor straightened Michael out, we went to the basement of the chalet to hear a presentation about the deal with Jürgen, which sounded promising. After the meeting, Michael and I went up to my room to get ready for dinner. Somehow I'd gotten my hands on two bottles of white wine. I wanted to review what we'd heard in the meeting, but Michael said, "Fuck it, let's enjoy ourselves." So we did. We talked about the beautiful home we were in, the stunning girl downstairs, and how we were going to conquer the world together. We were in a really good mood, and we ended up drinking a whole bottle of wine. Or maybe we were in a really good mood *because* we ended up drinking a whole bottle.

When it was time to go down for dinner, both Michael and I got dressed up. I put on a black suit. Michael wore a lime-green shirt with black pants and a black sport jacket. And sunglasses, which he eventually took off.

It was a very long, convivial dinner, and Michael was in rare form. He was usually very shy, but that night he made all sorts of conversation with people at the big table. We spoke about meditation, soccer, and music. In the middle of dinner, a family of local entertainers showed up to regale us with traditional folk music from their village. They looked like they'd walked straight out of a fairy tale, like characters from the Brothers Grimm who had strolled over from their gingerbread house.

Then there was the beautiful girl, Valerie. She was sitting across from me, and she had gorgeous sandy-blond hair, chiseled features, and remarkable blue-gray eyes. We didn't speak much at the dinner, but we made eye contact and silently flirted with each other from across the table all evening long.

Michael knew something was up. At the end of the dinner, when everyone arose from their chairs, Valerie and I happened to be standing under a mistletoe sprig. (I guess mistletoe is available year-round in the Alps.) Suddenly I heard Michael from over my shoulder.

"Frank, you need to kiss her!" he told me. "It's bad luck if you don't."

With that, he grabbed my head and Valerie's and pushed us toward each other. Michael was feeling exceptionally, shall we say, confident that night. I defused the awkwardness by kissing Valerie on the cheek.

It was past midnight, so Michael and I excused ourselves and returned upstairs, where our second bottle of wine was awaiting us. Everyone else went to the only disco in the village—a place called the Après Club. Michael and I drank and talked until we ran out of wine, at which point we realized that we had the munchies. We figured everyone was asleep, so we slipped downstairs to raid the kitchen, Michael limping on his one good foot. There, standing in the kitchen, was Valerie.

Valerie told us that we'd missed all the excitement. On the way to the club, her mother had slipped on the ice, hit her forehead, and been taken to the hospital. Later, Valerie had returned home to check on Françoise, but apparently she was still at the hospital with our security team. After we called to check on her condition and learned that she was fine, Valerie, Michael, and I stocked up on snacks and more wine and brought our stash upstairs.

Valerie and I sat next to each other on the top of the steps, while Michael sat in a chair in the wide corridor. We were all just talking and laughing when Michael suddenly said, "Come on, Frank, you know you want to kiss her. You should just kiss her."

I started blushing. Michael did this sort of thing to me frequently, and I was inured to it, but this time was different because I actually wanted to kiss Valerie. Trying to hide my embarrassment, I threw a pillow at Michael, stood up, and announced, "You've had enough. You are going to bed." I started to push him to his room, all the while saying, "You had too much to drink. You need to sleep."

I was joking, but Michael excused himself, saying, "I guess I'll leave you two alone." He instructed me to behave myself and warned Valerie to be careful. I knew Michael wanted me to be happy, but I also sensed, behind the teasing, a little bit of jealousy. It was great for me to be with a girl—so long as it didn't mean I'd be less available to him. I understood this, but I didn't worry about it. I was in the moment, and I was enjoying it.

Now it was just me and Valerie. She led me outside, where the air was as cold and clean as air can be. A famous mountain climber lived next door, and he kept a couple yaks in the fields behind the house. Valerie showed me the yaks, but I was unimpressed. I thought they looked like oversize cows. Still, they were a reminder that New York, with its everyday bustle and ringing cell phones and deadlines and general yaklessness, was far, far away. Valerie and I huddled near the yaks, with a blanket wrapped around us, watching the sunrise. At last, alone in the picturesque dawn, we kissed.

CHAPTER SIXTEEN

HITTING BOTTOM

T HE PROBLEM WITH FAIRY TALES IS THAT THEY exist only in contrast to the real world, and the real world isn't quite so pretty. After the magical time we'd spent in the Italian Alps, my return to New York proved to be the beginning of one of the most difficult times I would ever have with Michael.

While he and I had been shuttling back and forth between Neverland and Manhattan during the creation of *Invincible,* Court and Derek had been continuing their analysis and review of Michael's organization. In their ongoing study of his financial situation, they had discovered bad news about a deal he thought was nearly complete—the move to purchase Marvel Comics. As with the Beatles catalog, which he had acquired in 1985 in a brilliant business maneuver, Michael predicted the value of Marvel, especially the potential of Spider-Man, before the films based on the comic were made. The

Marvel deal had in fact fallen through, but Michael had been led to believe that the company was his.

Michael trusted me with his children, which meant he trusted me to the ends of the earth, but our most challenging moments came when I had the onerous task of being the bearer of bad news. I knew he didn't want to hear about the Marvel debacle, but I was compelled to tell him the unvarnished truth. Court, Derek, and I met with him and informed him that he did not in fact own Marvel Comics and never had. Michael refused to believe it, and was angry at me—at us—for delivering this news, but finally, he put his hands over his face and started crying.

"Why do I get used and lied to like this?" he kept repeating. "Why?"

It was a heartbreaking moment and pointed to an even more heartbreaking truth: as ill-placed as his paranoia could be, there were times when it was a legitimate and justified reaction. Time and time again, Michael would insist that there were forces working against him—mercenary people who wanted only to profit from their contact with him and would stop at nothing to exploit his best intentions and instincts for their own ends. Every time something like this Marvel Comics disappointment occurred, it deepened his inability to trust his closest advisers. More and more, automatic distrust became his only defense mechanism. And while the paranoia that came with it sometimes had a basis in reality, there were other times when it was nothing but paranoia.

I hated seeing the devastation caused by the Marvel Comics deal and I hated witnessing his paranoia, but I wouldn't soften or bend reality to cater to what he wanted to hear. If loyalty and truth would end up complicating and compromising our relationship, so be it. Protecting Michael was hardest when I had to protect him from himself, but for better or worse, the conviction that he needed to be protected was my guide.

IN APRIL 2001, MICHAEL WAS TRYING HARD TO FINISH up *Invincible,* but there were a lot of maddening distractions. His perfectionism was getting in the way of completing the project. He was increasingly frustrated with Sony, because they hadn't come up with the marketing plan he thought the album deserved. Meanwhile, his philanthropic instincts were pushing him to spend more time on Heal the Kids with Rabbi Shmuley. And of course, the presence of his kids continually reminded him that his heart lay elsewhere—with them.

Michael had never recorded an album under such circumstances, and it was apparent that he wasn't as clearheaded as he had been in the past, especially when one considered the impact that his medicine was having on him. *Invincible* was moving forward, yes, but it was moving slowly.

One of Michael's producers, Teddy Riley, was from Virginia, and during that spring of 2001, he wanted to return to his home studio, no doubt because he'd grown weary of producing out of that bus parked in front of the Hit Factory. Michael liked the idea of a trip to Virginia—maybe a change would do him good—so he, the kids, their nanny Grace, and the omnipresent security crew left for a two-week stay. I remained behind in New York to work. In the month since my trip with Michael to Oxford and the Italian Alps, Valerie and I had kept in touch, and we decided that with Michael in Virginia, which would leave my nights free to have dinner with her, it would be a good time for her to visit the Big Apple. (Most nights, when Michael was in town, I was with him—and if I wasn't physically with him, I was on call.)

Valerie and I had an amazing week. As soon as she returned to Europe, I flew to Virginia to give Michael a status report on our various projects.

When I got to Virginia, I was glad to see him, and he greeted me with a big hug. He was in a white V-neck, pajama bottoms, a fedora, and the same black penny loafers he always wore. For the first time in a while, he seemed very clear and focused: I could see, and was greatly relieved, that he was doing well. Grace said, "I'm so glad you're here with Michael. I think he was a little lost without you."

We'd been apart for a week, which doesn't seem like a big deal, but it was a long stretch for us. It had been nice for me to have a little break from him, only because when he was around I had to make sure everything was perfect. In his absence, I'd been able to relax in a way that I hadn't been able to do in almost two years. Michael, Grace, and the kids were staying in a two-bedroom condo that belonged to Teddy, so I slept in Michael's room. We stayed up late talking and listening to music.

Michael was happy to hear about the time I'd spent with Valerie, but he was not without reservations. He had met her and knew her family, had seen for himself what warm and gracious people they were, and he liked Valerie. But he couldn't help being paranoid, even when it came to my girlfriend.

"Watch what you tell her," he warned me. "Do what you want, but keep it separate."

I sensed that he worried that my being in a relationship might distract me from my work, though nothing could have been further from the truth. There was also clearly a tinge of jealousy. He'd had me all to himself for a long, long time. I clearly understood how he must feel, and saw that it was best to do as he asked and keep our work relationship and my private life separate. I was wrapped up in a brand-new relationship, the first serious one of my life, and already it was making some not very pleasant waves.

From the start, there were certain challenges in my relationship with Valerie. The first concerned secrecy. Michael expected me not just to keep my work with him separate, but to keep it confidential. Much as I trusted and loved Valerie, I couldn't come home and tell her what had happened at work that day. What could I say? "Michael was in the studio feeling unsatisfied with yesterday's work. I had a fight with the doctor who was trying to give him more pills. So that was my day, how did things go at your book club?"

Because of this limitation, it was impossible for me to be completely present and transparent with anyone. Indeed, if you didn't know me, you could easily have taken my extreme reticence for shadiness, yet that reserve had become a part of who I was, and even Valerie felt the distance. This is a characteristic I can't entirely blame on Michael. Certainly, it was triggered by his paranoia and the restrictions of his world, but ultimately I had to take responsibility for it. I'm much better now, but at the time I was simply shut down.

Another challenge for Valerie and me was my odd lifestyle. I was used to traveling first class or on private jets and having my own driver. After leaving my apartment in Santa Barbara empty for months while still paying rent on it, I had finally given it up and rented a place for myself in Manhattan . . . until I found it made no sense to keep that one either. I was on call with Michael twenty-four hours a day, so I just stayed in five-star hotels alongside him. If my phone rang at four A.M. and Michael said, "I can't sleep. What are you doing? Want to come over?" I always went. And let me be clear about this: it wasn't because I was stuck with a slave-driving boss. I went because I wanted to be there for him. There were no boundaries between me and Michael: the boundaries fell outside of our circle of two, and we both liked it that way.

I was in Virginia for only a couple days, but we had a really good time, being friends, catching up, and trying to forget about work for a little while. I had no idea how quickly the mood would turn.

Shortly after I flew back to New York, Michael, Grace, and the kids were scheduled to return as well. They had traveled to Virginia by train and were coming back the same way. Michael loved trains—they were a great way to see the countryside and relax—so he chartered a private railcar on Amtrak, which was souped up with bedrooms, bathrooms, entertainment systems, and so on.

Three or four days after my arrival in New York, Michael's driver, Andy, was due to meet Michael and his entourage at the train station. But before the train pulled in, I received a phone call from Skip, one of the security guys who was traveling with Michael.

"The boss is not doing well," he said.

"What do you mean he's not doing well?" I asked.

"Just be ready," Skip said. I had a sinking feeling in my stomach.

By that point in the spring of 2001, we had moved from the Four Seasons to the Plaza Athénée on the Upper East Side. (We moved a lot: we would be at this hotel for only a week.) As Michael and his entourage approached the hotel, I requested a wheelchair.

I met the car at the curb. It was evident that Michael was incapacitated. I didn't know what alcohol he'd drunk or pill he'd taken, but whatever it was, it had left him incapable of even walking.

I had never seen Michael in such a state. Never, ever in my life. He had been clear and focused when I was with him two days earlier. I had spoken to him just moments before he and the kids had boarded the train, yet now, after a mere six hours of travel, he was a mess. I was furious at everyone. I was angry at Michael for doing such a thing to himself, and at security and the nanny for doing nothing to keep it from happening, even though I knew it wasn't really their fault. Especially not Grace's. Mostly, though, I was pissed off at myself, for not being on hand to stop it.

I covered Michael's face with my jacket and loaded him into the wheelchair, and we all went upstairs: Michael in the wheelchair, Grace, Prince, Paris, the two security guards, and I. When everyone started to pile into the room, I suddenly felt like I couldn't take it anymore and I blew up.

"Grace, take the kids!" I demanded, and sent them away.

Security was trying to explain what had happened, but I didn't even let them get started.

"How could you let this happen?" I exploded. "He can't even fucking talk. His kids were on the train with him! His kids saw this! Everyone get the fuck out of this room." They had never heard me raise my voice like this before. Everyone filed out of the room, and once the door closed, I turned my attention to Michael.

I ordered some Gatorade from room service so Michael could start to hydrate. Then I turned to him and said, "Why the fuck did you do this to yourself? What did you take?"

Michael was honest with me. "I was drinking vodka—and then I took a Xanax."

"You're a fucking idiot for doing that in front of your kids," I fumed.

"It wasn't in front of them," he mumbled, which I guessed was possible. I got him situated, calm, and hydrated. Then Michael announced, "They are trying to fuck me."

"Who is trying to fuck you?"

"The Firm." He was referring to his managers. He told me to get one of them on the phone.

"You can't talk to them right now," I told him. Michael was drunk, but he was beyond persistent. Finally I relented and made the call.

"You shouldn't be speaking to anyone in this condition," I said to Michael. "Tell me what you want to say, and I'll let him know." But he grabbed the phone from me and proceeded to curse out the poor guy on the other end of the line.

"I'm the biggest artist in the world," he began. "And you're treating me like this? You're supposed to be working for me, fighting for what I want and what's best for this album. You haven't shown me a marketing plan. I've been asking for a plan for six months and I haven't seen a thing. Where's the plan? You're purposely trying to sabotage this album. You're fucking traitors." I kept trying to understand what exactly Michael thought they had done, but he was slurring his words and was not very coherent.

I'd never heard him raise his voice and yell at someone, but now he was screaming: "Fuck you, fuck you, you're fired. Stay out of my life. If you don't believe in me, there are other people who do."

Afterward, when Michael was more coherent, he explained to me what he thought was going on. He felt that Sony—his label—wasn't arranging any marketing or promotion for *Invincible,* and the Firm, his management company, wasn't fighting Sony on his behalf. Rather, he was convinced that Sony and the Firm were in cahoots, in a scheme to take control of his Beatles catalog from him. Sony, who owned a 50 percent share in the catalog, had an option to buy the rest of it from Michael. If the album flopped, Michael, in financial need, would be forced to sell his half to Sony. Michael thought it was a big conspiracy.

His anger about this situation was clearly the reason for his behavior on the train trip. Michael was almost done with the album. He had worked hard and wanted the album to have the ultimate marketing and promotion plan. In supposedly helping Sony come up with this plan, his managers would hardly be pushing for anything revolutionary. Since they weren't doing this, he didn't think they had his best interests at heart. I thought he was right . . . and yet not so right. I didn't believe that either the label or the Firm was out to get him. I just thought the guys at the Firm had no idea what to propose. They were managers, not marketers. They weren't really capable of coming up with an innovative marketing plan that they would then push Sony to implement. As for Sony, the label had already invested an enormous amount of money in the project. The hotels, the travel, the production: they were paying for everything and Michael had spent millions of their dollars. They had to cut the supply off somewhere, and the Firm probably understood this.

After Michael yelled at the hapless manager, he seemed a little better. Sometimes people go to a bar to drink and forget about their problems. Michael was doing a version of this, in his own dramatic way. After all, the stakes of his problems were quite high. The fate of the Beatles catalog was in his hands. After he'd settled down a bit, I tried to talk to him a bit more calmly.

"I understand if you need to let off steam. I'll be the first one to have a drink with you. We can have two bottles if you want. But you have to be careful. Don't you remember telling me, 'Have a drink, enjoy yourself, but if you can't walk out of a place on your own two feet, you're a bum'?"

At first, Michael tried to make excuses.

"Frank, you don't know what I'm going through. The stress. The album. People trying to take my catalog. Heal the Kids." He listed these and more obligations and issues, the to-do list that kept him awake at night, calling me and other staff members at all hours when the stress boiled over.

"This is going to pass," I said. "We'll move on. Everything's going to be fine. You need to stay focused if you want to be the best. You have to become one with yourself again." I tried to keep him calm and to reinforce what was important. "Your kids. You can't let your kids see you like that."

He winced, and took a deep breath. "I know, you're right," he said. There was a moment of silence, and he seemed to pull himself together. He gave me a hug. "I'm sorry, Frank. Thank you for being there for me, for everything you do." I pulled away to look at him. His eyes were filled with tears.

It was a rare moment. We were in the habit of saying "thank you" and "I love you" every night when we parted, but it was rare that he acknowledged the feeling between us in a deeper way. I knew I'd gotten through to him, and I hoped it meant that this—the furthest I'd seen him go—was a turning point.

I slept in Michael's room that night, almost feeling like I needed to stand watch over him. My week with Valerie seemed like a hundred years ago. Somebody with different wiring might have fallen in love and realized that he couldn't let life pass him by, that he didn't want to be in a job that required his full attention, twenty-four hours a day. But if I'd learned anything from this brief break Michael and I had had—and how miserably it had ended—it was that I couldn't have a life. I couldn't be away from Michael—not for Valerie, not for other projects, not for any reason. I couldn't let go. It was all on my shoulders. My life, my career, my relationship, they all came second because I myself came second—sometimes third or fourth. Taking time for myself was a luxury, and right now we couldn't afford it.

WE WERE SCHEDULED TO TAKE THE *INVINCIBLE* PROJ-ect to Miami, where we'd finish it up with Michael's producers, Rodney and Teddy. It would be another change of scenery that Michael hoped would help him to get done with the album once and for all. In the few days we had in New York before the move, he seemed to be himself again. Michael was excited, but with recent events still fresh in my mind, I was a bundle of nerves.

Before we went to Miami, I had a talk with Michael. I told him I wanted him to stay healthy, focused, and clear.

"Even if it's not a problem, things have to change," I told him. "You've been meeting with people, and they can see when you're out of it. People will start talking. You don't want that."

"Frank, I appreciate your concern," he answered. "But I'm still just trying to heal my foot."

I shifted tactics. "Don't fix things for me. At this point I'm not even going to tell you to do it for yourself. But you have children. You are responsible for them. I'm not saying that you should go cold turkey tomorrow. You can't do that. But let's find a solution, a plan, that will help you become healthy."

"Okay," he said, shaking my hand. He got it. I was certain of that.

I gave him a hug and said, "I'm going to go through this with you. We'll do it together."

When we got to Miami, I put his security guards on alert: because I wasn't around Michael one hundred percent of the time, they were to let me know immediately if any doctors came to see him. I was resolved to put myself between him and any doctor who might be willing to administer any medicines. I had been the one to hire these security guards: because of everything that had been going on between Michael and me, businesswise and personally, I felt more responsible for taking care of things, and that I'd become a more authoritative voice in his world.

We were staying at the Sheraton Bal Harbour in Miami Beach. Soon after we arrived, I was down in the restaurant, having a meeting with the concert promoter David Gest. In the middle of the meeting, one of the security guards, Henry, came up to me. Excusing himself, he took me aside and told me that the hotel's house doctor was, at that moment, with Michael in his room.

David overheard. He'd known Michael for many years, and knew something of his struggles with his medicine. He started freaking out. I said, "David, relax. Stay right here."

I had a key to Michael's room, but first I banged on the door. He didn't answer. I banged harder, saying, "Michael, it's Frank. Open the door." I was sick to death of these house doctors who, starstruck by Michael, heedlessly supplied him with whatever drugs he wanted.

"Hold on, I'm in a meeting," he said.

"Open this door!" I demanded, and then, without waiting for an answer, I started to use my key card.

As I slid the card in, Michael opened the door.

"Frank, calm down," he said as he let me in. Without my saying anything, he knew exactly what I thought and exactly how upset I was going to be.

The doctor looked like a quack to me. He had droopy eyes and thick glasses, and to my mind he had all the markings of a shady character. Of course, by this point I was starting to mistrust all members of the medical community. To say that I was in a state is an understatement: I was convinced that Michael was hurting himself and I was desperate to protect him. And it was on that poor doctor that I unleashed it all. As soon as I entered the hotel room, I blew up at him: "What are you doing here? What are you giving him? This is not happening."

The doctor was totally unfazed. "Relax, man," he began. "I'm not here to give your friend drugs. We're just talking."

"Frank," Michael interjected, "you're so out of line here. You have no idea what you're talking about. This man is going to help me with my foot." He told me that the doctor, Dr. Farshchian, was a specialist in the field of regenerative medicine. I wasn't buying it.

"I've said my piece," I told them both. "I'm going downstairs now. Do what you need to do. But you'd better not be giving him anything." I was pissed that Michael had gone and summoned a doctor behind my back even after we had talked about it and come to an agreement. I thought I'd gotten through to him.

The next day Michael called me to his room. The doctor was there, and Michael wanted me to apologize for screaming at him and attempting to kick him out. I explained to the doctor why I had done so.

"I may have been out of line," I said, "but you have to understand that these doctors keep giving Michael drugs he shouldn't be taking." Dr. Farshchian said he understood and thought it was very honorable of me to try to protect Michael.

The three of us sat down together.

"After you and I talked in New York," Michael said to me, "something snapped in my head. That's why I called Dr. Farshchian. Because I want to get better." As it turned out, the doctor really did specialize in regenerative medicine. Michael, who was still wearing an ankle support, needed his foot to heal as quickly as possible. But he also wanted to set up a program to detox and get off the drugs entirely.

"It's a process," Dr. Farshchian said. "Michael can't go cold turkey. But I'm going to come up with a plan to help his foot and wean him off the medicine."

I didn't know how much faith to put in this news, but I said, "Listen, I'm happy to hear this. I sincerely hope you can help."

Ironically, given the melodrama of my intervention, Dr. Farshchian turned out to be the only doctor who sincerely did his best to break Michael of his habit. He put a patch on Michael's stomach that was supposed to help suppress the urge to medicate himself. And in Miami, under Farshchian's care, Michael began to make a conscious effort to stick to the plan. Soon the doctor started traveling with us, even spending time at Neverland, because Michael wanted him there. Michael wanted to change.

I was immensely relieved. For the first time Michael had actually admitted that he had a problem and wanted to get better for his kids. I had been trying to make him see this for a long time, but unless the motivation sprang from him, all my words were useless. He had to come to it himself, and it seemed that at last he had done this. I felt the weight of responsibility on my shoulders lift slightly. Michael was getting help. And he was getting it from a doctor who clearly knew what he was doing.

At last, we were going to get Michael healthy again, and it was just in time for good news. While we were in Florida in May 2001, Michael called me to his hotel room. When I entered, he couldn't stop smiling.

"I'm going to be a father again!" he exclaimed, giving me a happy hug.

"Aw, I'm so happy for you," I said. "You deserve this."

Though Michael had been deep in the making of his album, building his family always remained a top priority. I can't say this often enough. Michael was a natural father, and he had always said he wanted ten kids. Debbie had had trouble during her pregnancy with Paris, so Michael sought an egg donor for his next child. Without Debbie as a familiar, willing volunteer, he resolved that his relationship with any prospective mother would be anonymous. I remember a day when he and I were in his suite at the Four Seasons, perusing a big binder full of pictures of potential donors. It was not unlike making our mind maps—flipping through pictures and imagining our future. The difference was that this choice was real, immediate, and serious. I flipped through the pages until the photo of one young woman caught my eye.

"This is the one," I said. I liked her eyes and her skin tone. She had beautiful black hair. The bio said that she was part Italian and part Spanish.

"You just like her because she's Italian," Michael said, seeming to dismiss my choice. But there was more to her than her Italian roots. She sounded like someone Michael would like. Describing herself, she said, "I'm a positive person. I see the good in people. I'm not judgmental . . . I'm very spiritual, do awareness work, and read a ton of books." I knew a match when I saw one, and ultimately she was the one he picked. He said, "Let's do it," and I called the doctor to give him the young woman's donor ID number.

Now, in the Florida hotel room, Michael was telling me that everything had worked out. A surrogate mother was pregnant with Michael and the donor's baby.

"This makes three of ten, Frank, three of ten," he said. Then he nudged me and added, "Come on, Frank, you're behind. When are you going to have kids? I can't wait to tell your kids stories about you. I'm going to embarrass the hell out of you."

Later, Michael told his kids that they were going to have a younger sibling. I wasn't there at the time, but afterward I saw how excited Prince and Paris were. They couldn't wait to help take care of the new baby.

AFTER YEARS OF ANTICIPATION, EFFORT, HURT FEEL-ings, frustration, and suspicion, Michael brought the finished *Invincible* album to Sony execs on June 12.

A musician's partnership with a record label is like a marriage. There is plenty of discussion and compromise over how the children should be raised. Sony was very happy with the album, and during that meeting they helped to narrow down the list of songs that would be on it. A conflict arose when Tommy Mottola, the head of Sony Music, didn't want "Lost Children" on the album because he was of the opinion that associating Michael with children would only serve to stir up unpleasant memories of the 1993 allegations. Michael thought this was absurd and was adamant that "Lost Children" stay on the album. It was a battle, but Michael eventually won.

Michael and Sony also disagreed about the order in which the singles would be released. Michael wanted to release the song "Unbreakable" as the first single, and was eager to make a video for it. (He never, by the way, used the word "video" when referring to one of his filmed songs. If anyone used the word, he would say, "Short film. It's a short film. I don't do videos.") Michael even knew exactly how he wanted to open the "Unbreakable" short film. He would be on the roof of a very tall building that was under construction, held over the edge by some thugs, and then they would let him go. He would go hurtling to the ground, seemingly dead, but slowly, his body parts would come together and he would turn into fire—dancing on fire from scaffold to scaffold as his body parts reassembled themselves. Michael envisioned creating a dance for "Unbreakable" that people would remember forever.

He fought for this vision, but unfortunately that's not how things finally went down. Sony wanted the first single to be "You Rock My World." Don't get me wrong: Michael loved "You Rock My World," but he wanted it to be the second single from the album. As a compromise, he thought "Unbreakable" should follow as the second single, but Sony wanted "Butterflies." Sony wasn't behind it. Ultimately, there were three singles: "Rock My World," "Butterflies," and "Cry," but the only one that would also be a music video was "Rock My World."

The summer of 2001 found us on the set for this video when John McClain, a long-term adviser to the Jacksons, called me. He had met with the director, he said, and reported, "They want to use makeup to darken Michael's skin for the video. They also want to fill in his nose with putty." He wanted me to suggest these cosmetic effects to Michael. He clearly didn't know Michael at all.

I was stunned. And I refused.

"John, I cannot have this conversation with Michael. There's no way he'll ever go for anything like this. If you need to, go ahead. But I'm not doing it." I didn't want to get involved.

A little while later I was back in my hotel room when the phone rang. It was Karen Faye, Michael's makeup artist, calling from Michael's room. She was supposed to be getting him ready for the video shoot, but he had locked himself in the bathroom and she had no idea why. She asked me to come to the room immediately.

When I arrived, I heard Michael inside the bathroom, freaking out and throwing stuff around. Clearly John McClain had talked to him about the proposed changes to his skin and nose, and he was extremely pissed off. I tried to get his attention, but the chaos inside the bathroom went on. Finally I heard him bang something with such force that I got worried. I started trying to break down the door.

At last, Michael let me in. He was sitting on the floor. He'd been in the middle of having his hair cut when he heard the news, so his hair was half long, half short. He was holding his hands over his face, sobbing.

"Can you believe it?" he said. "They think I'm ugly? They want to put putty on my nose? What the fuck is wrong with them? I don't tell them how they should look. Fuck them." Talking through his tears, he kept saying, "They think I'm a freak, they think I'm a freak, they think I'm a freak."

Seeing him crouched on the floor, sobbing and with his hair half cut, was devastating, to say the very least. This was the second time in recent days that I'd seen him break down. Although for years, the media had been mocking and attacking his appearance, Michael didn't always react so strongly to what people said about him. It depended on the day. Sometimes he didn't care what people thought. He was a strong guy. Then there were times when enough was enough, and he would break down. The fact that his supposed allies were criticizing his appearance at a time when he was in such a fragile state was too much for him to bear.

More and more often this man, who had once been a father figure to me, was starting to feel like a son. This wasn't the Michael Jackson that existed for the rest of the world. This wasn't Michael Jackson the icon. This was Michael Jackson at his most vulnerable, his most human, being pushed to the brink. While it had become a habit for me to force him to face painful truths, this time there was no truth at stake. There is no objective right or wrong to a person's appearance. Michael had been ignoring tabloid headlines about his appearance for years, so my advice to him now was simply not to listen.

"We can walk away from this," I said. "They need you, you don't need them."

I canceled that day's shoot and told everyone involved that we would start fresh the next day. Michael and I returned to our rooms and stayed in for the remainder of the day. Before leaving, I spoke to John McClain and the director of the video, Paul Hunter.

"John," I said, "I can't believe you said what you said to Michael. We're going to finish this project, but there will be no more conversations regarding Michael's appearance in the video. If that's a problem, we'll walk off the set for good and deal with the consequences."

I was always furious when people criticized Michael's appearance or his actions, saying he was strange or weird or a freak. I thought they should walk in his shoes, starting from the very beginning of his working childhood. From what he told me, and what I myself saw and absorbed, his life would have been a tough one for any person to have to live. Of course he'd had massive success, but the very enormity of that success put him in an extremely vulnerable position. People took advantage of him. There was nobody to trust. His money and fame were part of what made people so quick to find fault with him.

Don't get me wrong: Michael had his faults, but to my eyes, they were a good deal more mundane than the eccentricities that captivated the world. There were some hard times when I was the nearest person around, and had to take the role of the fall guy. He rarely lost his temper in my presence, but sometimes my phone would ring in the middle of the night and Michael would bring up low-priority matters, like phone calls that hadn't been returned yet, saying, "Frank, why wasn't this call made? Frank, why isn't it done yet?" If it took me a moment to wake up and he had a to-do list to rattle off for me, he'd say, "See? I told you you should always have a pen and pad next to you. Karen is always on it. You're not on it."

When those calls came I knew he was under extreme stress. The circumstances of his life were simply overwhelming. How was I to react? My response was to keep my dignity. I was the first to tell him when I thought he fucked up, and he did the same with me. For a while that worked for us.

I had many theories to explain why people needed to criticize Michael, but for the most part, seeing him as misunderstood as he was just made me angry and sad. The betrayals and cruel judgments affected him deeply. Michael's suffering was great, and while he was responsible for some of those problems, many of them were due to circumstances beyond his control.

Michael arrived in adulthood with missing pieces, with developmental deficits, as they are called, but he tried to compensate for this through the home he built, his appearance, his music, and his interests. What was Neverland but an over-the-top, even desperate attempt to find happiness? The beauty and peace to be found there were hard won. Every aspect of the ranch was evidence of how very, very hard Michael was trying to find a way to enjoy what he had achieved.

Michael's skin disease, along with his difficult childhood and the molestation allegations, were conditions or circumstances that he did his best to survive, and the plastic surgeries he had on his nose were, like so many of his eccentricities, attempts to exert some kind of control over his own destiny and happiness. Those surgeries didn't make him normal. And, in many people's eyes, they didn't make him beautiful. What they did do was make him Michael.

But the world passed judgment on every aspect of Michael's life, and while everyone loved his music, they deemed the rest of his life wacko, or worse. The trauma of the 1993 allegations still haunted him, and the fact that people condemned him as a child molester was beyond devastating. The combination of all these forces—the physical and psychological toll of his childhood, the public condemnation of his character and appearance, and above all, the pressure and desire to make groundbreaking music—was too much for one person to cope with, but because of his paranoia and his particular nature, he felt compelled to deal with much of it on his own. No wonder sleep eluded Michael, and no wonder he sought refuge in the "medicine" that granted him a few blessed hours of rest.

During the evening of the day we canceled the video shoot, Michael called me to his room. I opened a bottle of wine. We spent the whole night in our usual routine: talking, listening to music, and drinking wine. We reminisced about the past, the fun we'd had, the pranks we'd played on people. And we also spoke about the future, our immediate goals, and what we wanted to achieve.

We sat and listened to the songs he'd recorded for *Invincible*. We still had to decide which would make the album and which would not. That night, I wanted to listen to "You Rock My World," but Michael said, "Please, we are going to listen to that song all day tomorrow. Let's not listen to it now."

As we played various tracks that night, Michael said, "People will not understand this album right now. It's ahead of its time. But trust me, Frank, ten years from now they will understand and the album will live on forever."

Neither of us suspected that ten years later he wouldn't be around to see if his prediction came true. But I believed in the timelessness of his music, believed that all of his albums—*Off the Wall, Thriller, Bad, Dangerous, HIStory, Invincible*—would live forever. I believed it then, and I believe it now.

CHAPTER SEVENTEEN

THE SHOW GOES ON

ONCE THE VIDEO FOR "YOU ROCK MY WORLD" was taped, Michael began rehearsing for his thirtieth anniversary special—two multi-artist concerts at Madison Square Garden in Manhattan to celebrate Michael's thirty years in show business. The second would occur, as fate would have it, the night before two planes hit the World Trade Center.

The idea for the show had emerged over a year earlier, before we moved *Invincible* production to New York, when David Gest, Michael, and I traveled from Neverland to San Francisco on a memorabilia shopping expedition.

Michael collected entertainment and pop culture memorabilia. He had posters for Three Stooges and Shirley Temple movies, an Oscar someone had received for *Gone with the Wind,* a massive collection of Disney stuff including checks signed by Walt Disney, a first edition *Spider-Man* signed by Stan Lee, antique Radio Flyer wagons, anything to do with Charlie Chaplin, Marvel, *Star Wars,* or King Tut, and more. David shared Michael's interest, and his collection rivaled Michael's.

At the time Michael and I were at Neverland, taking a break from the album, and we arranged to catch up with a touring memorabilia sale that was coming to San Francisco. David joined us, which meant we were going to have a good time. To top it off, we decided to travel by bus—just the three of us and the driver, no security. We had wine and food, magazines, books, and movies; we were singing songs, reminiscing about the time Michael and I traveled by bus through Scotland, playing Name That Song, and so on. Michael, David, and I kept ourselves very entertained.

When we reached San Francisco, we checked into the Four Seasons. The hotel reservation was under my name, but we had people refer to us as Mr. Potter (me), Mr. Armstrong (David), and Mr. Donald Duck (Michael).

The next day we disguised Michael as an East Indian woman. He wore a sari and wrapped a turban around his hair, and we used lipstick to make a bindi in the middle of his forehead. I have to say we were very impressed with our handiwork. He was unrecognizable. So we hit the sale. There was a guy with a microphone, announcing what could be found in each aisle. I heard him trying to locate the owner of a lost purse. I said, "Michael, let's do something to David." A prank was in order.

Michael particularly liked to tease David, who, though he was balding, was meticulous about having every hair on his head in place. He'd say, "David, hair number forty-three is out of place. Let me fix it for you."

David hated this, but, well, he knew that we did it out of love.

So we marched up to the announcer and asked him to make the following announcement: "David Gest, you dropped hair fifty-four in aisle three. David Gest, you lost hair fifty-four in aisle three." The announcer wouldn't agree to do it, but he allowed me to do it myself. Michael was cracking up, and David was hopping mad, but it was all very funny.

The day after the memorabilia sale, we went to lunch at Shirley Temple Black's house. David Gest was a friend of hers, and he knew what a huge fan Michael was, so he arranged the meeting. She had a light lunch prepared for us—hors d'oeuvres and sandwiches. It was nice to see Michael and Ms. Black talking about being child stars and what they'd both gone through. Michael always connected with former child stars. That's why he was so close with Macaulay Culkin.

When we left, Ms. Black gave Michael a picture of herself as a child. From then on, Michael brought that picture with him everywhere he went.

It was on our way back to Neverland that the idea for the thirtieth anniversary special emerged. Michael, David, and I were in the back of the bus, having a little wine, when David, ever the collector, asked Michael to write song lyrics on a piece of paper and to sign it for him. Suddenly the deal maker in Michael reared its head. He wasn't about to sign a page of lyrics and give it to David unless David traded some of his newly purchased memorabilia for it. The two of them went back and forth, negotiating, and Michael managed to score a number of items. It seemed as if Michael made out better in the deal, but that day David walked away with signed song lyrics to "Billie Jean" and "Thriller," which are quite valuable today. I couldn't understand at the time why he would want handwritten song lyrics from Michael, but David was very smart. Crazy-like-a-fox smart.

On that bus ride back, David was talking about doing a special where stars would gather for a dinner or charity event to honor Michael. Listening to him, I said, "No, wait, let's do a tribute show where the stars perform Michael's songs." Michael had been performing as a solo artist since 1971, when, at age thirteen, he split from the Jackson 5. A year from now, 2001, would mark his thirtieth anniversary in the business.

David liked this idea, and there's something about his fast, authoritative delivery of decisions that is incredibly convincing.

"Michael," he said, "we're doing it. We're going to do a tribute to you. It will be the biggest show in the world." David was already running with the idea, and he wasn't stopping.

Now, the bus driver, for some reason, had decided to take the scenic route home, south on two-lane Highway 1. God knows why: it was all too clear that this bus was not made to drive on narrow, winding roads along rocky precipices with steep drops into the Pacific Ocean. We passengers were convinced we were going to die. At one point, as the bus was making a turn, we looked out the right-side window, and let out a collective gasp: there was no shoulder. All we could see was the ocean far below us. The roadside had disappeared. David cursed the bus driver, telling him he was the most incompetent driver in the world and that he, David Gest, was going to take over at the wheel. I thought to myself, *No matter how bad this driver is, I'll take him over David. With all due respect, you'll never catch me getting into a car that David Gest is driving, not for any amount of money.*

It was dusk, and Highway 1 was looking more and more like Mr. Toad's Wild Ride and less and less like a public thoroughfare. At a particularly narrow turn in the road, we encountered a car coming in the opposite direction, and we couldn't fit past each other. Traffic came to a halt. David was still swearing at the driver, and by this point he was also sweating profusely. As for Michael, he was in the back of the bus, laughing.

Maybe it was because we'd all had to face death during the drive, but by the end of the trip, David and I had sold ourselves and Michael on the idea of what came to be known as the *30th Special*. It wasn't too hard a sell, considering that we had Michael alone to ourselves, trapped for six hours. We played with ideas about the singers we'd ask to participate. At first Michael hesitated when we suggested that the show include a reunion with the Jackson 5. For all the love he felt for his family, he was careful to maintain a certain distance from them.

When my family first became friends with Michael, we saw Janet and La Toya occasionally. If they were in the New York metropolitan area, they'd come to our family's restaurant for dinner. If Janet was performing, we'd attend her show, and afterward we'd join her backstage with some cheese bread from the restaurant, which she loved. I grew up at Neverland with Jermaine's kids, Jeremy and Jordan, Tito's sons (3T), and Rebbie's son Austin, whom we called Auggie, and I always knew that generation of Jacksons better than I knew Michael's siblings.

When I started working for Michael, I asked him one day if he ever spoke with Janet.

"Yeah," Michael said. "We can go months without talking, but we're always there for each other."

And that was the sense I had as time passed, that he didn't communicate with his family members constantly, but he loved them, especially his mother, Katherine, who was his hero. His relationship with his father was always more complicated. The harshness Joe had displayed in compelling his children to perform had left its scars on Michael's psyche, but still he was grateful for everything his father had taught him. Throughout the years, Michael always had enormous respect for Randy's talent. Randy could play every instrument, and Michael put him on a pedestal when it came to his musical abilities. He said, "Randy can do whatever he wants; he can work with anyone," which was one of the highest compliments Michael could give.

Nor did he have anything bad to say about Jackie, Marlon, Janet, Tito, and Rebbie, but his relationships with La Toya and Jermaine were more complicated. He had been close to La Toya when they were growing up, but after her betrayal during the 1993 allegations, he had pulled away from her.

The situation with Jermaine was similar. There were occasions when, according to Michael, Jermaine entered into performance contracts committing Michael to appearances without checking with him first. Regardless of what really happened, Michael felt that much as he loved Jermaine, he had to stay away. Jermaine, in what must have been an angry, bitter moment, wrote the song "Word to the Badd," a swipe at Michael's "reconstructed" appearance and how he only thought about "number one." After that, Michael would have nothing to do with him.

Still, David and I thought the *30th Special* should include Michael's whole family.

"Michael," I said, "you're always talking about making history. This is going to be a historical moment. Do it for your mother. She'd love to see everyone on that stage together one more time."

"No," said Michael, "I'm not reuniting with my brothers. Jermaine's going to be a headache."

David knew the family very well. He said, "Don't worry, they're not going to be your concern. Leave it to me. I'll deal with them." By the time we got to Neverland, Michael was revved up and couldn't wait to get started.

So with Michael's blessing, David and I worked hard to turn the idea that we had on the bus ride into a reality.

From then—late summer of 2000—throughout the time when I was supporting Michael's labors on *Invincible,* David and I were constantly working on the show, lining up artists, negotiating contracts, and, eventually, negotiating a major deal to have the show broadcast as a two-hour special on CBS. The two-concert show was planned for September 7 and September 10, 2001. It would air soon thereafter.

David was great comic relief, and working with him was a blast. He taught me a lot, and although he drove Michael crazy, Michael respected and was fond of him. David was extremely superstitious about the show, and as far as Michael and I were concerned, this

214 / MY FRIEND MICHAEL

was an excellent attribute: it made him such an easy target for our childish jokes. I'd say, "David, I have a bad feeling about the show. It has something to do with the lights not working. I'm not sure where this feeling is coming from, but to be safe you need to cross the street and touch that red sign five times." Poor David was such a prey to his own obsessive fears that he actually complied with my instructions, and ran across the street to touch the red sign five times while Michael and I roared with laughter.

Once we had latched onto this particular form of harmless torture, Michael and I couldn't let it die. One night, after a meal in the private, downstairs area of a restaurant in London, we were halfway up the stairs to leave when Michael suddenly announced, "David. David, something is wrong. The show, David. Go downstairs and touch the picture three times with your pinkie. If you do that, the show will be saved."

David wailed, "You guys have to stop! This is not right!" He chastised us the whole way back down the stairs, continued his scolding while touching the picture with his pinkie three times, and was still at it as he trudged back up the stairs to rejoin us.

By the summer of 2001, the preparations for the show were in overdrive, and I had to juggle those duties with everything else I was doing for Michael. It was a tremendous amount of work, but it was rewarding on every level. Working on the concert was a turning point for me. Now my work wasn't just overseeing Michael's personal business. I was responsible for pulling off a major concert. Not bad.

AS MUCH AS I WORRIED ABOUT MICHAEL'S MEDICAL situation, I never imagined it would interfere with his performance at the *30th Special*. He was, after all, a consummate professional, and if anything, he used the medicine to help prepare himself for an appearance. But as the night of the first concert approached, Michael started seeing a new doctor. Although his health had improved under the care of Dr. Farshchian and he had successfully tapered off his medicine, there came a time when the good doctor had to return to his family in Florida. He couldn't babysit Michael, and neither could I. The doctor who replaced him was based in New York; he was a sweet man, with a nice family. Unfortunately, Michael, in spite of the progress he had made with Dr. Farshchian, requested the same old medications. Though he never appeared to suffer from any kind of stage fright, my only theory to explain this behavior was that he must have been anxious about the upcoming shows. The new doctor was naive, and complied with Michael's requests.

I tried to speak to Michael about it, but soon realized that I wasn't getting through to him and that I needed some help. His family was coming to town for their appearance in the special. There were ties that bound them—no matter how much time and distance was between them—and I hoped that they might be able to intervene. Who else could I trust? If Michael had known I was talking to any-one, even his family, about my concerns, he would have killed me. In general, he did not want his family to know his business—especially when it came to things that he was adamant about keeping secret.

But I was convinced that it was the right thing to do, and so I spoke with Randy, Tito, and Janet. Tito and I walked around the Four Seasons several times, just talking. I had a private conversa-tion with Randy. I didn't speak with Michael's mother: though I knew how much influence she had with him, it seemed wrong to burden a mother of a certain age with such distressing news about her beloved son. The family took my words seriously, and a couple of days before the show, they met with Michael to talk about the matter. But of course Michael told them that there was no cause for concern. He had barely acknowledged to himself that he had a problem. They wanted to be there for him, and they tried, but, as

I had feared, he wouldn't let his family into his life to help—not even for a moment.

Michael avoided confrontations. After the meeting, all he said about it was, "My family talked to me about my medicine. They were out of line."

I could tell from the way he dismissed the conversation that he was no more convinced by them than he had been by me. I'm sure his family persisted—Janet and I spoke several times after the special—but Michael simply pushed them away.

Though I was worried about Michael, I wasn't worried about the special. Michael was a showman. When it was time to perform, it was as if a switch in his head flicked to the "on" position, and he was transformed into another being. I knew that whatever the situation with his medicine was, it would not interfere with the responsibilities he felt he had to the audience.

When the morning of September 7 arrived, I woke up early, full of excitement. Tonight was the night of our first show. We had all worked so hard to get to this point, and I felt like I was giving birth to my first child. But there was still so much to be done before showtime that I couldn't allow myself to stop and dwell on my achievement.

Karen Smith, my devoted phone friend and colleague, was in town to help with the show. I had never seen her at a concert before; as far as I knew, this was her first, and I was happy that she'd made it. She and I had spoken up to twenty times a day over the last couple of years, but I had met her only once—when I was about thirteen years old. I had no idea what she looked like.

As it turned out, that morning I had to fetch something from her and so I went to her hotel room and knocked. When the door opened, the disembodied voice at last turned into a human being! She must have been six feet tall, a white, bespectacled brunette who struck me as the kind of straitlaced woman who'd gone to college, done all her assignments with admirable discipline, and followed

Michael in our hotel room during a trip we took to Euro Disney.

When Michael performed "Billie Jean," his transformation was awe inspiring. Part of the brilliance of the performance was that it somehow seemed simple and effortless. But behind the simplicity, I could see Michael's deep understanding of composition and storytelling.

My sister, Marie Nicole; Michael; and my brother Dominic in a hotel in Rio de Janeiro, Brazil. In this shot, he was teaching them a card game, after a long day of shooting his "short film" for "They Don't Care About Us."

Michael performing "The Way You Make Me Feel."

Listening to music with Michael at my parents' house in Franklin Lakes, New Jersey.

Michael had an incredibly silly side to him and we were always playing jokes on each other, which is why I am giving him rabbit ears in this photo. We were backstage before Michael performed a special concert for the Sultan of Brunei. From left to right: Eddie, Michael, Dominic, and me.

My mother, Connie, with Michael backstage before a concert on the *HIStory* tour.

I took this picture while Michael was on the phone at the Four Seasons Hotel, and it clearly shows the vitiligo on his arms.

Aldo, Marie Nicole, and Dominic with Michael in Brazil.

Marie Nicole and Aldo sleeping on Michael's lap in São Paulo, Brazil, during the video shoot for "They Don't Care About Us."

My grandmother Nicoletta Sottoli with Michael at my parents' house in Franklin Lakes, New Jersey. Michael loved my grandmother, and she loved him. He even went on to dedicate an award to her.

My family traveled extensively with Michael on the *HIStory* tour. It didn't matter where we were; the show was always amazing. The fans loved Michael, and the feeling was mutual.

Marie Nicole, Dominic, Michael, and Aldo sleeping in the back of the car on the way to our hotel while on the *HIStory* tour.

A candid shot that my father took from the side of the stage while Michael was performing "Beat It" on the *HIStory* tour.

Aldo, Dominic, and Marie Nicole backstage with Michael before a concert on the *HIStory* tour.

Michael would often go out in public, but never as himself. He always wore a disguise. One of his common ones was a turban-style headpiece that covered his face, like in this picture with my siblings and me at Disney World in Florida.

Getting off the Spider-Man ride at Disney World in Florida. From left to right: Dr. Alex Farshchian; Spider-Man; Joseph Farshchian (Dr. Farshchian's son); Michael; his son Prince and his daughter, Paris (in Spider-Man masks); and me.

"The Sleeping Prince," a six-foot painting that Michael commissioned, with my brother Eddie (*left*) and me (*right*) as royal guards protecting Prince as he sleeps in his throne.

Prince and Paris holding my dog, Gucci, and sitting by the fireplace at my parents' home in Franklin Lakes.

Michael performing "Smooth Criminal."

Michael and Marc Schaffel, the producer of "What More Can I Give," in the recording studio in Florida.

Michael was obsessive about every aspect of the recording process, paying attention to every detail of the song and frequently asking producers to start over from scratch when he wasn't happy with what he was hearing. It could be aggravating, but it was also brilliant.

Michael in the studio during the video shoot for "What More Can I Give."

Michael's playfulness wasn't reserved for members of my family. He liked to joke around with a lot of people and had the ability to make grown men act like kids, which explains why Marc Schaffel is giving Michael rabbit ears in this photo.

Me, Dieter Wiesner, and Michael at Neverland during a fund-raiser honoring the Brazilian artist Romero Britto, which was also Michael's forty-fifth birthday celebration. Michael was quoted saying, "It was the greatest party ever thrown at Neverland."

Romero Britto's birthday present to Michael.

Michael's birthday cake.

Michael started a food fight
earlier in the evening . . .

. . . but he was the one who ended up
with cake all over him.

Aaron Carter and Michael after the
cake fight.

Michael with Rodney Jerkins, the world-renowned music producer who worked with him on *Invincible,* at Neverland.

Michael, Chris Tucker, Aaron Carter, and Nick Carter at Neverland.

Mike Tyson and Michael at Neverland.

My family remained close with Michael up until the end of his life, and each of us feels his loss every day. This photo was taken at the Four Seasons Hotel at one of Michael's birthday celebrations. Back row, from left to right: Michael, me, my father, Dominic, Eddie. Front row, from left to right: Aldo, Prince, Paris, and Marie Nicole.

There will never be anyone like him. Ever.

all the rules. I had always teased Michael about his secretly being in love with Karen. She had such a lovely phone manner. In reality, although she was certainly attractive, she was not the blond bombshell I had envisioned. Be that as it may, we gave each other a big, long hug. We'd been in the trenches together, she and I, albeit via phone lines. Karen was the foundation of Michael's life. She had devoted her life to him.

Also on my to-do list the day of the first concert was a visit to the Bank of America offices. The jeweler David Orgell was lending Michael a diamond watch to wear for the show that was valued at about $2 million. An armed officer escorted me to the bank's offices, where I signed a bunch of papers pledging to return the watch or face some version of death by firing squad. I was due to return the watch to the bank—which was located in the Twin Towers—first thing on the morning after the second show—on September 11.

The watch wasn't the only item David Orgell had provided for the show. Michael had asked Elizabeth Taylor to attend the special as his date, but initially she declined. He was determined to change her mind.

"I know exactly how to get her to come," he said. He never had to buy Elizabeth's friendship or lobby for her presence at public events, but when the spirit didn't move her, Michael had a little trick up his sleeve, and it wasn't rocket science. All it took was . . . you guessed it . . . diamonds. When Michael wanted Elizabeth to join him for an award show, or in this case, his thirtieth anniversary special, she was there for him, contingent upon receipt of a diamond.

A couple of weeks earlier, we had gone to David Orgell in L.A., where Michael picked out a beautiful diamond necklace that must have cost over $200,000. Since Michael was such a good customer of the jeweler, he was allowed to take the necklace, along with the $2 million watch, without deciding to buy either. If he planned to keep the items, he would pay for them later. If not, he would simply return them.

We sent the necklace over to Elizabeth, and her response was swift.

"I absolutely love the necklace, Michael. And of course I will come to your show." Everybody knows how much Elizabeth loved her jewelry.

And so, back at the hotel, I carefully put the diamond watch in my little safe and decided to take a little nap before the show. I'd barely shut my eyes when I got a call from Henry, the head of security at the time.

"Karen needs to get in to see Michael," he said. "It's time for her to do his makeup, but he's not answering the door or his phone."

This wasn't anything new. I said, "Don't worry—I have the keys." I promptly let myself into Michael's suite, but quickly discovered that the door to his bedroom was also closed and locked.

It was a flimsy lock, so I broke it, sliding open the doors. There was Michael, lying in bed, sleeping. I went to wake him up.

"Michael! Do you know what time it is? You should have been in makeup an hour ago. You have to get ready! What happened?" He rolled over and moaned.

All at once I knew what had happened, and just like that, my naive belief that Michael wouldn't let his medicine interfere with the show blew up in my face. I can't begin to describe my feeling of disappointment and panic at this moment.

Shaking him awake, I asked, "The doctor was here, wasn't he?"— already knowing the answer.

In a very slow voice, he said, "Yeah, Frank. I was in so much pain. I couldn't do it. I was in so much pain."

"You did this to try to get out of the show," I fumed. "It was an excuse." Michael didn't say anything, but I saw from the look on his face that he knew that I was right and that he had let me down.

"My back was killing me, and I had to do the show," he said. "I'm fine."

We were running very late. David Gest was calling frantically.

I told him that Michael's alarm clock hadn't woken him up, so he had overslept.

This had never happened before. Michael had never taken medicine right before a show. He never let it get in the way of his work. This was a sign that his dependency had not only returned, it had grown. It was now causing him to screw up his priorities.

Somehow I had to bring his energy back, so I ordered gallons of Gatorade and some vitamin C pills from the concierge. Gradually, he seemed to return to normal, at which point I brought Karen in and she began to do his hair and makeup. I stood behind him as he was getting ready, finally able to relax and joke around with Karen. Because of the delay, the show would start over an hour late, but nobody questioned it. That's entertainment.

Before we left the hotel, I found myself with another fire to put out. It was Britney Spears. She was supposed to sing "The Way You Make Me Feel" with Michael, but she was having cold feet about performing live next to Michael.

This wasn't the first time I'd seen a seasoned professional get nervous in Michael's presence. Some even behaved like overexcited fans. Cindy Crawford had been so eager to get close to Michael that she all but pushed people out of the way and climbed over chairs to get to him. Justin Timberlake, even Mike Tyson, seemed humbled around him. Michael, who was actually nurturing a brand-new crush on Britney, was understanding about her nerves. In the business unfortunate things like Britney's stage fright happened sometimes. It wasn't anything horrible or new.

We headed to Madison Square Garden in two cars—Michael and Elizabeth Taylor in front, and Valerie and me in the car behind them. I was proud to be showing Valerie, at last, what all the fuss had been about.

By the time we entered the Garden, Michael was in good spirits. Marlon Brando kicked off the show with a speech about humanitarianism. It was a shaky start, not because anything went wrong with the speech, but because the crowd was simply too revved up. They didn't have the patience to listen to a speech, even one delivered by the likes of Brando, and booed the actor off the stage. Michael, who was sitting in front of me in the audience, tried to calm the fans in his immediate vicinity, but it was a waste of effort.

"Why would David put him first?" he whispered to me. "The people want to hear music." There was nothing we could do but wait it out. Soon Samuel L. Jackson kicked off the show by introducing Usher, Whitney Houston, and Mya, who sang "Wanna Be Startin' Something." The rest of the first hour included Liza Minnelli, Beyoncé as part of Destiny's Child, James Ingram with Gloria Estefan, and Marc Anthony.

At some point during the first part of the show, we all went backstage so Michael could get ready to appear with his brothers in the second half. Michael wasn't remotely nervous, and there were no traces of the medicine's effects. As usual, we stood in a circle and said a little prayer before he went out onstage. The prayer was pretty much the same every time: "God bless everyone up on that stage, and give us the energy to put on the best show."

Michael and his five brothers reunited for the first time in seventeen years to sing a medley of their hit songs. Then there was a brief intermission before Chris Tucker introduced Michael singing "Billie Jean."

Up to that point, I'd been backstage the whole night, but because Michael's performance of "Billie Jean" had long been my favorite, I went back to my seat in the audience. That night, more than ever, I was impressed with Michael's virtuosity. He was a natural, and the energy he was able to create was absolutely incredible. This guy made every single move look special, even just walking. Over the years, and in spite of all the mental and physical anguish he suffered, his talents hadn't faded in the least. This was the heart of what we were here for, what we were celebrating: Michael's massive talent and his years of complete dedication to his art. I watched him, as rapt as I had been during the *Dangerous* tour. So much had changed, but at this moment, this stunning moment, everything was suddenly remarkably familiar.

The second show was scheduled for three days later, the night of September 10. The first show had gone well, but during the second show everyone involved was better prepared, more confident, and more relaxed, especially Michael. There were no problems. Even so, I can't say I was able to sit back and just savor the moment. I was way too wrapped up in the details for that.

When the show was over, my family and Michael's all went up to his hotel room. His mother, Katherine, and oldest sister, Rebbie, were there. We were all excited. I could see that my parents were proud of me. They were probably about the same kind of proud as they would have been if I'd given a piano recital at age ten. That's one of the things I love most about my parents. They are proud of their kids for who we are and how hard we work. The rest is second-ary. Michael was joking around, laughing, clearly happy about the production. In front of everyone there he announced, "You have no idea how proud I am of Frank. He really worked very hard on this show." Then he turned to me and said, "Good work. You did great, Frank." That meant a lot to me. Although I was disappointed that I didn't get an official producing credit, it felt good to have Michael acknowledge my huge contribution to the shows and my instrumen-tal role in pulling it all together.

I decided to enjoy the rest of the night in my own way. So Val-erie and I met up with some German friends of ours. We went to a French bistro right down the street. Valerie knew it well and loved their *poulet frit*. By the time we arrived it was 1:30 A.M. There were only four in our group, but we must have polished off six or seven bottles of wine. It was a late, amazing night in a city that was about to change forever.

I had my alarm set for seven forty-five the next morning, because I was supposed to bring the $2 million watch back to the Bank of

America, but I slept through the alarm and awoke only when the phone rang. It was Henry, Michael's security guard. He said, "Hello, sir, I just want to let you know that planes hit the Twin Towers."

The night before, everybody had been joking about how I was going to take off with the $2 million watch. Still in a fog, I didn't properly understand what Henry was talking about and assumed it had something to do with the watch.

"Oh shit," I said. "I'm sorry. I forgot to bring the watch there. I'll go right now." I started to scramble out of bed. I was late! I had to get to the World Trade Center—to Bank of America.

"No, sir," Henry replied. "I don't think you fully understand. We need to get out of here. Do you have any idea where we can go?" I heard the panic in his voice and turned on the TV.

Valerie was next to me, saying, "What's going on? What's going on?"

In a matter of seconds, we packed up our belongings and met Michael, Paris, Prince, Grace, and my brothers Eddie, Dominic, and Aldo at the car. I suggested we head to my parents' house, but we soon realized that the bridges to New Jersey were closed.

Luckily, one of the security guards was a retired chief of police. He called someone in the police department and got us permission to leave the city. As we crossed the George Washington Bridge, we looked downtown and saw the smoke. The first tower had fallen.

"Wow," Michael said, shaking his head. He started to say something, then looked at Prince, whose eyes were wide and innocent, and closed his mouth. But I know what was going through his head, because soon after we got to New Jersey, he started talking about how he could use the song "What More Can I Give" to raise money for the survivors and the families of victims of September 11.

It had been such a calm, peaceful day. The concert had felt big, like an amazing spectacle. The next day the whole country changed. In an instant, my work with Michael Jackson felt insignificant and dispensable.

CHAPTER EIGHTEEN

INTERLUDE

ICHAEL'S RESPONSE TO SEPTEMBER 11 WAS swift and generous. He organized a star-studded charity concert called *United We Stand: What More Can I Give,* in Washington, D.C., with performances by Beyoncé, Mariah Carey, Al Green, Justin Timberlake, Destiny's Child, Reba McEntire, and twenty-seven other brilliant performers. It took place on October 21, just five weeks after the attacks. The plan was to release the song "What More Can I Give" as a single to benefit the victims of 9/11, but Tommy Mottola was worried that this would compete for attention with *Invincible.* Nonetheless, immediately after the concert, Michael brought in Marc Schaffel, an experienced producer, to make a music video. He knew he wouldn't be bound to the label forever.

Invincible was released on October 30. Despite mixed reviews—*Entertainment Weekly* thought it sounded like "an anthology of his less-than-greatest hits"—and the fact that it was coming out on the heels of a tremendous national tragedy, the album debuted at No. 1 on the *Billboard* 200 chart. In its first three months it was certified double platinum with sales of two million. "You Rock My World" peaked at No. 10 on the *Billboard* Top 100 and was Michael's highest-charting single since "You Are Not Alone" had hit No. 1 in 1995. Michael didn't read the reviews, but we got *Variety* every day and watched the album's performance. *Thriller* had sold twenty-nine million copies in its first nine months on the market. *Invincible* was an album that would have been deemed a massive success for any other artist, but in Michael's eyes, the numbers were a disappointment.

The album was done. The anniversary special was over. But there was no calm after the storm as Michael's business and legal issues, which we had kept at bay until now, came raging back with inescapable force.

For one thing, Michael's relationship with Rabbi Shmuley and Heal the Kids came to an abrupt halt. Whatever happened there, I never doubted Rabbi Shmuley's honorable intentions. I believe part of the rift had to do with Michael's advisers, who were not big fans of the foundation. Michael had been accused of child molestation, so no matter how important the work was to him, they didn't want him to be involved in children's causes. I was disappointed.

But Heal the Kids was just the tip of the iceberg. Michael's legal issues were building in number and intensity. Marcel Avram's lawsuit over the canceled millennium shows was still hanging over our heads. On top of that, there were issues with the jewelry we had borrowed from David Orgell for the thirtieth anniversary special. After September 11, I had sent the $2 million watch back to L.A. with Michael. He was supposed to return it to the jeweler, but this didn't happen. Nor was the diamond necklace he had purchased for Elizabeth Taylor paid for.

As a result, David Orgell threatened a lawsuit. Michael decided to return everything, but Elizabeth still had her necklace, of course, since she'd understood it to be a gift. One of Michael's lawyers phoned

Elizabeth's people and requested that she return it. She was not at all pleased. Not only did she love the necklace, but it bothered her that Michael hadn't made the call himself. She ended up returning the piece, but she and Michael didn't speak for about a year. Eventually, he sent her a simple letter, asking for forgiveness. Later, he would put the blame on his financial advisers, saying he had had no idea how they had handled it. Elizabeth forgave him.

Though all of this was bad, there were personal issues that loomed even larger.

Michael and Debbie Rowe had divorced in 1999, but suddenly she was back on the scene and began seeking visitation rights for the children she'd once said she never needed to meet. When Michael got the phone call from his attorney about Debbie's custody suit, he was livid. He called her every name in the book. But once he got this reaction out of his system, he just collapsed in tears.

"See, Frank?" he said. "You can't trust anyone. She was my friend. I trusted her so much that she carried my children. Now look what she is trying to do to me."

"Debbie knows you're the greatest father in the world," I told him. "This must have come from lawyers, whispering in her ear." Later, I would find out from Debbie's camp that I wasn't far off the mark. The truth of the matter was that the divorce settlement called for Debbie to receive alimony. When, because of Michael's cash-flow issues, the alimony went unpaid, Debbie's lawyers started playing hardball. They took aim at the most important thing in Michael's life: his children.

"She is going after my children," Michael lamented. "I promise you, she will never take my kids from me. No one will ever take my children away from me!" Once he paid his debt to Debbie, the issue was eventually resolved, but Debbie was miffed that Michael had failed to keep his promise to pay her alimony, and Michael was miffed that Debbie's lawyers had taken the matter so far. It put a serious strain on their relationship.

Bad as all these developments were, they didn't impact my relationship with Michael, but there was something else that did.

Ever since I'd brought in Court and Derek to clean up and oversee Michael's organization, they had been doing just that. The three of us had begun to make drastic changes in the way day-to-day business was handled that would ultimately help him cut expenses and earn more money. Between closing offices, shutting down charge accounts, and consolidating personnel all over the country, we were able to get rid of a lot of redundancy and unnecessary expenditures. There were recently negotiated contracts that were not in Michael's best interests financially or otherwise that we renegotiated or terminated.

We felt good about what we had accomplished so far, and there was more work to do, but Michael's organization was large, and it was full of very powerful players who felt threatened—even accused of impropriety—by me, Court, and Derek—three young upstarts who seemingly had the power to upset the applecart. Some of them banded together to force Michael to get rid of Court and Derek and bring them back into power. There were threatening letters from attorneys, even anonymous, physical threats against Court and Derek.

Finally, before the special, Michael's attorneys called a big meeting at the Four Seasons in New York. They told Michael he was making a big mistake, putting control of the company in our hands. Court and Derek were not present at the meeting to defend themselves, and in the end, Michael caved to the pressure and was convinced that we weren't the right people to run the business.

"Do what you're doing," Michael said to me. "Everything's under control. You don't have to get involved in my finances. Let's just stay creative."

Okay, if this was what he wanted, I washed my hands of the whole matter. Michael knew that we were right. My daily life didn't change dramatically. I was busy trying to pull off the *30th Special*.

The problem came when Michael's attorneys terminated Court and Derek's contract (which, full disclosure, included me) without paying them. Now Court and Derek were coming after Michael for unpaid fees. They were young, but they were brilliant. They were competent and had integrity. Court would go on to run an investment firm for Eric Schmidt, chairman of Google, and Derek continued as a very successful entrepreneur and filmmaker. Both advise several other ultra-high-net-worth families. I'm not saying that as a twenty-one-year-old, I knew how to fix Michael's financial problems, but if there's one thing I'm good at, it's finding the right people for any given job. I had chosen my partners well.

They had legitimately fulfilled the terms of their original contract with Michael, and they were refusing to walk away unpaid. So they sued Michael for damages. I was horrified and dismayed. They were my friends. They were suing Michael. My efforts to help him out of a mess had themselves turned into another complicated mess. And I was in the middle.

Court and Derek had first filed their lawsuit right in the middle of the *30th* concerts. Days later, in New Jersey, Michael, my parents, and I sat down in my father's office to talk about the situation, and the tension was practically palpable, with Michael leading the charge.

"Frank brought these people in," he said bluntly.

"I was trying to protect you," I shot back. "I wanted to help you."

"I know you always have the best intentions," Michael said, "but you've gotta be careful as to whom you bring into our world."

"But *you* brought them in!" I said. "I met them through you. You thought they were smart, motivated entrepreneurs."

"I know, but you brought them back, and look what they did now."

At that moment I felt horrible. I couldn't believe that my good efforts and intentions had led to such an impasse. I was really sad, even broke down crying at one point. Michael already had enough trouble. I had never wanted to add to it. I resolved to do everything I could to make peace between him and my friends.

Though I walked away from that conversation with my tail between my legs, a few days later I realized that while I had deep regret about the circumstances we found ourselves in, I had no real reason to apologize for my own actions. I hadn't done anything wrong. Neither had Court and Derek. In fact, our projections—that if he kept on the same path, without straightening up the organization, Michael would fall into a deep financial hole—came to pass, quite publicly. No: what had happened was simply that Michael had changed his mind about paying them for their good work. He had brought this lawsuit on himself. Still, I wanted to fix things.

Court and Derek's lawsuit wasn't the only turbulence I felt in my relationship with Michael. Before the *30th Special,* the people who had maneuvered to get rid of Court and Derek had also begun to turn their attention to me. To them, I was trouble, too, and they sought to discredit me.

In truth, the tensions surrounding me had been building for some time. They had largely begun when John McClain, who had grown up with the Jackson family, was brought in as one of Michael's managers, primarily for *Invincible.* John, you will recall, was the one who'd wanted me to tell Michael to put putty on his nose and darken his skin for the "You Rock My World" video. John took control, and, in what I view as a misguided attempt to clean up Michael's organization, he immediately tried to fire two people who were among Michael's most loyal supporters.

First, before the special, while we were still working on *Invincible,* John had tried to fire Brad Buxer, who had been with Michael since *Dangerous.* Brad loved Michael and would have done anything for him. He had a keyboard set up next to his bed so that if Michael called at three in the morning, he was ready to comply with any request or answer any question. When John tried to fire him, Brad called me, crying.

"I'm not going to let this happen," I promised him.

I went to Michael and said, "You can't do this." Brad never took advantage of Michael. Many people did, but Brad was not one of them. Thankfully, in this case, Michael listened to my appeal and agreed with me.

If this wasn't bad enough, what made things a whole lot worse was that John McClain then wanted to fire Karen Smith, and it seemed like he wanted to handpick Michael's assistant. I was appalled.

Again I went to Michael. "You can't fire Karen just because John McClain wants to put his own assistant in her place," I told him. Once again, Michael heeded my words and Karen stayed.

In a way, I can't blame John. Maybe he was truly trying to save Michael money. There were definitely people who had to go. But while Court and Derek were doing what I thought was needed to put Michael's organization back on track, I felt that John was fingering all the wrong people. Though these people were certainly remunerated for their hard work, their relationship with Michael went deeper than money. The same was true for me.

While I'd helped save the jobs of Brad and Karen, I had gotten in John's way twice, and for that, I knew, a price would have to be paid. When John realized that I was a problem, he turned his ax toward me. I heard from my parents that he told Michael that I was the devil and that he should get rid of me. Apparently my parents weren't the only ones to whom Michael mentioned this flagrant claim, because word got around that John McClain was calling me the devil. Instead of believing his warning about me, however, after the *30th Special,* Michael had me fire John. It bothered Michael that although John hadn't been involved in planning the concerts, he had been quite happy to take a standard manager's cut of the proceeds, and then hadn't even shown up at the events.

Still, the firing never fully materialized, and after speaking with Michael, John was soon back, muddying the waters again. As the one who'd actually been responsible for his firing, I felt like I had a big target on my back. The fact that Michael was in the middle of a dispute with two people whom I'd brought in meant that now, more than ever, I had to watch myself.

I wasn't sure exactly when trouble would come knocking on my door again, but I knew that it would, and sure enough it did.

In February 2002, my parents went to Neverland for Blanket's birth and Prince's fifth birthday. My mother was with Michael when he picked up the baby from the surrogate's representative at a hotel. They brought baby Prince Michael Jackson II back to Neverland on a private luxury bus.

"Look, look, look! How beautiful," Michael kept saying. He was thrilled.

The baby was wrapped in cozy blankets, and my mother said to his proud daddy, "He's so cuddly, he's like a blanket." Somehow, the nickname stuck. The baby was "Blanket" from then on.

Back at Neverland, even amid the excitement and joy of the occasion, Michael took my parents aside and spoke to them confidentially.

"You will not believe what Frank did," he said. He seemed furious.

"What did he do?" my father asked.

"Frank wanted some development group to pay him one million dollars before he would introduce them to me. Can you believe that?" He was very, very upset. As indeed he should have been—if the allegation had been true.

My father knows me. I'm not motivated by greed. I had never taken money or any kind of bribe (and, believe me, since I'd refused that first briefcase full of cash, I'd had many opportunities).

"I'm sorry," my father said. "I'll put my hand in the fire. I know my son. You know him, too. He would never, ever do that."

My father called me later that day to tell me what he'd heard. These accusations outraged me. I had never asked for money. I could not believe what had been said and done.

I'd had my suspicions before, but here was evidence that people were flat-out trying to destroy my relationship with Michael. I was twenty-one years old, and in my dealings on Michael's behalf, I had been fearless because the only person I cared about was Michael himself. So when I saw something that didn't seem right, I was the first one to bring it to his attention. It didn't matter if the problem seemed to be caused by someone who'd been in the business for twenty years. I didn't care. Now, though, the ante had been raised drastically. What had been targeted in this instance was the one thing I cared most about—Michael's opinion of my character.

I immediately called him at the ranch, outraged that he would even remotely entertain the idea that the accusation could be true. Michael's paranoia, which seemed to wax and wane over the years, was at a notable peak at this time. He was doubting me, and he had never doubted me before. I had never given him reason to do so.

"I would never take money," I told Michael. "You know that."

"I got this letter," Michael said. A person on his management team had written an official letter to him, asserting that I had said, "If you want to get anything done, deal with me. You don't need that guy in Florida, Al Malnik." Al Malnik was a well-respected businessman who had been advising Michael, and I thought very highly of him. It was clear to me that Al wanted to help Michael as a friend, not to serve his own interests.

"I trust and admire Al. I never said a word against him!" I protested.

When the conversation ended, I still couldn't tell if Michael believed me, yet soon I was back at Neverland, helping Marc Schaffel with the "What More Can I Give" video. We all went to David Gest and Liza Minnelli's wedding in March, but through it all I was mulling over the accusations that had been levied against me, Michael's lack of faith in my integrity, and the pall that had fallen over the friendship I had so valued for so long. Much as I tried to shake it off, the bad taste of recent events stayed with me. Between the Court and Derek mess and now the baseless accusations against my character, I had no choice but to accept that some pretty ruthless people wanted me out of Michael's world, and the stress and pressure were starting to take their toll on me.

My job or role or whatever I called my working relationship with

Michael was not a normal situation. It was not like most people's first jobs, and I knew this and accepted it, with all its anomalies. The learning curve was steep, and it was a game for serious players. Michael, as a guide, was great and difficult, but his biggest blind spots had to do with controlling his paranoia and discerning the often less than idealistic motives of those around him. Without him to guide me through those areas, I was still figuring out how to play in this murky world I found myself in. I had Michael's best interests at heart, this was something I never doubted, and it seemed like it should be enough, but it wasn't. I never imagined the degree of dirtiness that the politics would reach, and even if I had, I never thought they would come between me and Michael. I knew that Michael was going through a very rough patch, financially and emotionally, and it was hard for him to trust anyone. But my professional life with Michael was testing our personal relationship. I didn't want to lose our friendship. I thought long and hard about what to do.

After we returned to Neverland from the wedding, I told Michael we had to talk. We sat in his room, and with a heavy heart, I told him that I needed a break.

"You raised me," I said emotionally, even a little teary-eyed. "You know everything about me. And I don't want these people to come between us. I have no agenda here. My agenda is to make sure you're not being fucked by these people. But I feel attacked and accused, and it's affecting our friendship and our family. I think I need a break."

"Are you sure you want to do this?" Michael said. In truth, I didn't know what I wanted to do. All I knew was that I needed time to think and be away from this ugly situation. For so long I had lived for Michael and his work. I put myself second. It wasn't worth it anymore. I just wanted to walk away.

"People around you can't stand me, and you're believing some of the things they're saying."

"I always stand up for you," Michael said. "I have your back. I don't believe those people."

"But you did," I said. It killed me to have my integrity challenged, and I knew it could and would happen again.

"Well, you're still here," Michael said. "Nothing's changed."

"I know," I said, "but I need to do this right now."

"Listen, you have to do what's best for you, what makes you happy." Although Michael spoke calmly, I could see that he was distraught. We both were. But he understood and respected my decision, difficult as it was. Afterward we hung out, had dinner, and watched movies. A couple of days later I went back to New York.

It was March 2002. I had been working for Michael for only three years, but it felt like a century. For the first time in my adult life, I took a break.

I LEFT NEVERLAND AND WENT BACK EAST. I'D PULLED myself out of the whirlwind of Michael's life. Now it was time for me to venture out into the world, figure out what I wanted to do with my life, and establish an independent career. I stayed with my parents, partied with friends, and set up shop in a friend's office trying to figure out my next move. There were no quick answers. I made an effort to give myself time. To all appearances, I was fine, but the truth was that I was aimless. I felt lost. I had no plan. I missed my best friend. I missed my life. Working with Michael was more than a job to me. It was more than what I did. It was *who I was*.

Uncertain of just about everything in my life, I did the best thing a man can do in such a situation. In May, I took a vacation in Italy with a beautiful woman. Valerie and I went to her family's house on isola d'Elba, the beautiful Tuscan island to which Napolean was famously exiled. The escape of kings. Then we went to Florence, where we rented an apartment. We cooked, drank wine, and watched a TV show called *Saronno Famosi* (If I Were Famous) that had us obsessed.

Every escape has to come to an end, and after three weeks, I returned to New York. Back in the city, I ran into an old friend of mine, Vinnie Amen; his father and my uncle had worked in a restaurant together as teenagers, washing dishes. Both our families owned popular restaurants a few towns apart, and Vinnie and I had played soccer together (and against each other) since we were thirteen. In high school, we'd go out to dances, but we were always in a hurry to get back to our families so we could drink wine and eat antipasto, both of which were in abundant supply in our homes. Most kids went out for pizza. Not us.

I knew I wanted to be in the entertainment business, but my ideas were all over the place. Vinnie had graduated from Carnegie Mellon. He was smart and a hard worker. And he was very organized, the kind of person, it seemed to me, who could help me get my head straight. So I brought Vinnie on, and convinced him to change his last name to Black. Don't ask me why. I guess I just had a thing for last-name changes.

I never really took a break. I didn't know how to relax. Instead, Vinnie and I furiously mapped out our plans for taking over the universe.

While I was off taking my break, Michael started making news with Al Sharpton, protesting Sony Music's exploitation of him and other black artists. When *Invincible* didn't perform as Michael had wanted—after all that hard work—he pointed the finger of blame at Sony and its executives. He thought the label was failing to promote the album. Sony certainly had a conflict of interest in this instance because of their interest in the Beatles catalog. Back in the fall of 2001 when the album was released, Michael had done a promotional event at the Virgin Megastore, signing autographs while the store sold albums. I sat on one side of him, my brother Eddie on the other. I knew that Sony wanted Michael to do more such promotions—they wanted him to tour as he had with his past albums, a surefire way to drive sales—but Michael was tired of all that. He'd been touring his whole life. He wanted Sony to find an innovative way to promote the album, but he didn't want it to include their most powerful asset: him.

All along, Michael had the power to turn the situation around. But he was so outraged that he made all his efforts contingent on Sony's commitment to a marketing plan that never materialized. Ultimately, Michael's and Tommy Mottola's egos got in the way of promoting a great album.

Then, in June 2002, Michael chose to take a somewhat perverse course of action: he stood atop a double-decker bus and held up "Go to hell, Mottola" signs as it circled Sony's headquarters. Just because I was no longer officially working for him didn't mean I had to keep my opinions to myself. Protecting Michael was a habit I couldn't break. Hoping I still had some influence, I met with him in his hotel room at the Palace.

"What are you doing?" I said. "You're Michael Jackson. You're better than this."

Michael was sitting at a desk. He'd just gotten off the phone with the president of his fan club, making plans to rally his fans to his cause.

"Frank," he replied, "these people, they're trying to take my catalog. I'm tired of being taken advantage of. We have to expose them."

"I'm not disagreeing with you about Sony," I said, trying to be as supportive as I could. Try as I might, I just couldn't see the point in parading around with the signs. "But I'm against the bus."

Michael looked tired. And angry. This kind of public display was out of character for him, but he was at the end of his rope. He'd hoped and expected that this album would bail him out of his financial troubles—and the lawsuits that plagued him. He was taking out his disappointment on Sony. If I'd been working with him, I would have done everything in my power to cool him down, talk it out, and avoid this kind of undignified acting out. I don't know who had Michael's ear at the time, but if anyone was urging him to fight in this way, I thought it was bad advice. Sony's marketing plans for *Invincible* had nothing to do with race, and trying to make it seem like they were was, I believed, beneath Michael.

"I want no part in this," I said. Of course, since I wasn't working for Michael at the time, I actually didn't have to worry about having a part in it. But it didn't feel that way to me. I was, by force of habit, with Michael in everything he did. This was the first time I'd ever told him that I didn't support him.

A couple of months later, I spoke out again. I couldn't help myself. It still didn't matter that I wasn't officially working for Michael. I couldn't keep my mouth shut.

By that point Michael and I were talking and seeing each other as each of our travel schedules allowed. Trudy Green, Michael's manager at the time, told him that at the upcoming MTV Music Awards, which fell on August 29, 2002, Michael's forty-fourth birthday, MTV wanted to present him with an "Artist of the Millennium" award, an honor they had never bestowed before. When Michael first mentioned it to me, it sounded great. He was honored and excited about receiving such an award.

Then I heard from a friend of mine at MTV that no such award existed. In reality, MTV had no plan to offer any such award to Michael. They were just going to bring him out to celebrate his birthday. When I told Michael what I'd heard, he called Trudy immediately. He put her on speaker so I could hear the conversation. Trudy told him that I didn't know what I was talking about. And, she wondered, what was I doing talking to MTV in the first place? (I was being a pain in her ass, that's what I was doing.)

"Yeah," Michael said, "Frank probably mixed up his facts."

When he got off the phone, he told me that I needed to be sure of what I was talking about before I started making problems. So I had no choice but to believe that the information I had been given had been wrong. When I got back in contact with my friend at MTV, though, he stuck with his story. According to him, it was Trudy who'd been misinformed . . . or worse. Again, I reported to Michael what I had heard. But Michael had had enough. He wanted me to stay out of it.

"You are still young," he said. "You have to listen and learn from these people and from myself. Trust me, Frank, if I did not have a good feeling about this, I would not do it. It's the Artist of the Millennium. It's important."

"Okay, no problem," I said. But I couldn't let it lie.

The night of the award show, I warned him for a third time. Now Michael had really had it with me, and he told me so in no uncertain terms. Even if I'd still been working for him, it would have been pushing him too far. He was excited about this award and he didn't want to believe the negative things I was saying about it. I hoped I was wrong, but I was pretty sure I wasn't. Michael had invited my whole family to attend the ceremony, but I couldn't bear to watch it all go down live and in person.

"I think it's best that I not go with you tonight," I said. "You go. We can meet up afterward." So Michael took the rest of my family to the auditorium, and I went off on my own.

That night, when Britney Spears introduced Michael, she called him "the artist of the millennium" and presented him with a birthday cake. There was no award. Nonetheless, Michael delivered the acceptance speech he'd prepared all the same. It was a very awkward moment, and as always, the press had a field day with it.

I had hoped that I was wrong about the award for Michael's sake, but at the same time I felt vindicated when the truth came out. The next day, an MTV spokesperson would say that "some wires got crossed," and I was pretty sure I knew exactly where they'd crossed: Trudy's office.

Michael and I met up in his suite after I got home. He wanted to share some Jesus juice before bed. He opened the door in his pajama bottoms, V-neck shirt, and fedora. As he led me into the living room, he said, "Yeah, yeah, yeah," which was his way of saying, "You were right." He had already ordered two bottles of white wine.

As we sat and drank our first glasses of wine, I said, "I will say this once, and then we do not have to talk about it . . . I told you so." I smiled.

"Yeah, yeah," Michael said, "don't let it go to your head."

"Too late," I said, and we both started laughing.

Outspoken though I was, Michael was used to it and didn't seem unduly bothered by it. Therefore I was shocked when a few weeks later, out of the blue, I received a letter from Brian Wolf, one of Michael's attorneys. The letter said that he was writing on behalf of Michael to tell me not to contact any of Michael's friends or associates that I'd met during my tenure with Michael, and further informing me that I was not to represent myself as working for Michael. It was a very official-looking letter, and on it were copied Michael, John McClain, Trudy Green, John Branca (another of Michael's lawyers), and Barry Siegel (Michael's accountant). *What the fuck?*

My mind reeled for a moment, but then it came to me. I knew exactly what the letter was about, and it had nothing to do with Michael and me. I had been here before: this letter was just like the one in which I'd been accused of soliciting bribes, but this time, instead of a letter full of lies going to Michael, it had come to me. No bones about it: this was a bully letter. The people cc'd on it were still pissed off at me for questioning their decisions and threatening their positions. Now they were attempting to cut me off from Michael altogether.

After all our years together, this is what it had come to.

PART THREE

MICHAEL AND ME

CHAPTER NINETEEN

METHOD TO MY MADNESS

A FEW MONTHS HAD PASSED SINCE I RECEIVED A letter telling me not to contact Michael. But in November 2002, I came to Los Angeles to meet with the producer Marc Schaffel in order to discuss one of my projects. Around that time, in spite of the letter, I had arranged for Michael to receive a Bambi Award for "Pop Artist of the Millennium" in Germany, and Marc was creating a video montage for the song "What More Can I Give." I knew that Michael would be leaving soon for Europe, so I called him and said, "Michael, I'm in L.A. I'd love to come see you." He invited me to Neverland, where I still had a bedroom and an office filled with clothes and papers and God knows what else.

It had been a while since I'd seen Michael and I was looking forward to the visit, but I'd brought with me the letter I'd received from Brian Wolf, and it was burning a hole in my pocket.

After I arrived at Neverland and was escorted to the library, Michael entered the room and we gave each other a big hug. We were both happy. Michael was enjoying some downtime. He seemed clear and relaxed, and I hoped that the paranoia and anger that had surrounded the release of *Invincible* were at last behind him.

Michael thanked me for arranging the Bambi, and after we'd caught up on each other's life, I got to what was, for me, the elephant in the room.

"I have to be honest with you. I'm really upset and disappointed about something. Why would you send me this letter?" I handed it to him. He read it. As he read, his eyes widened.

"Frank, I didn't send you this letter," he said matter-of-factly.

If I had any suspicion that he was feigning ignorance, it was dispelled by what he did next. He picked up the phone and called Karen.

"Why would anyone send a letter to Frank without my permission?" he asked. "Have Brian Wolf call me immediately."

Karen hadn't been cc'd on the letter. This was the first she was hearing of it, but she was Michael's central contact—the person he called whenever he wanted something to happen immediately. Michael was fuming. He was clearly telling the truth: he had never seen the letter before. Phone still in hand, he said, "Do your parents know about this?"

"Yeah, I told them."

He immediately called my father and said, "I had no idea this letter went out to Frank. I didn't authorize this, and I'm really sorry it happened."

Ever since I'd received the letter, I hadn't known where I stood with Michael. Now, after seeing his reaction, I gave a huge sigh of relief. We were back to normal. Still, it was clearer to me than ever that I had made some powerful enemies in the organization who were gunning for me, and while this was apparent to Michael, too, he wasn't about to fire anyone over it. Sure, I thought the letter was grounds for dismissal, but over the years there had been plenty of things I'd thought he should do, and if my past experiences had taught me anything at all, it was that Michael made his own decisions. So I took a deep breath and let the matter go.

This proved easier to do than I expected because I was dying to see the new baby, Blanket: I couldn't believe he was already eight months old. Michael led me to the nursery, the same nursery that Prince and Paris had used before they moved to their own room on the same floor. Blanket was sleeping, and as Michael and I looked in on him, I could see that he was just as adorable as both Prince and Paris had been at that age. As I glanced over at Michael, the look I saw on his face made it apparent that the eight months since Blanket's birth had done little to lessen his enthusiasm for fatherhood.

Back in the library, Michael casually mentioned two people who, unbeknownst to us, would soon cause him untold damage. The first was a man named Martin Bashir, who, as Michael told me that day, was filming a documentary about him. Michael's friend Uri Geller, a psychic who was famous for his ability to bend spoons with his mind, had proposed the idea to Michael, telling him that doing an interview with an esteemed journalist like Bashir would help people understand him, and thereby revolutionize his image. Michael was particularly impressed when Uri told him that Princess Diana had done an interview with Bashir.

In the years to come, numerous people, including myself, would question every aspect of Michael's decision to participate in Martin Bashir's documentary. Truthfully, I don't know the exact conversations that convinced Michael to go ahead with the documentary, but based on how Michael spoke about it with me, I imagine Uri and Bashir appealed to his ego, saying, "Michael, look at all these other people who've been interviewed. You're the King of Pop. The world knows your music. They should get to know you. Your life is fascinating and enlightening." Skeptical though he may have been, that sort of appeal would have had an effect on him. In addition, it's not hard for me to see Michael hoping that the documentary would put an end to the "Wacko Jacko" press that had plagued him for so long. After all, I can imagine him thinking, people had responded so well to the self-revealing speech he delivered at Oxford University; perhaps by allowing himself to open up again, a wider audience would see and understand who he really was.

"Are you sure about this?" I asked him, not even trying to hide my unease.

Michael was used to my cautiousness.

"Yes, Frank," he said. "I have everything under control. He can't release anything without my approval." Hearing these words made me feel somewhat reassured. He'd given Bashir, who would be accompanying him to the Bambi Awards, a lot of access, but at least Michael would be able to approve the final product. After all, if he himself had final say, how could he be misrepresented?

"Frank, do you know who you just missed?" Michael asked, pulling me away from my doubts about Bashir's intentions. "Gavin was up at the ranch a couple of days ago."

The Gavin he was referring to was someone I hadn't thought about in a while, which was probably for the best. In 2000, when Gavin Arvizo was ten, he was diagnosed with cancer. Michael had heard of his case and arranged a blood drive for him. In response, Gavin voiced his wish to meet Michael, so Michael invited him to Neverland on several occasions that year. At the time the boy walked with crutches and was weak from chemotherapy. Michael tried to help him by giving him affirmations to say every day. He encouraged him to fight his cancer, promising him more visits to the ranch if he got well enough to handle the travel. In addition to the moral support that Michael provided, he also gave financial support to Gavin and his family.

Gavin was only one of many children Michael tried to help, and while most of the kids' parents were extremely kind and thankful for his efforts, Gavin's parents had given me the creeps from day one. Initially I couldn't put my finger on anything specific; it was just a gut feeling. Then, however, on one of the family's first visits, David, the father, asked me for money to buy a car. Though they'd only been to Neverland a couple of times, Michael had already done a lot for the family, and I knew that handing out cash was a very tricky business.

"We're not going to give you money," I said, "but I'll talk to Michael about whether there's an extra car we can lend you." As it turned out, we actually found one—Michael gave the family a beat-up truck that wasn't being used. But the very fact that I had had such an exchange with David was a big red flag. After all that Michael had gone through with the Chandler family, I was always wary of families wanting to exploit him.

The next year, 2001, Michael had been busy with *Invincible,* and as a result, he had kept his distance from the Arvizo family. When we were working on the album in New York, Gavin went to considerable lengths to reach Michael, calling me, calling security, and persisting until Michael finally took the call. We put the phone on speaker, and as Michael and Gavin talked, we could hear the mother whispering in the background.

"Tell him we want to see him," she hissed. "Say 'You're our family. We miss our daddy.'" Gavin parroted back the lines his mother fed him.

At the time I reiterated my anxieties about the Arvizos, telling Michael in no uncertain terms, "I don't want to have anything to do with this family."

Michael agreed with me but felt bad for Gavin and his siblings.

"Be nice," he responded with a dismissive wave of his hand. "It's so sad. Parents ruin everything. Poor Gavin's an innocent kid."

Given his experience with Jordy Chandler, Michael and I were both wary about the dangers that continued contact with a family like this posed for him. But at the same time Gavin was a safe distance away, and Michael had a hard time refusing to take a phone call from a boy who claimed to love and need him. He didn't see what harm could come of it.

Throughout 2001 and 2002, I hadn't heard Gavin's name mentioned, and as far as I could tell, Michael hadn't seen the family again—until now. When I heard that Gavin, who was now thirteen, had recently been at the ranch, my skepticism instantly came flooding back.

"So I didn't miss much, then," I said.

"Come on, Frank," Michael said, echoing his words from two years earlier. "He's a sweet boy. Don't blame Gavin for the faults of his parents."

"Yeah, you're right," I said begrudgingly. I agreed with him in principle, but Jordy, too, had been a victim of a parent's ulterior motives. The similarity wasn't lost on me. In an attempt to convince me of Gavin's good intentions, Michael explained that the boy had even done an interview with him for Bashir in which he told the camera how much Michael had helped him.

"Great," I said, genuinely pleased by Michael's words. "Everyone should know how much you help people all over the world." Wary as I was about the Arvizos in general, the videotape appearance sounded okay to me, since again Michael had approval over the final product. Since Michael had been so supportive of Gavin and his family, there didn't seem to be anything wrong with Gavin saying so on camera. If Michael had liked what he heard, what harm could it do?

Famous last words.

Before Michael left for the Bambis in Germany, he was due to make a court appearance to deal with Marcel Avram's charges regarding the millennium concerts. As so often happened, Michael didn't sleep at all the night before his appearance. The next morning he was a mess—unshaven, his hair disheveled. He walked from the car to the courtroom wearing tape over his nose. The tape helped him breathe, but it wouldn't have been most people's choice for what would inevitably be a much-photographed few minutes in the public eye.

The media accounts that immediately followed the appearance focused on Michael's appearance. Despite the fact that Michael had been open for years about his struggles with vitiligo, journalists speculated that he was trying to be white, and then, taking this kind of offensiveness to a new low, they also made the ridiculous claim that his nose was falling off from excessive plastic surgery.

This wasn't the first time that the press had reacted so dramatically to Michael's appearance. Maybe it was because I saw him so frequently, but strange as it may seem to some people, to me he looked normal. His progressively lightening skin color was not mysterious to me, and it shouldn't have been to anyone else. This was an issue he'd addressed numerous times, but somehow the media still had not gotten it, or they simply didn't believe it. As for his plastic surgeries, most of them had been performed before I started working for him, and I never paid much attention to what happened after that. We never talked about the surgeries—not because the subject was forbidden but because he never brought it up, and I accepted Michael as he was. If he wanted to make changes, that was up to him. I imagine that what was ultimately behind it all was his damaging childhood. Michael often mentioned his father making fun of him for having a big nose when he was a kid. I thought Michael was perfectly good-looking before he changed his face, but I believe that when he looked in the mirror, he didn't see what everyone else saw. Now his nose was smaller, but it still looked big to him. But his appearance wasn't his focus during our time together, so even if he did have a distorted perception of himself, it didn't dominate his thoughts and energy. It didn't represent a broader disconnect with self-perception and reality. Truth be told, I dismissed the surgeries as a rather typical Hollywood practice. If he went too far by some people's standards, well, that was par for Michael's course.

Maybe I was too close to the situation, and it was hard to have perspective, but when I'd watch Michael struggle with his body image, it was hard not to have sympathy for what he was going through. My focus was on helping Michael through the negative reporting in the media. He hated the dumb, even cruel stories the tabloids made up about him. He liked his nose, and as far as his appearance at the Avram-case hearing was concerned, that people would actually say in all seriousness that his nose was about to fall off was absurd.

"Why are they giving me such a hard time?" he said. "See, Frank? See what they do to me? If it were anyone else, this would be perfectly normal. You can buy these strips at any pharmacy. They help me breathe. If it were anyone else, people wouldn't say a word, but they're always trying to find something wrong with me." He was right, of course, but that wasn't going to stop the tabloids from speculating about the oddity behind his wearing a nasal strip to court. And in spite of the media's comments, he kept wearing them. When it came down to it, he wasn't going to change his behavior just because he was mocked for it.

The next day, before they left for Germany, Michael introduced me to Martin Bashir. I looked him right in the eye and shook his hand firmly, as I do when I meet people. His handshake was weak—never a good sign. And as I looked deeply into his eyes, it seemed to me that he kind of looked away.

"So I heard you're doing an interview. Tell me about it," I said.

"It's going to be great," Bashir said. "We're going to show Michael in the best light." He was perfectly polite, but somehow I didn't trust him. There was no way that I could foresee, however, the devastation his so-called documentary would cause Michael, nor that my own reputation would be threatened in the process.

Though he was leaving for Germany, Michael encouraged me to stay at the ranch until his return. That sounded nice. I was still meeting with Marc Schaffel, who was in relatively nearby Calabasas, so Neverland was a perfect base for me.

Shortly after Michael's departure, a video from Germany appeared on the news. It showed Michael dangling baby Blanket over the balcony of a hotel room. Instantly I was fixated on the screen, my jaw dropping open in shock. I could see the headlines forming before my eyes, and the only thought going through my mind was *This is not going to be good.*

I tried to imagine the context of the video. The fans had wanted to see Blanket, so Michael complied with their wish and held the baby out to them. He lifted the baby over the balcony edge to give them a better view. When Blanket kicked his little feet, Michael drew him back over the rail, maintaining, I was sure, a firm grip on him, as he always did. He would never drop him, not inside the hotel room, much less outside on the balcony. He would never do anything to harm his children or put them in danger. Michael had been communicating with his fans from hotel balconies for years and years. To him, it was perfectly natural to share his beloved new son with them.

At the same time I instantly saw how careless and dangerous Michael's behavior was. It was foolish to hold a baby at such a height, even with a firm grip. If Michael had seemed unhinged when he was riding a double-decker bus around the Sony building or when he'd worn "tape" on his nose, now he appeared to have gone off his rocker entirely by putting his baby son at risk.

From the outside, things looked bad. This was a serious lapse in judgment, and coming as it did on the heels of the speculation about his physical appearance, people around the world started to seriously doubt his sanity. I knew better than anyone that Michael was not crazy—eccentric yes, but certainly not crazy. But the truth of his mental state didn't matter. What mattered was how that moment on the balcony would be perceived, and what began as a lapse in judgment quickly turned into a full-fledged tabloid scandal. Like most of Michael's mistakes, this one was caught on camera and recycled for judgment a hundred million times. Now instead of focusing just on his nose, people were focusing on whether he was fit to be a father.

There is no doubt that Michael did a lot of good in the world, and although people were aware of this, it was still difficult for them to reconcile his generosity and philanthropy with the rest of his public persona. This contradiction was on full display the next night when Michael accepted his Bambi Award, and Marc Schaffel's video of "What More Can I Give" premiered. Taken by itself, it should have been an emotional, dramatic moment in the long career of a talented musician, but occurring right after the Blanket incident, it didn't make any sense. Those two events juxtaposed, with elemental force, the conflicting images of Michael that the public was struggling to reconcile: on the one hand, the strange-looking, unpredictable man who kept his children's faces covered and recklessly dangled one over the balcony of a hotel; and on the other, the musical genius who sought to use his work for the benefit of all of humanity. People loved the second Michael, but for some reason they felt compelled to assume the worst about the first.

After Michael and the kids came home from their trip, we had dinner, put the kids to bed, and talked about the trip. Michael had issued a statement saying that the dangling episode was a "terrible mistake," and he had gotten "caught up in the excitement of the moment," but that he would never "intentionally endanger the lives of [his] children." He said much the same to me, but with a slightly defensive tone.

"The fans wanted to see the baby," he said. "I showed them. I had a firm grip. I wouldn't ever put my child in danger." Period. End of discussion.

But of course, just because it was over for Michael didn't mean it was over for everyone else. For many people, the damage had been done.

Soon after his return from Germany, Michael had another court date for his ongoing lawsuit with Marcel Avram. His last court date had been followed with a round of press regarding his appearance.

Then there was the hotel incident with Blanket. And now, Michael skipped a court date claiming he was suffering from a spider bite on his leg. There was much speculation in the press as to whether this spider bite was real. In truth, Michael had checked himself into the hospital to receive nutrients and vitamins by IV, as he sometimes did. In the middle of the night, he'd woken up to go to the bathroom. Forgetting where he was and that he was still hooked up to IVs, he stood up. The needles tore out of his leg. By way of explaining his absence in court, he showed his injured leg to the judge and made up the story of the spider bite. The judge looked at it and didn't say anything. He probably knew it wasn't a spider bite but, judiciously, decided to let it go.

DESPITE THE MEDIA CIRCUS UNLEASHED BY THE HOTEL incident with Blanket, Christmas 2002 at Neverland was a great one. My family was there, as were Omer Bhatti and his family, a family from Germany whom Michael had befriended, even Dr. Farshchian and his family. We all loved big Christmases with lots of food and presents and kids running around.

For years we had the same Christmas ritual. In the months leading up to the holiday, Michael and I always shopped for the gifts together, sometimes enlisting Karen to help find what we had in mind. We stored everything we'd purchased in the firehouse. (Because of Neverland's size and isolation, insurance regulations or California state law required that it have its own fire department on the premises, with a small fire truck boasting a Neverland logo and full-time firemen.) The staff would wrap all the presents, labeling each with its contents. Then, on Christmas Eve, Michael and I would write names on the presents and put them under the tree in preparation for the morning. On Christmas Day, we all slept in, knowing that we wouldn't open the presents right away. Because my father always had to work on Christmas Eve, present opening never began until his flight from the East Coast arrived. Everyone got dressed up . . . and then waited. Prince and Paris were very patient, not only because they were used to the ritual, but also because their father had worked hard to instill in them a sense of gratitude and respect. When my father arrived, Michael took his place beside the tree, handing out every gift, Santa style.

A few days after New Year's Eve, when everyone was gone, Michael and I spent the day watching movies and doing some work in his office. In the late afternoon we decided to go down to the wine cellar, which was our hideout—it was cozy and secreted away below the game room. The door looked like part of the wall, so you had to know where it was in order to find it.

Down in the cellar, we opened a bottle of white wine. I love my red wine, but Michael preferred white. That afternoon Michael and I spoke about the future, and what our goals for this next year were going to be. From the start, his words were bold and ambitious, but I could tell that he meant them.

"I'm going to get myself out of this financial mess that everyone has made of my life," he stated.

This was the first time Michael had openly admitted to me or, as far as I knew, anyone, that he was in financial trouble. The fact that he was finally willing to face the music was astounding.

"Yes, it's their fault," I replied. "But it's your fault, too, for allowing it to happen."

"I needed to focus on being creative," he said, with a hint of defensiveness in his voice. "You know, when I made *Off the Wall* and *Thriller,* I was the one who signed every single check that went out to anyone. Everything ran smoothly back then."

"What changed?" I asked, honestly wanting to know. "Why did you start letting other people handle your money?"

"It got too big. It was too much for me to handle," he said.

While it may seem obvious, this admission was one of the only times I'd heard Michael accept responsibility for the situation he was in and for the dysfunction of his organization.

Even now, years later, it's hard to understand why he was so hesitant about discussing problems like these—not just with me, but with anyone. Of course, some of it boils down to his distrust and paranoia, but to me those were only part of the equation. As a person who struggled with accepting reality, Michael could isolate himself, he could stay in Neverland, he could indulge his whims, but all those elements of his lifestyle were enabled by his finances. Saying out loud that the latter were in disarray made it a real problem, one that he could no longer avoid.

When Al Malnik took charge of his finances, he assured Michael that he would get him out of the mess he was in. But Al told me that he also had said, "Michael, I can't do this unless you do your part." Now it looked like Michael had taken Al's words to heart. He had to, in order for things to change. The continued well-being of his children, more than anything, compelled him to face what he had been avoiding for so long.

We spoke a bit about my plans. I was still trying to figure out what I wanted to do with my life, but now Michael said, "You know I can always use your help. You're the one who left, remember? We can work together again."

"Yeah," I said, "we could do that." In that moment I realized that the majority of people in the organization with whom I'd had issues were no longer in the picture; Michael and Al Malnik had gotten rid of them. Michael and I didn't make any decisions, but the reality was that when I was with him, at Neverland, I was back in my comfort zone, and I'm not just talking about the wine cellar, although I was certainly comfortable there. I knew the ins and outs of the job, exactly what Michael wanted and how he wanted things done. Working with Michael was my comfort zone.

It was a nice moment. Both of us, in some ways, were at a crossroads. I had branched out since leaving Michael's employ, but now I was finding my way back. He had finished an album and was facing the hard truths of his financial situation while feeling energized about starting anew. We sat in the quiet familiarity of the wine cellar, ruminating over our lives, how we had gotten where we were, and where we would go from here.

SHORTLY AFTER NEW YEAR'S DAY, MICHAEL AND THE kids headed off to Miami. Michael suggested that while he was gone, I should have guests over if I liked. For years, I'd loved sharing Neverland with a few pals, and when Michael left for Miami, I had a kind of bold idea: I decided to invite Court and Derek to the ranch.

While this sounds presumptuous of me (and perhaps it was), I had my reasons. At this point the lawsuit the two men had brought against Michael was in the process of being settled out of court. Much as I knew Michael was at fault for reneging on the stipulations of the contract, his view of it was simpler. Over Christmas, when we'd talked about it, he said, "You brought them back into my life. Now they're suing me, so fix it."

"Okay," I'd said to him, "I've been talking to them behind the scenes. I'll do everything I can to make sure the deal goes through and the lawsuit goes away."

"Tell them I said hi," Michael added, "and that it's a shame things went this far, but I still like them."

Both sides were eager to reach an agreement. Michael liked and respected Court and Derek, and the feeling was mutual. I knew this, and thought that the lawyers were dragging out the suit unnecessarily, as lawyers always want to do. As the opposing legal teams went back and forth, I'd been talking to both sides. I kept reassuring Court and Derek that the delays weren't coming from Michael, and I kept reminding Michael that he'd signed a contract with them and owed them money.

I felt partially responsible for the situation. A settlement deal was on the table, but it hadn't been signed. Michael always said that the best way to close a deal was to bring people to Neverland. It occurred to me that if Court and Derek returned to the ranch as guests—as they had been many times before—they would see that the days of acrimony were over. Of course, it was pretty radical to invite people who were suing Michael to be guests at his house, and I knew that Michael's attorneys would think I was nuts. But lawyers tend to ignore the human element of negotiation.

And so, for better or worse, Michael's two former associates came up to the ranch. We had a nice evening. Court and Derek made it clear that they hadn't really wanted to sue Michael. They just wanted to be paid for the work they had done. They left the ranch understanding that Michael liked and respected them and hated that things had come to such a pass. Everyone agreed that we should all put our emotions behind us and move ahead with the settlement.

That night, while Court and Derek were still there, I got a call from Michael. He was in Miami with Aldo and Marie Nicole, my brother and sister, and he'd heard about Court and Derek's visit.

"Frank, why the fuck would you have those people at Neverland?" he demanded. Michael only swore when he was really upset or joking around. I was pretty sure he wasn't joking around this time.

"You don't understand. Let me explain . . . ," I began. I thought it would be obvious to him that I was doing as I had promised—trying to make the lawsuit go away. Why else would I invite the two to the ranch? How could this possibly serve my own interests? "Don't you realize your attorneys want to drag out this conflict?" I said to him. "The longer it takes, the more money they make. You can settle now, and get it over with."

Not surprisingly, Michael's attorneys saw it differently, and as far as they were concerned, my invitation and the subsequent visit only reinforced their belief that I was a liability. Thus they pounced on the opportunity to share their view with Michael, convincing him that I was screwing up. Apparently I was the only one who thought I had saved him millions of dollars by soothing egos and encouraging Court and Derek to compromise.

I tried to calm Michael down, but he was very angry. As I spoke, I could hear him talking to my siblings in the background, saying, "You won't believe what Frank just did." When I started to explain myself, he interrupted: "Why don't you ever listen?"

"Why don't *you* listen?" I retorted. Then I gave up. "Fuck this. Obviously you don't see what I'm trying to do for you. I'm your friend, just trying to help because I feel responsible for the mess. But go ahead. Keep spending attorney fees fighting something that doesn't need to be fought. I give up." I hung up the phone.

I'd known all along that what I was doing was unorthodox, but I was confident that it would work. I didn't really care what Michael's attorneys—or anyone else in his organization for that matter—thought of me. I had already made enemies in the organization by speaking out and doing what I thought was best for Michael. Michael was the one who mattered. Maybe it sounds like hubris, but I genuinely thought what I was doing was within the bounds of his instructions. He had instructed me to do whatever it took to reach a settlement. He had said he didn't want to hear any more about it, he just wanted it done.

I went out to the pool and ran into Macaulay Culkin, who happened to be visiting the ranch with his friends Mila Kunis and Seth Green.

"What did you do?" Mac asked, before adding, "Michael's really pissed at you." Wow. News travels fast. I realized Michael must have just spoken to Mac.

"I really don't care," I said, and explained to Mac what was going on.

Ten minutes later I got a call from Karen. In her calm, sympathetic way she said, "Michael thinks it's best if you leave the ranch."

"No problem. I'm packing my bags."

I'd been kicked out of Neverland.

I didn't say anything to Court and Derek. When Michael was angry, he sometimes went for the jugular. I had a feeling he'd calm down. Sure enough, ten minutes later my phone rang again. It was Michael. I was angry and I was hurt, and I was going to let him know it. Before he could get a word out, I cut him off.

"You want me to leave? I'm leaving."

"I don't want you to leave," he said calmly. "I want you to come to Miami tomorrow."

I'm not sure why, but I wasn't surprised to hear this. Fighting with Michael was like fighting with my father, right down to the siblings chiming in on the other end of the line. Angry as I was, I knew just from hearing his voice that he'd forgiven me. Looking back on it now, I have to wonder how we could go from one emotional extreme to the other in a matter of seconds. We'd been screeching mad at each other just moments before. And yet neither one of us could find it in his heart to stay mad. It just wasn't the nature of our friendship. We always forgave each other.

So what did I do? I hopped on a plane and flew to Miami.

CHAPTER TWENTY

MISUNDERSTOOD

ON THE PLANE TO MIAMI I WROTE A LONG LET-
ter to Michael in which I explained my reasons for bringing
Court and Derek to Neverland. I reminded him that he
had told me to do whatever I could to fix the problem. I said that I
was following his advice about how to close a deal. I had used my
judgment, as he always asked me to, and unorthodox as my actions
may have been, they came from the right place. The letter was not
just a self-defense. I also waxed sentimental about our friendship. We
had been in such a good place when we talked in the wine cellar, and
now look what happened. I told him how painful it was for me to
be in the middle of the lawsuit, how much the feelings of both sides
mattered to me, and how determined I was to see the case resolved.
I wanted to prove to myself that I could clean up the mess I'd inad-
vertently helped create.

The last time Michael had been this angry with me dated back to the days when people had told him lies about me asking for money in order to arrange a meeting with him. Now he was mad about something that I had in fact done. I had taken things too far in my eagerness to smooth things over. I had overstepped my bounds because, truth be told, I was having trouble maintaining those bounds. I was young, and I thought that my good intentions gave me carte blanche.

When I arrived in Miami, I asked a security guard to give Michael my letter. Half an hour later, he called me to his room, gave me a big hug, thanked me for the letter, and apologized for overreacting, a rare occurrence.

"You gotta tell me these things," he said. "You can't just bring people to my home like that. You have to tell me."

"I'm sorry about this, about all of it," I said. "All I wanted to do was clear up the situation with Court and Derek. It never should have come to this. Upsetting you was the last thing I wanted."

"I know you always have good intentions, but you have to be careful. If anything goes wrong, it comes back on me," he said. "I love you, Frank. Let's put this behind us and move on. Your brother and sister are in the other room. Go say hello to them."

From this point on, we picked up where we left off at Neverland. Michael was in great spirits, and it felt like we had, so to speak, rebooted our relationship. Unfortunately, just as we'd put out one fire, another one was beginning to flare up.

The Bashir interview, *Living with Michael Jackson,* was set to air on TV in Europe on February 3, 2003, and in the United States three days later. A couple of days before the telecast, Michael decided he wanted to talk to a foreseer. He put some faith in spiritual advisers, and he was curious about what lay ahead. At Dr. Farshchian's recommendation, we called a woman from abroad on the phone. Michael, the kids, Dr. Farshchian, and I listened while Mrs. Farshchian translated what the spiritual adviser had to say.

There was bad news right off the bat.

"You will be accused," the spiritual adviser said. "There is someone trying to sabotage you. Be careful." Then she said, "You have nothing to worry about, everything is gonna be fine in the end." Michael freaked out. He couldn't bear the idea that he would be accused of wrongdoing, that his intentions would be questioned again. He stormed to the bathroom and proceeded to smash a mirror, which, to me, said everything that needed to be said. He was furious at the image of himself, the reflection that people saw. He'd brought in Bashir to help people begin to know him better, but instead the spiritual adviser was predicting that things would only get worse before they got better.

Soon enough, those predictions came to pass. First, though, came the sabotage.

For months, Michael had been saying that he had final approval over the content of the documentary. The plan, therefore, was that Martin Bashir would come to Miami to prescreen *Living with Michael Jackson*. But Bashir didn't show up at the designated time, and then kept delaying his trip. By the time it was clear that he was giving us the runaround, it was too late. We tried to halt the interview from airing in the United States, but it was past the point of no return.

Aldo and Marie Nicole, who were still in Miami, watched *Living with Michael Jackson* in his suite, but Michael refused to join them: he never liked seeing himself on TV. As my siblings watched, Michael popped in and out of the room asking them, "Are you sure you want to watch this? Why do you want to watch this?"

Meanwhile, I watched the interview in my hotel room with Dr. Farshchian, feeling a mixture of dismay and resignation. The interview didn't capture the Michael I knew, to say the least. That Michael was humble. He was a humanitarian. He was a talented musician. He put money and energy behind children's causes. Bashir didn't care about any of that. He was a sensationalist, interested only in the shallower elements of Michael's life: shopping excesses and plastic surgery.

All that was bad enough, but by far the most damaging part of the interview was the moment when Bashir spoke with Michael about his relationships with children. Michael had brought Gavin Arvizo into the documentary because he wanted to be understood, and sharing his efforts to help children in need would help bring about this understanding. Gavin was a prime example of this.

In Bashir's interview, Michael was shown holding Gavin's hand and telling the world that kids slept in his bed. Anyone who knew Michael would recognize the honesty and innocent candor of what he was trying to communicate. But Bashir was determined to cast it in a different light.

What Michael didn't bother to explain, and what Bashir didn't care to ask about, was that Michael's suite at Neverland, as I've said before, was a gathering place, with a family room downstairs and a bedroom upstairs. Michael didn't explain that people hung out there, and sometimes wanted to stay over. He didn't explain that he always offered guests his bed, and for the most part slept on the floor in the family room below. But, perhaps most important, he didn't explain that the guests were always close friends like us Cascios and his extended family.

One of the biggest misconceptions about Michael, a story that plagued him for years following the Bashir documentary, was that he had an assortment of children sleeping in his room at any given time. The truth was that random children never came to Neverland and stayed in Michael's room. Just as my brother Eddie and I had done when we were younger, the family and friends who did stay with Michael did so of their own volition. Michael just allowed it to happen because his friends and family liked to be around him.

What Michael said on Bashir's video was true: "You can have my bed if you want, sleep in it. I'll sleep on the floor. It's yours. Always give the best to the company, you know." Michael had no hesitation about telling the truth because he had nothing to hide. He knew in his heart and mind that his actions were sincere, his motives pure, and his conscience clear. Michael, innocently and honestly, said, "Yes, I share my bed. There is nothing wrong with it." The fact of the matter is, when he was "sharing" his bed, it meant he was offering his bed to whoever wanted to sleep in it. There may have been times when he slept up there as well, but he was usually on the floor next to his bed or downstairs sleeping on the floor. Although Bashir, for obvious reasons, kept harping on the bed, if you watch the full, uncut interview, it's impossible not to understand what Michael was trying to make clear: when he said he shared his bed, he meant that he shared his life with the people he saw as family.

Now, I know that most grown men don't share their private quarters with children, and those who do so are almost always up to no good. But that wasn't my experience with Michael. As one of those kids who, along with his brother, had any number of such sleepovers with Michael, I know better than anyone else what did happen and what didn't happen. Was it normal to have children sleep over? No. But it's also not considered especially normal for a grown man to play with Silly String or have water balloon fights, at least not with the enthusiasm Michael brought to the activities. It's also not normal for a grown man to have an amusement park installed in his backyard. Do these things make such a man a pedophile?

I'm quite sure that the answer is no.

The bottom line: Michael's interest in young boys had absolutely nothing to do with sex. I say this with the unassailable confidence of firsthand experience, the confidence of a young boy who slept in the same room as Michael hundreds of times, and with the absolute conviction of a man who saw Michael interact with thousands of kids. In all the years that I was close to him, I saw nothing that raised any red flags, not as a child and not as an adult. Michael may have been eccentric, but that didn't make him criminal.

The problem, though, was that this point of view wasn't represented in the documentary. Listening to Michael talk, people who didn't know him were disturbed by what he was saying, not only because his words were taken out of context but also because Bashir, the narrator, was telling them they *should be* disturbed. The journalist repeatedly suggested that Michael's statements made him very uncomfortable. Michael was quirky enough without the machinations of a mercenary newshound, to be sure, but there's no doubt that Bashir manipulated viewers for his own ends. His questions were leading, the editing misguiding. As I watched the broadcast, it seemed to me that Bashir's plan all along had been to expose Michael in whatever way he could in order to win the highest ratings he could for his show.

Luckily, Michael frequently had a videographer traveling with him, and his personal film crew had also recorded the Bashir interviews as they occurred. Those tapes of the unedited footage showed a bigger picture—providing insight into the kinds of questions Bashir had asked, how he had framed them, and the views he offered at the time about Michael's life (which, not surprisingly, were all glowingly positive). In this larger context, it is instantly apparent just how opportunistic Bashir had been, editing the material in the most sensationalistic way imaginable.

This was true not just in the documentary itself, but also in how Bashir promoted it. For example, in an interview about the documentary, Bashir said: "One of the most disturbing things is the fact that a lot of disadvantaged children go to Neverland. It's a dangerous place for a vulnerable child to be." This however, was a far cry from what he'd said to Michael during the actual interview. Talking about inner-city kids visiting Neverland, what he'd said to Michael was, "I was here [at Neverland] yesterday and I saw it, and it's nothing short of a spiritually [uplifting] kind of thing."

Even the *New York Times* recognized Michael as a victim of what their reporter called "his interviewer's callous self-interest masked as sympathy." Michael answered Bashir's questions honestly, explaining his unusual but harmless inclination to play with kids as just another one of their peers. He had been open about this in past interviews, telling *Vibe* that the inspiration for the song "Speechless" came to him after a water balloon fight. In that interview he said, "Out of the bliss comes magic, wonderment, and creativity." Nobody questioned Michael back then.

Yet what Michael never seemed to be able to grasp was how the public's shifting views of him caused the intentions of people like Bashir to change along with them, making him vulnerable to the scandal-hungry media in a way he had never been before. Through the baby-dangling episode, the masks his kids wore on their faces, the confusing marriages, Michael went about his life much as he always had: on his own terms. He lived in his own world and behaved with the same naïveté that had been a characteristic of his for years. He had no awareness of how his words and actions would be perceived, nor did he ever really try to understand how his behavior appeared from the outside.

For years, he'd been generally avoiding the press, but when he passed a newsstand or caught a glimpse of a magazine that referred to him as "Wacko Jacko," he was hurt.

"What makes me Wacko Jacko?" he would ask. "Am I wacko to you?"

"No, you're not wacko," I would say. "Just crazy. And your breath stinks."

We'd laugh it off, but we both knew that Michael cared what people thought. It upset him, but he always saw the aspersions that were cast on him as examples of false judgment, never true reflections of who he was. In a way, I agree with him. I saw this dynamic at work in the Bashir interview the same way I saw it in the treatment of the infamous baby-dangling episode. Brief glimpses of a life, taken out of context, can easily be manipulated to make a person look crazy. None of us are subject to the type of harsh scrutiny that Michael faced every day of his adult life, and sadly, the effect of that scrutiny only served to intensify the eccentricities.

Perhaps the biggest tragedy of the Bashir video was that Michael had entered into it with the best of intentions. His willingness to do the interviews showed his optimistic belief that given the right context and the right explanation, the public would love and accept him as he was. In the same way he wanted to straighten out his finances by taking them back under his control, perhaps he had also wanted to straighten out the false impression the world had of him by communicating directly with his audience. He had hoped the Bashir interviews would connect him with his fans and the wider public. He wanted to be open about his life and to be understood. He thought the interview would be something he could be proud of, something he would show to his children one day, a part of his legacy.

Instead, for the second time in his life, the world took Michael's greatest passion—helping kids—and accused him of doing the opposite—hurting kids. I thought this was beyond fucked up. It was horrible. I had known Michael for most of my life. He was the most magical person I had ever met. And the world had a completely distorted picture of him when it came to his relationship with children.

When we learned about the press's and public's responses to the video, Michael was disappointed more than anything else.

"I trusted Uri," he said. "I trusted Martin Bashir. I can't believe this is happening. It's all twisted. I was supposed to have final edit."

Michael never spoke to Uri Geller again, but he blamed himself for trusting the wrong people. He didn't say so, but I saw in his disappointment the realization that, at the end of the day, the disaster was his fault.

In the past, Michael's disdain for people's opinions would have prevented him from responding publicly, but now that he had children, he was determined to set the record straight. He issued a statement saying that he thought the video was a "travesty of the truth." Then Michael and I spoke to Marc Schaffel. Michael knew Marc would get the job done, but he also liked working with him because he could joke around with him. Marc added levity to every challenge.

We decided to make a rebuttal video, showing the real Michael and exposing Bashir's vicious misrepresentations.

My focus now became using that footage Michael's crew had taken in order to clear Michael's name. I immediately began working with Marc on *The Michael Jackson Video: The Footage You Were Never Meant to See.* We scrambled to release a film that showed Bashir's manipulative editing, then the real version, so viewers could see exactly how Michael's words had been blatantly twisted to show him in a negative light.

Around this time, Marc Schaffel asked Debbie Rowe if she wanted to participate in the rebuttal. Marc had known Debbie for years. In fact, it was through her former employer, Dr. Klein, that Marc and Michael had first met. Debbie wasn't happy with the press coverage of Michael, herself, and the children. Some stories—like the baby dangling—clearly put Michael's competence as a father into question. Others criticized the family structure, accusing the children's mother of heartlessly selling her offspring to Michael. Debbie was frustrated that she was unable to defend her decisions and Michael's parenting skills because of the confidentiality clause in her divorce decree.

"I don't like how the media is portraying Michael," she told Marc. "I don't have a problem expressing that if Michael would be willing." So Michael and Debbie signed an agreement giving her permission to speak about him as a father. It didn't dictate what she would say; it merely freed her to voice her opinions in an interview with Marc. It had been a big point in the divorce that she be forbidden to say anything about the kids and Michael, so she wanted to be sure that Michael was sincerely willing to let her speak. And so, before the interview, Debbie and Michael talked several times. Their conversations were friendly, and I could see that Michael was glad to be back in touch with her. They had been friends for years before the media and the lawyers complicated matters. In her interview, Debbie said, "My kids don't call me Mom because I don't want them to. They're Michael's children. It's not that they're not my children, but I had them because I wanted him to be a father. I believe there are people who should be parents, and he is one of them."

In the midst of working on the rebuttal, we moved back to Neverland from Miami to deal with the post-Bashir media onslaught. There was so much going on that I called Vinnie, who came to help me out. And Gavin Arvizo and his family joined us as well, seeking a haven from the ravenous press. It reminded me of how the media had surrounded our house when Eddie and I returned from the *Dangerous* tour. I didn't love the Arvizo family, but having been through a similar experience myself, I thought they deserved some shelter from the storm.

At Neverland, the Arvizos did an interview for the rebuttal video in which they stated, in no uncertain terms, that Michael's behavior had never been inappropriate. The boys said that when they had slept in Michael's bed, he had slept on the floor. On February 20, the L.A. Department of Child and Family Services interviewed the Arvizo family in response to a complaint filed by a school official who had seen Bashir's video. The entire family, one by one, again asserted that Michael had never initiated any inappropriate contact, and the case was dismissed.

Three days later, on February 23, 2003, our rebuttal aired, just three weeks after the telecast of Bashir's documentary. It was well received, and there was a flood of press condemning Bashir's journalistic tactics.

We were all doing our best to clear the air, but aside from these efforts, I have to say that the Arvizos were a handful to have around. They were rude and disrespectful. The children drove golf carts wildly around the property, crashing them into things. (I guess they mistook Neverland for the bumper car pavilion.) The behavior of Gavin's mother, Janet, was erratic. She was either demanding to be chauffeured somewhere or locked up in her room all day, ordering various services from the staff. It was like babysitting, and because I was working on other projects, Vinnie was stuck with the thankless task of dealing with it.

Janet Arvizo's bizarre behavior soon became a subject of concern for me and Vinnie. The first cause of alarm came when she approached Vinnie and accused one of Michael's business advisers of sexual harassment.

"He wanted to sleep with me," she told Vinnie. "He was all over me, ask anyone." Vinnie came to me, deeply concerned. It was a shocking and upsetting accusation, and he and I took it very seriously. When we started to investigate, however, talking to the accused and to the people who Janet claimed had seen the adviser's behavior, it quickly became evident that nothing had happened.

Another time, I was at an Outback Steakhouse with Janet and her three kids when the two boys announced that they wanted to be in the movies when they grew up.

"Do well in school," I told them, "and one day we'll help you fulfill your dreams."

Then Davelin, their sister, declared, "I want to be a dentist." Janet leaned over and whispered in the girl's ear, and suddenly Davelin started to cry. Then, in a somewhat less than convincing manner, she announced, "I want to be an actress, too." I had no idea how soon all the Arvizo children would be practicing their acting skills.

Soon thereafter, Vinnie was at a mall with Janet and her three children, Gavin, Star, and Davelin. They saw some celebrity pass by and suddenly Janet was galvanized into action.

"Gavin!" she called. "Gavin, go up to him and tell him who you are. Tell him you're the kid in the Michael Jackson video."

Gavin wasn't especially eager to do this, and turning to Vinnie, he said, "I don't want to go up to someone I don't know and tell him I'm friends with Michael Jackson." He successfully stalled until the celebrity had disappeared into a store. But Vinnie told me the story later. Janet clearly liked her children to cultivate friendships with celebrities. All I can say is that it was gross.

Then came the night when Gavin and his brother Star pleaded with Michael to allow them to sleep with him.

"Can we sleep in your room tonight? Can we sleep in your bed tonight?" the boys begged.

"My mother said it's okay, if it's okay with you," Gavin added.

Michael, who always had a hard time saying no to kids, replied, "Sure, no problem." But then he came to me.

"She's pushing her kids onto me," he said, visibly concerned. He had a strange, uncomfortable feeling about it. "Frank, they can't stay." He was absolutely aware of the risks he ran in agreeing to share a room with these boys, especially because this was the very issue that had provoked such a furor in Bashir's video.

"No," I said flatly, "they can't stay. Their family's crazy."

But Michael didn't know how to say no to Gavin, so he asked me to handle the situation.

I went to the kids and said, "Michael has to sleep. I'm sorry, you can't stay in his room."

Gavin and Star kept begging, I kept saying no, and then Janet said to Michael, "They really want to stay with you. It's okay with me."

Michael relented. He didn't want to let the kids down. His heart got in the way, but he was fully aware of the risk. He said to me, "Frank, if they're staying in my room, you're staying with me. I don't trust this mother. She's fucked up."

I was totally against it, but I said, "All right. We do what we have to do." Having me there as a witness would safeguard Michael against any shady ideas that the Arvizos might have been harboring. Or so we were both naive enough to think.

That night we watched movies and hung out. At some point Michael and I went down to raid the kitchen. We came back to the room with Doritos, vanilla pudding, some cans of Yoo-hoo, and peanuts.

Michael had just given Gavin a laptop as a gift, and when we returned to the room, we were greeted by the sight of a thirteen-year-old boy ogling an Internet porn site. I don't think the kid had a porn habit or anything. He was just a teenager exploring the Web for the first time. He kept saying, "Frank, look at this. Frank, look at that."

I didn't pay much attention, but when Gavin and Star tried to show Michael something on the screen, he said, "Frank, they can't do that. I don't want this coming back on me," and left the room.

At some point I made the boys stop watching the porn. I hadn't introduced them to it, suggested it to them, or shown them anything in any way. As far as I was concerned, they were just being boys . . . doing what boys with access to the Internet tended to do. Later, Michael came back to the room and put on a movie, some kind of cartoon.

That night, he and I made our beds downstairs, but the two boys wanted us in the same room with them, so they took the bed and Michael and I slept on the floor next to it.

The next day Michael told me it was a good thing that I had stayed in the room.

"I don't like the mother," he said.

"I'm happy you finally see it. She's sick in the head," I said.

"I always saw it," he told me, and then, repeating a sentiment I'd heard many times, he added, "These innocent kids suffer because of the parents."

As the unsavory aftermath of the Bashir interview continued, we decided that it might be wise to take a vacation. We would all relax on the beach while everything died down. Marc Schaffel had access to an apartment in Brazil, so we decided to go there. Personally, I was looking forward to the trip. Beaches . . . girls . . . a two-week vacation. I couldn't wait to leave. But Gavin had doctors' appointments, and it became clear that the Arvizos were reluctant to go, so we canceled the trip.

Eventually, the media circus died down. One day, Janet called and said the children's grandfather was sick and they wanted to go see him, so in March 2003, we sent them on their way. They had been at the ranch for less than a month, and everyone at Neverland—both residents and staff—was delighted to see them go.

THERE WAS RAMPANT SPECULATION IN THE MEDIA about the huge emotional toll that Bashir's video had taken on Michael, with reports declaring that he'd never recover from it, but this absolutely wasn't so. In the months following that savage telecast, Michael was in great spirits.

For the next six or seven months he stayed at Neverland. Vinnie and I were there, too—back and forth between Neverland and Marc Schaffel's house in Calabasas—and everyone had a fun time. Energy was high. At Neverland, Vinnie and I were helping the filmmaker Brett Ratner put together a longer version of the rebuttal, *Michael Jackson's Private Home Movies,* which incorporated footage from the Bashir video, Michael's own videos, and new interviews with Michael's friends and family in the hope of creating a true portrait of him—the one he had wanted to show the world. Every now and then, Brett would bring some beautiful women to visit, which kept things interesting. The actor Chris Tucker, a close friend of Michael's, was living in a huge bus parked on the ranch.

We filmed the whole project on-site—we didn't want anything to leave the ranch; so there was an entire production team at Neverland—me and Vinnie, Brett Ratner, Marc Schaffel, and others. Together we weeded through hours and hours of footage.

When it came to putting together the private home videos, Michael was hands-on. We showed him cuts; he gave notes. He'd always been interested in filmmaking, and the collaboration gave a much-needed boost to his sense of controlling the way he was represented to the world and ensuring that it was accurate.

On April 24, 2003, when *Home Movies* aired on Fox as a two-hour special, many viewers tuned in and Michael felt vindicated by the ratings. Of course, positive images don't get as much attention in the press as the negative ones. We had to rely on people taking the opportunity to form their own opinions. We hoped they would.

After the home videos were released, Vinnie and I began work on a new project. As part of the effort to fix Michael's image, we were going to relaunch Michael's brand and merchandising. If handled properly, the licensing of Michael's name and image could be a billion-dollar business all to itself. Though I'd used the break I had taken from working with Michael to explore other opportunities, the truth was that this was where I most wanted to be. It was exactly the role I wanted to play.

A lot of my enthusiasm came from knowing that there was a great team in place. Al Malnik continued to run Michael's operation from Miami, and let me tell you, Al ran a tight ship. Everything went through him. But regardless of where we were, everyone shared the same vision. We may have subsisted on two or three hours of sleep a night, but it didn't matter because everyone's adrenaline was up. We were all working hard and having fun. We believed in Michael and what we were doing. It felt like a machine had been put in place in order to rebuild Michael's business, career, and image.

Meanwhile, Michael was off his medications, and Dr. Farshchian had him on a program of vitamins and supplements that looked like it was working. Al Malnik was running his organization, and he was on track to get Michael out of every lawsuit. Al put Michael back on track to start making money again. He was the best thing to happen to Michael. Michael was traveling back and forth to Miami, where he met with Al and checked in with Dr. Farshchian. He was working on a new album—*Number Ones,* a greatest hits album. In the studio, he'd been playing around with some new tracks, one of which, "One More Chance," would end up on the album. He spent time with his kids. Blanket, who was a year and a half that summer, was developing a funny personality. He loved Spider-Man. (Michael loved Spider-Man and all Marvel comics, so of course his boys did, too. That year, for Prince's sixth birthday, he had thrown a Spider-Man party.)

"I'm Spider-Man," I'd tell Blanket.

"No, I'm Spider-Man," he would reply in his funny little-kid voice.

"But I'm Spider-Man," I would insist. After going back and forth like that for quite a while, Blanket would pretend to fire web at me.

"Frank, you have to fall," he would say. "I got you."

"No, you missed," I'd say. He'd shoot again and this time I'd crumple to the ground, struggling against the invisible web as I went down.

The press during that period portrayed Michael as a man trapped in a downward spiral. The bus-top protests against Sony, the baby dangling, the Bashir video, his changing appearance . . . To the outside world, these issues had come to overshadow Michael's life, his talent, and his career.

But to those of us who actually knew Michael, such a portrayal couldn't have been further from the truth. There was no sign that he was losing control, no sign that he was heading downhill. In reality, he was more vibrant and engaged than he had been in years. I felt like he'd turned a corner, and I wasn't the only one. Everyone around him felt the same way.

If you compare the footage of Michael in *Home Movies* to what you see of him in Bashir's video, you can get a sense of what we saw: how much happier he was during that spring and summer at Neverland. In *Home Movies,* he is back to being himself again. He is joking around and happy. His whole demeanor is relaxed. Working on music in the dance studio with Brad by day, he had dinner and socialized with everyone at night—Brett Ratner, Chris Tucker, me, Vinnie, some of Michael's cousins, and Brett's beautiful female guests. He would join us in the game room or lead everyone to the movie theater to watch music videos. Sometimes in the past, when Neverland was full of people, Michael had retreated to his bedroom, but not this time. He was absolutely present, a proud host.

On August 30, Michael celebrated his forty-fifth birthday with his fans. He didn't perform—the fans performed his songs—but when he thanked them, he mentioned some of the projects that he was looking forward to: the new merchandising line that Vinnie and I were developing, resort hotels, and a new charity project that involved mentoring. He pledged to make Neverland more accessible to his fans; that announcement got the biggest cheer, of course. He was also studying 3-D technology—he knew that was where movies were going next—and planning a huge charity event at Neverland to be held in September 2003. The next chapter in Michael's life promised to include his diverse interests, which extended far beyond the hit albums the world expected from him. He was back to his dynamic old self. He was in command of his life. And I, for one, could not have been more excited to be a part of it all.

CHAPTER TWENTY-ONE

FALSE CHARGES

O N NOVEMBER 18, 2003, *NUMBER ONES* WAS RE-
leased, but the album's debut was immediately trumped
by bigger news.

The day after the release, I was back in New Jersey, working with
Vinnie on Michael's new merchandising initiative. Michael himself
was in Las Vegas, where he had been shooting the music video for
the song "One More Chance," but production had been halted after
another conflict with Tommy Mottola arose. Michael wanted my
brother Aldo and my sister, Marie Nicole, both dancers, to perform
in the video, but Tommy Mottola didn't want any children to appear
in it. Marc Schaffel overheard Michael's side of the heated conversation between the two.

"Screw you guys," Michael said through Marc Schaffel, who was
serving as his middle man with Tommy. "I'm not going to do it
without the kids. We're shutting down."

"One More Chance" was one of the new tracks on *Number Ones,* and Sony needed the video to promote the album. Months of labor and preparation had gone into setting up the studio in Vegas.

"I don't like the concept anyway," Michael told Tommy. "It looks too much like 'Smooth Criminal.' We gotta do something new and fresh anyway. We'll shoot it ourselves, on the road."

So the video production was canceled. Through Marc, Michael planned a six-month trip to Europe, Africa, and Brazil, during which he would shoot the video. He and his entourage were scheduled to depart the next day, but their plans were about to change.

I was officially homeless, as I had been most of my adult life. Michael had conditioned me into being a hotel guy. So Vinnie and I were camped out at my parents' house, working with the TV on, when we noticed a news ticker running across the screen. It said that Michael's ranch was being raided by police. An aerial shot of Neverland came up on the screen. The ticker told us that there were allegations that Michael had committed "lewd and lascivious acts" with a minor under the age of fourteen.

Vinnie and I looked at each other in horror, then back at the screen. *Holy shit.*

"Who did this?" Vinnie asked. "Who accused Michael?" The news didn't give the name of the accuser, but I didn't need one. I knew this had come from the Arvizos.

I called in my parents, and we tried to reach Michael but failed. All our phones were ringing—a mix of concerned friends wondering what was going on and colleagues filling us in. Someone confirmed that the accusers were the Arvizos. Of course; who else could it have been?

We'd been here before. I was young at the time, but I'd seen the years of damage those first accusations had inflicted on Michael's heart as well as his public image. Again, he was being attacked by liars. We had never trusted the Arvizos, and now the worst had come to pass. Why hadn't Michael severed ties with the family back in 2000?

Why had he invited them back into his life for the Bashir video? Why had we taken them in to help them deal with the aftermath? I was angry with Gavin's mother, of course, but I was also angry at Michael for foolishly allowing her to get away with her manipulations of her kids and angry at myself for failing to act more aggressively. After all, we had ample reason to doubt Janet's intentions from the start, yet we had stood by while she set up this situation.

The allegations were all bullshit. There was nothing ambiguous about the whole thing. These people were after Michael's money. But he was innocent, and we were going to destroy them in court. I felt confident of that. What I didn't realize at the time was how great a battle we would end up having to fight, and how heavy a toll it would exact. I had no idea it would drive a wedge between me and Michael that most friendships couldn't hope to survive. Ours just barely would.

Michael, Aldo, and Marie Nicole were spending their last day in Las Vegas when they received the news that the ranch was being raided again, and immediately they went to their hotel. But the hotel wouldn't admit them for fear of the impending media onslaught. They drove to another hotel but were turned away there as well. Hotel after hotel turned them down for fear of the media storm. The three of them circled Vegas, with no refuge, while Michael grew increasingly agitated. Finally, Karen was able to secure them a hotel room.

From what my brother and sister told me, once he got to the room, Michael lost it. He could not believe this was happening. Again. He went ballistic, overturning tables, throwing chairs, destroying everything in sight. If Aldo and Marie Nicole hadn't been there, I would have been concerned for his safety. The trip abroad was canceled, the video shoot for "One More Chance" was never rescheduled, and Aldo and Marie Nicole went home to New Jersey.

Michael didn't want to return to Neverland, which he felt had once again been violated by a police raid. Instead, he rented a house up Coldwater Canyon in L.A. A week or so later, I went to visit him, but because the DA was looking to subpoena me and there was speculation about a warrant for my arrest, I wanted to stay under the radar. So I flew into Las Vegas. Michael's driver picked me up and brought me to L.A.

When I arrived, Michael's brother Randy was in and out of the house. In all my years with Michael, I'd never really spent any time with Randy, and I was a bit surprised to see him there now, though it was clear that he had stepped up to support Michael. He was trying to help his brother and to get a handle on things, and Michael, who could be resistant, was grateful. The three of us sat down at the kitchen table to catch up. It was nice spending time with Randy. I really like him, and Michael was clearly happy to have him around. I assured both of them that I would do anything I could to help and that I was there with Michael till the end.

We just hung out for the next couple of days, trying not to think or talk about what was at the forefront of all our minds. There was a bowling alley in the house, so we bowled. Gary, the same driver Michael had had for years, took us out to do a little shopping, and we grabbed some Kentucky Fried Chicken takeout. After the kids went to sleep, we'd open a bottle of wine and joke around. All our other business had come to a standstill—our first priority was to get through the trial—but we were optimistic.

Michael was keeping it together, hoping and expecting the best, but I could see that he was not himself. There was sadness in his eyes.

After my stay at Neverland, I returned to New York, supposedly to get back to my life. Obviously, I couldn't work on relaunching the Michael Jackson brand. Instead, I started producing a tribute to Patti LaBelle for UPN, assembling an all-star performance in the Bahamas to celebrate her forty-five years in the music industry. I moved into an apartment in midtown Manhattan.

Just before Christmas, on December 18, 2003, Michael was officially charged with seven counts of child molestation and two counts of administering an intoxicating agent, that is, the Arvizos were claiming that he got Gavin drunk in order to molest him. According to the legal documents, these crimes had occurred in February and March 2003, when we were all at Neverland following the Bashir fiasco.

Not long after the official charges were filed, Vinnie and I started getting calls from the district attorney's office saying they wanted to speak to us because we'd been staying at Neverland during the time in question.

"Frank," Vinnie said. "Look, I don't know our position, but I think it's time we got an attorney." I called Al Malnik, who gave me some names, and I wrote them down, not totally processing everything that was going on.

After meeting with a few superlawyers, Vinnie and I walked into Joe Tacopina's office in Manhattan. There in the waiting room, the first thing I saw was a picture of the lawyer with his wife and kids. A family man. I liked that. Then, on a TV that was on in the background, I saw Juventus, my favorite soccer team, playing a match. Joe told me it was his favorite team, too. All three of us had soccer in common. That settled it. He was our lawyer.

Joe spoke to the district attorney's office. They indicated that they were going to a grand jury—which meant they believed they had enough evidence to warrant a trial. Their story was that Michael and I had formed a conspiracy in which I helped him gain access to Gavin, then covered up various nefarious activities and tampered with witnesses.

Over several meetings, Vinnie and I gave Joe a detailed history of our interactions with the Arvizos. I made sure Joe understood that I believed that the Arvizos were liars, that we had nothing to hide, and that I wanted to do everything I could to support Michael. Joe thought that we had considerable evidence showing that there had been no conspiracy, but this was a high-profile case with, as he put it, "a rabid prosecutor with a clear agenda." He worried that Vinnie and I would be dragged into it because the idea of there having been a conspiracy made the case sound even more sinister. He would work with Michael's lawyer, supplying him with our evidence to support his case wherever he needed it.

That Christmas, Joe didn't want me to see Michael. We didn't know if charges would be brought against me, and any further contact I had with Michael would be used against me. So my brothers Eddie, Aldo, and Dominic went to L.A. to spend Christmas with Michael at the Coldwater Canyon house, while I had a quiet Christmas with my parents at home. Michael, playing Santa even from so far away, sent gifts for me: a digital camera and an iPod. I was grateful, even more so because I took it as a sign that he was still his same old self.

One morning in January, I walked downstairs to get a coffee and cigarettes at the corner deli. I had long hair at the time, and I was wearing my usual sunglasses and a hoodie. A TV was on in the deli, playing a show called *Celebrity Justice*. As I waited to pay for my stuff, a picture of me came up on the screen. I watched in horror as the TV narrator made me out to be a mobster from New Jersey and alleged that I had attempted to kidnap Gavin Arvizo's family and hold them hostage at Neverland. The press was even reporting that I'd attempted to kidnap the Arvizos and take them to Brazil, possibly to make them "disappear." That would have made for a great movie. Back when I absorbed Michael's advice to be like Jonathan Livingston Seagull, to lead an extraordinary life, being falsely accused of kidnapping wasn't exactly what I had envisioned.

A cute little old lady was in front of me in line.

"I hope they get that bastard," she said.

"Me, too," I said.

I thought of all those times that Michael and I had gone out into the world, assuming disguises that he needed and that I wore just for fun. Now I had a real reason to shield my identity and it felt simply horrible. There were people all over the world listening to these ludicrous accusations, forming opinions about me. Since they didn't know the truth, whatever reason would they have not to believe what they heard? And so I had a taste of what Michael lived with every day of his life. The only saving grace was that in all the news reports, and even in the court papers, I was named Frank Tyson (aka Cascio). My early efforts to separate work and family had a beneficial side effect I never could have imagined. My family name remained untainted, which not only meant that my parents were somewhat protected, but that I had a place to go. In my business life, I went back to being Frank Cascio. It had been a while, but I was myself again.

I hadn't been charged with any crime, but we knew from the leaks to *Celebrity Justice* and other news sources that I was somehow involved. Later in January 2004, when Michael was arraigned, Vinnie and I were named as unindicted co-conspirators. As Joe explained the co-conspirator charge, it meant that we weren't being charged with any crimes and that the prosecutors had no evidence against us. We were safe—for now—but if Michael was convicted, they would probably charge us. My fate, as it had been for most of my life, was tied to Michael's.

Soon after the arraignment, I checked in with Michael. He and the kids had returned to Neverland. I asked to say hi to the kids, and Prince came on the phone.

"Frank," he said, "Daddy is sad. Are you going to come here? Is Daddy going to be okay?" It broke my heart.

"Of course Daddy's going to be okay," I assured him. "Everything is perfect. I'll be there as soon as I can."

The fact that I hadn't been charged at the arraignment meant that I wasn't about to be subpoenaed or arrested, but Joe still didn't want me to be in touch with Michael. Against his advice, I flew to L.A. with my father and Eddie to visit Michael for a couple of days at the ranch. On the plane, I sat with my brother; my father sat alone. Ten years earlier the three of us had flown to Tel Aviv to reassure Michael that he had our support in the Jordy Chandler case. Now we were back to do the same. As kids in 1993, Eddie and I had been blissfully oblivious to Michael's circumstances. This time, we were adults, fully aware of the gravity of the accusations and the toll they would take on Michael.

When we walked into the main house, my father greeted Michael by reassuring him that we were all there for him and the kids ran up to us and hugged us. In spite of Prince's call, they seemed happy and carefree. They knew that their daddy was in trouble, but Michael was careful to shelter them from the specifics. He was always scrupulous about protecting them from both the good and the bad of his fame. He didn't want them to be swarmed by his fans or to see him perform in a sold-out stadium. He didn't want them to go on the Internet, for fear they would do a search on his name and see rumors about their father that they were too young to process. And now he did his best to protect them from the madness at the door. Once the kids were out of earshot, we talked about the upcoming trial—we had to—but then we tried to have some fun.

In 1993, on the *Dangerous* tour, we had distracted Michael by exploring foreign cities, throwing water balloons out of hotel windows, and trashing a hotel room (once, just one time). As adults, we resorted to watching movies and hanging out. We always said, "Let's sit around and just stink," and that's exactly what we did. Although we didn't say it outright, whatever we did was an effort to demonstrate to Michael that everything was going to be okay.

Still, as upbeat as we tried to be, it was evident that the weight of these new allegations was oppressive. Michael was mentally and physically drained. He slept a lot. I found myself thinking back to the lessons he had taught me about controlling the outcome of circumstances. I didn't know if he was visualizing the outcome he wanted in order to make it happen. We weren't talking that sort of talk. What I did know was that, more than anything I'd been through with him, this would be a test of his will and of his faith in himself.

One of the first things I'd done when I'd arrived at the ranch was check to see if my small stash of pot was still in its hiding place in my room. I was worried that the police might have found it in the raid and that somehow it would be used against Michael.

Michael had always been against pot and other illegal drugs. But back in Miami, a year earlier, Michael had spent some time with two of the former Bee Gees, Maurice Gibb, who was on his deathbed, and Barry Gibb. When Barry told Michael that he had recorded his greatest songs when he was smoking pot, Michael was intrigued. He was a big fan of the Bee Gees. The songs "How Deep Is Your Love," "Stayin' Alive," and "More Than a Woman" were among his favorites. And so Michael smoked pot with me when we were at the ranch working on the home videos, for what I think was his first time. I remember how, in that state of mind, the lights of Neverland came to life.

"Ah, now it all makes sense," Michael had said, as we drove through the property. "This is exactly what the Indians were doing when they passed around the peace pipe." He liked that pot came from the earth—it helped him justify something he'd always been against.

Over the past year, we had gotten stoned on a few occasions up in the mountains. Michael was extraordinarily discreet—he didn't want a soul to know about it. And the good news was that the secret was safe. As it turned out, the police had not found my stash, and one afternoon, in an attempt to cheer both of us up, I rolled a joint and found Michael in his office, which was an extension of the main house, a warm room with dark wood floors, a beautiful desk, and a couch. Six flat-screen TVs lined one wall—each playing different cartoons. On the wall over the fireplace was a six-foot-tall portrait of Prince at age two or three, asleep, with me and Eddie standing on either side of him, keeping guard.

"Come on, let's take a break," I suggested.

"Yeah, okay," he said. We walked outside and got into Michael's golf cart.

We drove up to the mountains, and passed the joint back and

forth, quieter than usual. It's not that the conversation lagged, exactly, but we didn't want to talk about the looming allegations, and we couldn't come up with any other subject to discuss. I wanted to say, "I told you so," but I didn't. And Michael wanted to ask, "How did this happen?" but he didn't. Instead, we were mostly quiet, and every so often I would say, "Can you believe this fucking family?"

"I can't believe this shit," Michael would respond. We would look at each other and shake our heads. It felt like a bad dream. Ordinarily we would have driven around like this, with or without the pot, taking in the beauty of our surroundings and just relishing the moment. Now we were trying, and failing, to distract ourselves from reality. To my knowledge, that was the last time Michael smoked pot—it was a short-lived phase for both of us.

When the time came for me, Eddie, and my father to leave, I went into Michael's room to say good-bye. Though Michael had come back to Neverland, he refused to stay in the main house because he felt it had been defiled by the police raid. Instead, he decamped to a guest unit where he stayed with all three kids. It was early in the morning, and Michael was still in bed. The three kids were sleeping in the adjoining bedroom, so we spoke quietly.

"We gotta pray," I told Michael. "God knows the truth, and the truth will prevail. You don't have to think twice. I'm here for you. My family's here for you. I love you. I love your children. If you need anything, *anything*, just let me know. We'll make them look like the idiots they are."

"Don't worry," Michael said. "Just make sure you stay strong." That was his way of acknowledging that I had my own worries about the trial. "Pray," he said, "and we'll celebrate when it's all over."

At his arraignment on January 16, 2004, Michael had pleaded not guilty on all counts. Then he walked outside and danced on the roof of his SUV for the hundreds of fans who had gathered, to acknowledge them and to show that he was going to fight with all he had. I'd seen it as the kind of performance that only an innocent man would give. Now I told him, "When all this is over, I'm going to get up on the car and dance with you." I was energized by my anger. They thought they could get away with this? Bring it on.

"Okay, Frank," Michael said, laughing. "I love you. Have a safe flight."

"Make sure you shower and brush your teeth before going to court so you don't kill any of the jurors," I said through a big grin. I kissed the sleeping children's foreheads and slipped out of the room. My father had said good-bye the night before, but Eddie went in after me to take his own leave.

I had said good-bye to Michael, but I wish I'd slowed down on my way to the car, taking a moment to look around at the beautiful house, the grounds, the lake, the paths, the mountains. I had no idea it would be the last time I would ever see Neverland.

AFTER THAT TRIP, BOTH MY LAWYER, JOE TACOPINA, and Michael's lawyer, Tom Mesereau, firmly instructed me not to have any further contact with Michael. If I was called to testify, and the DA asked, "When was the last time you spoke to Michael?" they wanted me to be able to say that we hadn't spoken since the charges were filed. Even though I hadn't been charged, Janet Arvizo was making criminal allegations against me as well. If any evidence developed during the trial to support her ludicrous claims, it would be better if I hadn't communicated with Michael. The lawyers didn't want us to appear to be in cahoots.

The reasoning made perfect sense to me, but a forced separation from Michael was a blow. We had experienced the Arvizos together; we had been accused together; and now we wouldn't be able to support each other through the trial.

I had confidence that our attorneys would reveal the truth, but our trial in the court of public opinion was a separate matter. A journalist named Roger Friedman was covering the trial for a Fox News entertainment blog called FOX411. He had tried to get in touch with me through mutual friends, but I hadn't responded. I had never spoken to the press about Michael before, but this Roger Friedman was writing daily stories and his information was wrong. Now, frustrated with what I saw in his columns, I decided that if they were going to write about me, they might as well have accurate information. I wanted to get the truth out.

Vinnie and I met Roger at a coffee shop on Seventy-sixth and Broadway. Vinnie put a big metal briefcase on the table and unsnapped it. He opened it wide, and Roger leaned forward for a closer look. Inside were piles of receipts. We explained to him that these were receipts from everything we had spent money on when we were taking care of the Arvizos during their stay at Neverland. There were receipts for hotels, movie theaters, restaurants, and spas. The press had been accusing us of kidnapping her, but, as was instantly clear to Roger, these were not the expenditures of kidnappers and their hapless victim. We had kept her comfortable and entertained while waiting for the media surrounding the Bashir video to die down. After this meeting, the tone of Roger's writing seemed to shift. I wasn't as powerless as I had thought. I could support Michael without even talking to him.

That spring, before the indictment, Joe spoke to Tom Sneddon, the district attorney of Santa Barbara County.

"Listen," Sneddon said, "Frank's on a sinking ship. He can take our lifeboat or go down with the ship." He offered me immunity if I came into the DA's office to testify against Michael. I know people who watch shows like *Law & Order* are used to thinking that the DAs are the good guys, but this time they were on the wrong side of the case. Even if I were to be completely honest, they would look for ways to use whatever I said against Michael.

Joe explained to me that this was a common prosecutorial ploy. He had met with these people, and was certain they had no evidence

As much as I accepted his logic, talking to the DA was like talking to the devil in my eyes. They were building a case against Michael and against Vinnie and me. They were already going to trial. The truth was irrelevant to them now; what mattered to them was building their case and winning. I couldn't believe he had done this. I felt betrayed. I thought we would go through this together, but for the rest of the trial, and afterward, I wouldn't speak to Vinnie. Eventually I understood that Vinnie didn't have the same history with Michael, or the same loyalty to him. Whereas I was willing to sacrifice anything for Michael, Vinnie wanted to make sure he didn't see any jail time and if talking to the DA ensured that, then he would talk to the DA. I was so pissed at Vinnie that I didn't speak to him for years. Eventually, he and I would talk things out and I would forgive him. Vinnie needed to do what was best for him. At the end of the day, he was still my friend from eighth grade. Our families went back a long way. It wasn't worth losing him. We would make it through this.

When I returned to the United States, I continued working on the Patti LaBelle show, but I fell into a serious depression that lasted for much of 2004. I didn't want to leave my apartment or to be around anyone. I didn't even want to talk to people on the phone. It affected my work. I had recently figured out that I was at my best when I was working alongside Michael. All that was gone, our connection was gone, and my life was on hold. I lost track of me, of what made me *me*.

As time went by, my depression morphed into a state of what you could call calculated caution, even paranoia. I was always thinking ten moves ahead. I felt like I had everything figured out, but needing to maneuver with so much calculation wasn't a good feeling. It seemed as though every step I took provoked ripples of change that I had to predict and control, yet this need for control was the only way I could combat the helplessness of waiting in limbo for the trial to be over. I finally understood Michael's endless paranoia. Being falsely accused, being judged by the public—it made a person desperate to regain control.

Needless to say, this was a difficult time for my relationship with Valerie. We loved each other, and we cared about each other. She was going to school, living her happy student life, while I was depressed and miserable. Valerie and I were young, we still had some growing up to do, and we were already geographically far from each other. Trouble had been brewing for a while. Besides the long-distance factor, there had always been issues between us—the secrecy of my job, the unusual lifestyle it involved, the full-time commitment. The trial and my state of mind at the time were the last straw. During the trial, I felt like my whole world was coming down. My relationship now turned out to be another casualty.

CHAPTER TWENTY-TWO

JUSTICE

THE TRIAL PROCEEDINGS WERE FINALLY KICKED off on January 31, 2005, when jury selection began, followed, a month later, by the trial itself. Not surprisingly, a media circus sprang into frenzied life outside the courthouse, with thousands of reporters running about and round-the-clock coverage on all news stations.

Joe and I paid scrupulous attention to every bit of testimony that was heard, and I tried to recall every detail of the events the prosecution brought up, in case I myself was called upon to testify. Along the way, Joe and I had to assemble a defense in case we needed it. After all, my case was tied to Michael's. If he was cleared of the charges against him, I'd be in the clear as well. So Joe worked closely with Tom Mesereau, Michael's lawyer. If a witness for the prosecution made any kind of statement that I could refute, Joe passed my evidence along to Tom. We did everything we could to help them win their case.

The molestation allegedly happened between February 20 and March 12, 2003, when all the parties in the case were staying at Neverland immediately after the Bashir videos. Even had I not known Michael as I did, it seemed absurd to me that anyone would choose that particular moment to molest a child: Michael had just been pilloried in the press for holding Gavin's hand in front of the cameras on the Bashir video. Why, of all times in his life, would he choose that moment of extreme vulnerability and visibility to do his nefarious deed? It simply didn't add up.

In addition, it was only too apparent that the Arvizos had been up to no good from the very start. Time and time again during the period when they regularly visited Neverland—in interviews that we taped for our rebuttal video and, even more critically, in the official interviews conducted by Child and Family Services—they had spoken out in support of Michael. Because this support had been repeatedly documented, the DA had to prove that each time the Arvizos appeared to support Michael, they were being coerced into doing it.

Every detail of the prosecution's case was a warped version of the truth. I was accused of showing porn to Gavin and his brother on the night when the boys had begged to sleep in Michael's room. The truth of course was the exact opposite: the boys had found the porn themselves, and Michael had left the room to make sure that he played no part in it.

The prosecution claimed that Michael served the boys "Jesus juice" disguised in soda cans, when in fact he used soda cans when he himself drank alcohol in order to avoid modeling alcohol consumption to kids. And he certainly never gave them any.

The list of lies grew longer and longer. As if the press's treatment of Michael over the years hadn't already been infuriating and outrageous, we were now subjected to hearing and watching the lies and misrepresentations put on the record in a court of law, knowing all the while that we would soon be obliged to defend ourselves against each and every one of them. It was a travesty.

After the DA delivered the prosecution's closing arguments, it was time for Michael's defense team to argue the case. Thankfully, no sooner had Tom Mesereau taken the stand than the Arvizos' house of cards came tumbling down. This was a she said/he said case—Janet Arvizo against Michael—and it didn't take very long for the entire Arvizo family to be discredited.

While on the stand, Janet was revealed to have had a long and not very savory history of using her children, and Gavin's cancer, to exploit celebrities, including Jay Leno, Chris Tucker, and George Lopez, attempting to milk them for all they were worth. Even more preposterously, she had twice in the past made claims of sexual abuse and imprisonment—once against her ex-husband, and once against the department store JCPenney. As this litany of past complaints rang out, item by sleazy item, I found myself recalling my earliest interactions with her and asking myself why, since I had known from the start that she was bad news, I hadn't trusted myself and taken swift and decisive action. Why hadn't I spoken up more forcefully when Michael had attempted to defend the family? How had we ever let this woman into our lives?

The climax, for me, was when Janet testified that she believed Michael's associates—that included me—planned to make her family disappear.

"And someone mentioned to you a hot air balloon?" Mesereau asked.

"That was one of the ways," Janet confirmed. The courtroom erupted in laughter. Things didn't look good for Janet.

The boys, Gavin and Star, despite the fact that they had obviously been coached by their mother, contradicted each other and themselves in their testimony, and the prosecution's case was revealed to be the travesty we had known it to be from the start. Not only was the testimony we heard riddled with inconsistencies, but a good deal of it just plain didn't make sense. The Arvizos were not credible people, and their story wasn't credible.

There was, however, one poignant moment in the trial: it occurred when Debbie Rowe was called to take the stand. She and Michael had resolved their custody issues a couple of years before, and now Debbie came forward to support him, as she had done in the rebuttal video. Her testimony was truthful, she was courageous enough to openly admit to mistakes she'd made in the past, and she did her best to help Michael. I was glad to see that her relationship with Michael was again on firm ground. They cared for each other; they had children together; and with this gesture, their mutual trust and love were affirmed.

MICHAEL AND I HADN'T SPOKEN SINCE THE LAST VISIT that Eddie, my father, and I had made to Neverland. As I mentioned before, we weren't allowed to, because if Michael was convicted then I might face conspiracy charges. Over the course of 2004, Eddie had started spending time talking on the phone with Michael, and as time went by, it seemed that Eddie had stepped in to fill the role that I had been forced to vacate. Michael was used to having a friend beside him, an ally he could trust, and in a way Eddie was a very appropriate choice: he was the next in line, a sort of heir apparent, if you will. I was happy that Michael had someone in the family to talk to, since I worried about him, remembering with a sad wistfulness the wonderful times we'd shared at Neverland in 2003 before the allegations in November cast such a pall over our lives. I knew that these allegations would set Michael back for years to come, if not forever, and I hated that I couldn't be there to support him.

Then, toward the end of the trial, my parents delivered some shocking news. They told me that Michael was upset with me. Apparently, he had been told that I hadn't been willing to testify on his behalf. This was ludicrous, and nothing could have been further from the truth.

One of Michael's nephews, Auggie, called me to report the same news. Michael had told him I wasn't going to testify, and was upset, stomping around and saying, "Can you believe Frank is not here for me in my time of need? He was like a son to me. He betrayed me."

"Auggie, I would never do that," I said.

During the course of the trial, I had done an interview on a *20/20* special hosted by Catherine Crier and had also appeared on *Good Morning America*. In the interview, I defended Michael and discredited the Arvizo family. I was one of the few people who came forward in order to defend Michael publicly, and I did so at my own risk. If the verdict didn't go in Michael's favor, it was I who would bear the consequences of my public stand. But I knew the truth, and I believed that the world needed to know it. I couldn't stand around passively.

The truth is that I was eager to testify. I of all people knew exactly what had happened during the Arvizos' visits to the ranch, and I wanted to see justice served. I was never called by the prosecution; after all, I would have been a hostile witness. Originally, the plan had been for me to be one of the last people who would be called to the stand for the defense, near the end of the testimony. But as the date for me to appear approached, Joe Tacopina called me and told me that he and Tom Mesereau no longer thought that having me testify made sense for the case.

"Tom thinks he has this case right where he wants it," he said. "He doesn't need to put you up there." Tom didn't want to bring me in, opening up the twenty years I'd known Michael for questioning. Besides, Joe said, the reasonable doubt that needed to be established in order to win the case was already proven.

The problem was that Michael hadn't heard it that way. He had been told that I refused to testify. If I'd ever thought that my suspicions that someone in Michael's organization was out to get me were mere paranoia on my part, here was irrefutable evidence that they weren't. This was the ultimate sabotage. *But who had it come from?* I asked myself. When nobody could give me an answer, I became obsessed with finding the source of the betrayal. I must have asked my lawyer a hundred times, "Joe—you didn't tell them I didn't want to testify, did you?" It drove me crazy at the time, and it haunts me still.

I was furious that someone was lying about me to Michael again, but even worse than the lie (we'd weathered those before) was the fact that Michael believed it. That he'd once believed I was capable of using my influence to ask for a kickback was bad enough, but this was leagues beyond that. The idea that I wouldn't support Michael ran counter to everything I believed about myself, about who I was, about all that mattered to me. How could Michael, after all we'd been through together, after all we'd done for each other, been to each other, shared with each other . . . how could he believe something that was so totally antithetical to my character? He had raised me, for heaven's sake. He knew everything about me. My whole life I had done nothing but support and protect him. I knew that I wasn't perfect, that I'd made mistakes, but I also knew that my intentions had always been good and my priorities always clear. Michael knew this, too. Yet in spite of all this, Michael turned on me, and did so with ease and assurance. Michael was going around saying to his family members, my family members, and mutual friends, "Can you believe what Frank did now? He's not defending me in my time of need."

Words that Michael had spoken when I first came to work for him replayed in my head: "Frank, you're in a position of power. People are going to be jealous of you. People will try to pit us against each other. But I promise you I will never let that happen." These words turned out to be prophetic, but instead of standing by me, as he'd promised he would do, he seemed to have forgotten his own prediction. When push came to shove, Michael didn't have faith in me. That betrayal was absolutely devastating.

I knew that Eddie had Michael's ear, and when Michael doubted me, I expected Eddie to set him straight. But Eddie decided that he, too, felt I wasn't supporting Michael. When I appeared on *20/20,* he thought I was trying to get attention for myself. This made no sense. If I wanted attention, it was in my own self-interest to take the stand and testify, not refuse to testify. And so I began to hold my brother partially responsible for my alienation from Michael. Whether he provoked it or not—he would later insist he didn't—my brother still could have said, "Michael, you know very well that Frank did not do these things. You're wrong. He loves you." Eddie didn't.

My brother was caught in the middle. Eddie, like me, had grown up with Michael. But unlike me, his idealized childhood image of Michael was still intact. Over the course of my years with Michael, I had accepted his imperfections. I was the first to defend him, but that meant accepting and protecting him from his faults. Michael had never showed his darker side to my family. Eddie hadn't seen him in full paranoid mode, impulsively cutting people out of his life. He didn't see Michael's struggles with prescription drugs or how hard it was for him to face his financial troubles. As a result, when Michael turned on me, Eddie trusted Michael's judgment the way a dutiful son trusts a father's. My brother and I had always been close, but the trial pulled us apart just as it pulled Michael and me apart. I'd lost Vinnie, I'd lost Michael, and now it felt like I had lost my brother.

It was inevitable that the conflict between Eddie and me and the difficulties of the trial would spill over onto the rest of my family— my lively, fun, restaurant-business family. They were overwhelmed, and as much as they loved me, they had no idea how to relate to me. Frankly, I don't blame them. Things had become far more complicated than I could ever have anticipated. My mother likes to keep her life simple: she wants to hear that I'm fine, and for the most part our dynamic was that I never went into details of a problem with her until the problem was already solved. She didn't know or understand why my brother and Michael bore such animosity toward me. We had many conversations about it, but I myself couldn't really explain what had gone so terribly wrong.

My father was the only one who really seemed to understand what I was going through. I went to him when I was upset or needed to talk. Nonetheless, without Michael, without New Jersey as the safe haven it had always been, I felt isolated and alone. If I had learned anything in my years with Michael, it was to separate myself from the world in order to protect myself, and so at this time I instinctively retreated deeper into myself. The depression that had begun during 2004 settled in for a long stay during the last months of the trial. I became a recluse.

THE VERDICT WAS DELIVERED JUNE 13, 2005. I WAS AT my parents' house, watching TV with my whole family, and for some reason that I can no longer remember, I was standing on a chair. Michael was found not guilty on all counts, and I was free.

Michael's good news was my good news. If he had been found guilty, the DA probably would have indicted me on conspiracy charges and I would have faced the possibility of two to six years in prison. But in the span of a few words, the whole ugly mess became history. We all started crying, jumping up and down, and hugging one another.

After the verdict, Michael called our house in New Jersey to talk to everyone. His conversation with me, it will come as no surprise, was a little strange.

"Are you okay?" I asked.

"I'm happy to hear your voice," Michael replied. "We got through this, but it was not good. It wore me out, Frank. I gotta get out of here. I want to get out of the country. They don't deserve me. Everyone can go fuck themselves. I want nothing to do with the United States. I'm never coming back."

We didn't talk about his belief that I had refused to testify in his behalf. And there was no acknowledgment of the ordeal that I myself had gone through during the trial. I felt like he was making the call because he needed to do it, but I could tell from his tone that this was not the right moment to deal with the elephant in the room.

After the not-guilty verdict, Michael went to Bahrain. Part of his reason for going abroad was that he no longer felt like he had a home in the United States. He said, publicly and privately, that he felt that Neverland had been violated by the police raid. Neverland, his beloved home, represented Michael's love for purity and innocence—and these were the very qualities that the trial had cast into doubt. So he abandoned the ranch, and in doing so, he abandoned one of his most cherished dreams as well.

An All-Star Salute to Patti LaBelle: Live from Atlantis aired on November 8, 2005. Sitting backstage, watching the Bluebelles reunite, was a musical pleasure and a career high. After the show was over, I felt a moment of pride and happiness. But it didn't last long. The show went well, but its success was small comfort to me. I was out of touch with my own emotions. I felt numb.

Michael invited my family to Bahrain to celebrate Christmas with him, but I didn't go. I was negotiating with Russell Simmons, one of the founders of Def Jam, to do a tribute concert celebrating his contributions to hip-hop. I used that as an excuse not to go, but the real reason was that I was angry. As much as I wanted to put the past behind me, as much as I believed in being magnanimous, the fact was simply that I wasn't. I still couldn't believe that Michael had doubted me, doubted my unwavering loyalty to him, especially after all of the fear, anxiety, and depression that I'd been through since November 2003. I didn't want to see him or speak to him.

Part of me wanted to clear the air, but the years had made me stubborn. When Michael had first asked me to work with him, I knew he was inviting me on a wild ride, and I went willingly. In the process, I'd had the time of my life, and though I'd suffered through Michael's episodes of doubting me, I'd ridden that roller coaster with as much patience and forbearance as I could summon. But for all the craziness we shared, the trial was the roughest ride I'd ever taken. I endured it because of him, because of our association, because of my loyalty. After living under the shadow of it for over two years, I thought I deserved a "real" phone call, a true clearing of the air. A conversation with a friend, not some pat response.

After the trial Michael didn't seem to want to have any contact with me. And it's not as though he disappeared into thin air. He was in regular communication with the rest of my family; he just avoided me. Given his easy acceptance of the lie he was told about my unwillingness to testify, I didn't necessarily expect a simple and joyous reunion. But I expected us to talk. I expected to have a chance to defend myself. And I expected, at some point, an apology. Maybe I was being self-centered or inconsiderate. Certainly what he'd been through was bigger and harder than what I'd endured. However, what Michael didn't realize was that I'd been through it with him; I, too, had experienced one of the most difficult times of my life.

Michael was a lot of things to me—boss, mentor, brother, father—but more than anything else, he was my oldest, closest friend. When he discarded me, I felt confused and lost. I'd seen him do this to so many other friends and colleagues, but I'd always thought the combination of my loyalty and our history made me exempt. Clearly, I was wrong.

Russell Simmons aside, I didn't know what to do with myself. It had been tough to look for more work while the trial was going on. And I wasn't sure where to begin. I had no intention of pounding the pavement for a job. For all my experience, there were some fundamental gaps in my work history. I wasn't used to showing up at a certain place at a certain time, and I wasn't accustomed to having a boss—a real boss—tell me what to do. I thought I wanted to continue producing concerts and shows, in theory, but I didn't feel like myself. I had always been a bit detached, but now I was virtually impervious. I came across as arrogant, stuck-up, even a little strange. Perhaps the worst effect of my unhappiness was that I'd picked up Michael's paranoia. I didn't trust anyone. The truth was, dramatic as it sounds, I had lost my faith in humanity.

Within a few months, I pulled myself together and set up shop in an office on Fifth Avenue, the first office I'd ever had. I started to rebuild. It turned out I did have skills, and I had acquired a reputation as a guy who could get things done. I knew how to forge relationships, make deals, and bring in financing. People came to me to handle various deals, and I started taking consulting fees. I began to see that stepping away from Michael was the only way to discover that I could succeed and thrive without him. It was an important lesson. My own identity, which had been wrapped up in his for so long, started to emerge. For the first time in my adult life, I was putting myself first.

CHAPTER TWENTY-THREE

RECONCILIATION

ICHAEL AND I KNEW WE WERE DUE FOR A real rapprochement, but direct confrontation wasn't Michael's style. Instead, the restoration of our friendship was allowed to evolve over time. It wasn't what it had been, but we eased back into it, talking occasionally throughout 2006.

Michael was spending time in Las Vegas with his children, occasionally returning to Los Angeles to appear in court to defend himself in the various lesser lawsuits that continued to plague him. Every time he called, I sensed that there was still a distance between us. He wanted to talk, to hear my voice, but the time wasn't right for the conversation I needed to have with him. We both avoided the topic. He'd ask what I was working on, what I was doing. I told him about my office in Manhattan and filled him in on some of the projects I had on my plate. I always made it a point to thank him, saying, "I wouldn't be able to think the way I do and do what I'm doing if it wasn't for you."

I remember him telling me, "Frank, just get one thing done. Finish one thing. Don't work on three hundred things. Nothing will get done."

He was right. I was working on three hundred things. I thought that was normal, because that's what he and I had always done. But Michael was like a mature Fortune 500 company, while I was just a start-up.

Our conversations were brief. He didn't want to talk about the trial, our conflict, any of it. There was no resolution, but the more we spoke, the more I started to understand that the trial had been so difficult for him that he couldn't bear to revisit it. Whereas I needed to talk about things in order to move on, Michael was too traumatized by those things to discuss them. Talking to me meant dealing with that pain, and he simply wasn't ready to do this yet.

But soon he started telling our mutual friends how much he missed me and how well I was doing. He told people that he talked to me all the time and everything was great. It wasn't the truth, but Michael knew that what he said would get back to me. Since I knew how nonconfrontational Michael was, I understood that this was his way of reaching out to me . . . without actually picking up the phone to reach out to me.

Calls from Michael usually came out of the blue. One day, in the spring of 2007, the phone rang and it was him, asking me to join him in Ireland. Two years had passed since the verdict, and we still hadn't talked through any of the problems the trial had engendered. Michael was on the phone for only a moment, but this was, I felt, the first time since the trial that he had truly reached out to me, asking to see me in person. I told him that I would be glad to join him. He said, "Okay, I'm going to have someone call you to work out the logistics."

Two days later I got a call from Raymone Bain, Michael's publicist and personal general manager, who was (briefly) running his world. (She, too, would eventually sue him.) Her words were shocking and unforgettable:

"As per Mr. Jackson," she announced, "if you come to Ireland, we'll have you arrested."

It took me a moment to register what she had said. Could I have heard her right?

"Hold on a second," I said. I was in my office in the city, and in a flash, I conferenced in my father. I was tired of it being my word against everyone else's. I wanted a witness. Raymone Bain also brought someone else on the phone.

"I'm a deputy," the new voice said. "If you go to Ireland, you'll be arrested."

"Are you kidding me?" I said. "What are you talking about?"

"Michael says you're calling him at the studio and harassing him," Raymone Bain replied.

This was too much. I didn't even know where Michael was working! My father spoke up.

"I don't know who you are," he said, "but this is Dominic Cascio. I expect Michael to call me in the next twenty-four hours. After a twenty-year relationship? This is unacceptable."

Michael called my father the next day and apologized. He said he hadn't known about the call. To this day, I honestly don't know if Raymone, for some reason, hadn't somehow done the opposite of what Michael had asked her to do, or whether, in his paranoia, he had changed his mind about inviting me to Ireland.

Michael told my father that he was going to apologize to me, but that call never came. He may have been embarrassed, or he may have decided that he would just come to see me in person.

WE THREW A SURPRISE PARTY FOR MY MOTHER'S FIF-tieth birthday in New Jersey on August 19, 2007. Later that evening, when the guests had gone, Michael appeared at the house. He had his three kids in tow, as well as his black Lab, Kenya, and a cat. My father called me in the city and said, "I think you should come home tonight, but make sure you come alone." As soon as he said that, I knew Michael was at the house.

I hadn't seen my old friend for three years—not since I'd gone to Neverland when the allegations were first announced. I went to New Jersey that night, and it was good to see him and the kids. But there was no way I could pretend that bygones were bygones and everything was fine. I said to Michael, "We have to talk."

"Okay," he replied.

Eddie, who by that point saw himself as Michael's protector, jumped in: "You have five minutes," he announced self-righteously. My brother truly believed that I had betrayed Michael. I would have behaved the same way if I'd thought the same of anyone.

"Really? I have five minutes with Mr. Jackson?" I returned. I was outraged, and turning to Michael, I continued, "That's it? I get five minutes with you?"

"I never said that," Michael said, and with that, he followed me to my old room, which had been converted into Eddie's recording studio. Eddie was right behind him. I asked my brother to leave, but he refused.

"No, it's better that you go," Michael said, and reluctantly Eddie complied.

"First of all," I said to Michael, "if I want to speak to you for four hours, I will."

"Frank, calm down," he said. "You know how your brother is."

Eddie, who was standing right outside, knocked at the door, wanting to come back in, but Michael said, "No, it's okay. We need to speak."

I looked at Michael . . . and simply broke down crying.

"How could you let this happen?" I demanded. "You know me better than anyone else. You know where my heart is. How could you let these people come between us? Why did you believe them?

Why did you want to believe them? You say I betrayed you. How did I betray you?"

All the questions I'd kept buried for almost three years came pouring out, each one practically running over into the next. In the middle of this torrent I told Michael, "For the record, I have a clear conscience. I have done nothing wrong. I don't regret anything that I did. I was one hundred percent there for you in every way anyone could ever be there for another person. You've told me how you've been betrayed by so many people. You taught me to be loyal, and I was. I always have been and I always will be. Where was your loyalty?"

Michael was calm. "Well, I was told you didn't want to testify. You weren't going to testify in my time of need. That hurt me, after all I've done for you," he replied.

"Who told you that?" I asked angrily. "It's not true. Your attorney, Tom, told my attorney, Joe, that they did not need me to testify."

"I don't remember who told me. That's what I was told."

"By whom?" I insisted.

"I don't remember. It was said." As he spoke, Michael was lying down on the bed, feet up, chilling out while he let me vent.

"By *whom*?" I repeated vehemently. It was driving me crazy. It had been for years. I tried to calm myself down and fought to keep my emotions in check, but it wasn't easy.

"You said this wasn't going to happen," I was finally able to say quietly. "From the first time I started working with you. Now you're telling people that I betrayed you, that I didn't stand by you." I was pacing, like I do, back and forth in front of the bed. "That wasn't the case. And you didn't call me to find out the truth because you believed what you wanted to believe—that I betrayed you. You wanted to be the victim, to say you helped me and I fucked you over, but I never did that to you. What did I do to make you hate me so much? You have no idea how you hurt me. I know how you get. Why didn't you just call and ask me for yourself instead of letting your imagination run away with you?"

At this point I was feeling like my impassioned words were finally beginning to sink in. Michael got teary, stood up, and gave me a hug.

"I'm sorry," he said. "You know I love you like a son. I'm sorry that I made you feel this way. Let's just move on from this. I could have gone anywhere in the world, but I'm here, with you and your family. I want to move on." He apologized for the insane call threatening to arrest me if I went to Ireland.

Explanations were something I never expected to hear from Michael Jackson. I was familiar with his paranoia, had been dealing with it for years; what I couldn't accept was that it had been directed at me, and I was never really sure whether or not he himself understood his own fears and defenses. He had been through a lot in his life, and I reminded myself, as I always did, that I hadn't walked in his shoes. And so I decided that enough was enough. I saw that he was truly sorry. His apologies, regret, and peace were all I wanted.

"I don't want to have a working relationship with you," I told him. "I just want to be your friend, and I need you to be my friend. I need you in my life."

"I want the same," Michael said.

We'd been friends for over twenty years, and yet somehow we'd forgotten how all the history we lived through bound us together. I knew Michael's flaws, but I still blamed the people around him for his excesses. I couldn't help wanting to take care of him. Old habits die hard.

"You're surrounded by idiots again," I said. "You need to get yourself away from these crazy people. Do me a favor, start working. Get back to what you do best." He nodded, a slight smile on his lips. He liked the sound of that. I went on: "Look, there's a studio in my family's house. Start working, start writing, start producing."

"It's funny that you should say that," Michael said, "because I just had that very conversation with your brother."

In the end, Michael and I talked for two full hours. At first, Eddie interrupted us every ten minutes, thinking Michael was being forced into a conversation he didn't want to have. But Michael kept telling him we were okay, and finally he stopped trying to control the situation. We didn't speak about the trial. I could tell Michael didn't want to go there. Instead, we stayed in neutral territory, chatting about his villa in Bahrain, a new record label he wanted to form with the prince of Bahrain, and how well the children were doing. I sensed, in Michael's tentative and cautious plans for the short term, that he was still getting his footing. The aftermath of the trial was apparent. But I could tell he would rebound from this. Michael was like a cat with nine lives.

When our conversation came to an end, I opened the door and said, "You can come in now, Eddie," as if we were ten years old.

Michael and I went from there. He and his family spent the next four months in New Jersey, and during that time we started rebuilding our friendship. We hung around talking about music and memories, just talking as we always had.

I was working in Manhattan, but I was back and forth to New Jersey frequently to see Michael and the kids. We celebrated Michael's forty-ninth birthday, which fell ten days after my mother's fiftieth, with a big family dinner. My mother cooked, and we also ordered in some pizza because Michael loved pizza.

The time he'd spent in Bahrain after the trial had been a good break for him. He had needed time away, time for himself, and he seemed rejuvenated. He was alive and excited, getting back into being creative and free. He and Eddie were working in the studio during the day, and he was playing with an idea for an animated cartoon he hoped to produce. He was happy to be around my family, with whom he could be himself. There was no sign that he was on any sort of medicine. He was back to being Michael.

One of the upstairs bedrooms had been turned into a classroom, and a tutor came to the house every day. Late as he went to sleep,

Michael made it a point to wake up early every morning to help his kids get ready for school. My mother fed them, but Michael was the one who got them dressed—nicely, as if they were going to school outside the house—and made sure their teeth were brushed.

During our long conversation, Michael and I had talked about working on our friendship—no business, just friendship—and we were true to our word. Any outstanding issues were finally laid to rest. We joked around, reminiscing about old Gary and the nutty songs he used to write and about the time Michael and I were at Disneyland Paris, taking the Peter Pan ride, when we paused in front of the animatronic Wendy.

"She's so beautiful," Michael had sighed, and then we looked at each other and instantly knew what we had to do. I'm not proud of it, and it was wrong, but it had to be done. To show our admiration, we lifted up Wendy's skirt and left our signatures on her, shall we say, animatronic person. And I am sure that, to this day, on the Peter Pan ride in Disneyland Paris, if anyone should ever be so bold as to lift poor animatronic Wendy's skirt, they would find my signature and Michael's signature, staking our claim. Actually, I lied when I said I wasn't proud of this moment. I actually am.

Meanwhile, things were going well in the studio with Eddie. Just as Michael had groomed me to do business with him, he had mentored Eddie's musical talents from a young age, always promising that if he worked hard, one day he would have his chance. Even though Eddie was my younger brother, I had always looked up to him in many ways. I was happy that they were working together, and happy that Michael was making music again. The two of them, along with our close friend James Porte, wrote twelve songs, three of which ("Breaking News," "Keep Your Head Up," and "Monster") would appear on Michael's last album, *Michael*.

Things seemed to be on the right track—in Michael's life, in my life, and in our friendship. But the months and months of simmering resentments and acrimony came with a heavy price, and despite the changes for the better in other areas, my brother and I remained unable to reconnect. Each of us held a grudge against the other, and though we kept them in check for Michael's sake, it was apparent to anyone who spent time around us that things between us were not at all the way they used to be. We were civil to each other, but we still hadn't made our peace. It was unclear if we ever would.

CHAPTER TWENTY-FOUR

THE UNTHINKABLE

OVER THE NEXT COUPLE YEARS MICHAEL AND I were in regular phone contact—as friends. He was working on *This Is It*, a series of fifty concerts that were to be held at London's O2 Arena starting in July 2009. The shows would be his swan song. Even his children, who had never been allowed to see him perform live, would be in attendance—for the first and last time.

At my suggestion, Michael brought back one of his former managers, Frank DiLeo, who hadn't worked with him since I was a kid and Frank was on hand for the *Victory* tour. At some point Frank got in touch with me to ask that I join him in London to work on the concerts. He was getting older and felt he needed some help.

"You'll have to discuss it with Michael," I said, "but if he's open to it, I'm open to it." The timing was right for me. I was looking for my next gig, and I felt close to Frank, who'd been a great mentor to me. But I left the decision in Michael's hands. I didn't want to force myself into the job.

Soon after this, Michael and I had a brief conversation. He told me that my brother Eddie and James Porte were flying out to London and were planning on working hand in hand with him on his days off to produce the album they had begun in New Jersey. Michael enjoyed the creative synergies between the three of them and was enthusiastic about making music again. He was giving Eddie the chance he'd always promised him. This was Eddie's moment.

Michael said how happy he was to have Frank DiLeo back in his life, and then he got to the point of the call: he wanted me to join them in London.

"Frank will get in touch with you," he said. "Just work everything out with him and keep it confidential. Don't say anything to anyone." I smiled when I heard that. Some things never change.

"I'm really proud of you," I said. "I love you."

"I love you, too," he said. "And now I gotta get going. We're heading into rehearsal now."

It would be a baby step for me and Michael in our journey to reconciliation, and for all the bitterness and strife of recent years, I knew how great things could be. It was his final series of concerts, and I wanted to be a part of it. I was in Italy, on hold, waiting and expecting to go to London, when Michael died on June 25, 2009. It was ten years, to the day, from the night of the *Michael Jackson & Friends* concert in Seoul. Ten years exactly since the night I'd started working with Michael.

IN CASTELBUONO, AFTER I LISTENED TO THE NEWS OF Michael's death on my cell phone, I walked up and down the cobblestone streets by myself for some minutes while a friend drove my car home and my cousin Dario waited beside his car, letting me process my shock and grief. I was in a mental fog, and it felt as if the world were spinning around me. Random memories rose up from the depths and then melted back into them. Brief moments from the past, some happy, some sad, some small or big, some heartbreaking or funny, swirled up then vanished. I was still in this state when I climbed into Dario's car.

Part of me even hoped that this was another ruse of Michael's. Michael had a history of missing concert dates. He'd ended the *Dangerous* tour early, of course, and later he'd canceled the Millennium concerts. But I was thinking particularly of a time in 1995, when I was fifteen. Michael was supposed to perform in a special for HBO, and I was looking forward to going to the show. But a week before the special, he said, "Frank, I have to tell you something. The show's not going to happen." A spiritual adviser had told him so. Indeed, just before the show, he collapsed in rehearsal. The show was canceled. Now I couldn't help hoping that this was some kind of elaborate scheme to get out of the concerts.

As my cousin drove me home, I called my family back in the States. Everyone was crying, but nobody could believe that Michael was gone. His death was surreal. I even spoke to my brother Eddie, our differences dissolving in the tears of this tragedy. There were no words any of us could find for each other. I sat there on the phone with my family, trying to make sense of everything, when one of them informed me that Michael had died of a drug overdose. When he was at our house in New Jersey, I knew that he hadn't been on anything (he didn't even want to touch wine), so the news came as a surprise to me. But at the time of his death, he'd been under pressure to perform, and I had seen that trigger his issues in the past.

So many times Michael had told me that he would die from a shot. That was always the word he used, and whenever he said it, I inevitably thought of a gunshot, but in the end he was killed by a different kind of shot. To my mind, the biggest difference between being shot and dying of an injection was that the latter involved a choice, a conscious decision. Michael had called doctors to ask for an injection on countless occasions. He had always had the option to stop this kind of shot from coming. At that moment it all seemed like such a waste to me.

And yet I knew that it was too easy to blame Michael for bringing this on himself and, even more, that it was unfair. Michael's pain and suffering were real and ran deep. Yes, there were safer ways for him to alleviate the pain, and he tried many of them. His studies, his meditation, his songwriting and performing, his humanitarian efforts, his creation and enjoyment of Neverland, and, above all, his children were all efforts to diminish the pain, and, in the case of his children, to transcend it with a love that meant more to him than all the other activities put together. But in the end, physical and mental anguish prevailed, and Michael died in his endless quest to attain some inner peace.

Certainly he hadn't been planning to die for a long time. He loved every moment he spent raising his kids, and was far from done in his creation of his family. He wanted more kids. Moreover, Prince, Paris, and Blanket had a lot of growing up to do, and he anticipated sharing in all of the milestones that would mark their futures.

"Frank," he would say, "can you imagine when Prince is old enough and we can have a glass of wine with him and just talk?" He also spoke about meeting Paris's future husband and making sure he was the right man for her. He joked with his children, saying, "Each of you is going to give me ten grandkids." There was no way Michael would ever have deliberately left his kids behind. He even imagined meeting his great-grandchildren. When it came to family, he was thinking long-term for both of us. He would say, "Frank, I can't wait to tell your kids stories about you."

In the days after his death, my anger turned to the people around him. Where were they? I wondered. Why didn't they make sure this didn't, this *couldn't* happen? Someone should have protected him.

I should have protected him. But I never imagined that something like this would happen. As I can't stop repeating, the last time I'd seen Michael was in New Jersey, and although almost two years had passed since then, he was completely clean at the time—not even drinking alcohol. His entire focus had been on getting back to work.

I remembered a conversation I had with Frank DiLeo, just a month or two earlier, during which he said, "We've got to make sure he's eating more. He's too skinny." But he also told me that Michael was performing well, that he had great energy, and that the show was going to be incredible: "It's amazing," Frank exclaimed, "what he can still do at fifty years old. We've just got to keep these crazy doctors away, and everything will be great." Then I knew Frank was battling with the doctors as I had.

Of course I had my suspicions about the dangers of the medicines that Michael was using, and I knew from the anesthesiologist who had been so forthcoming with me in New York that propofol was safe—*if the dosage was properly monitored.* The doctors Michael had seen were always specialists, experts in their fields. But Conrad Murray, the doctor who administered the propofol that killed Michael, was not an anesthesiologist; he was a cardiologist. It never occurred to me that anyone but an expert would administer such a drug, and this belief allayed any fears I had about the risks Michael was running. He was a person with a serious sleep disorder, who'd been led down the wrong medical path. Propofol was not a safe way to find sleep, but it was the only solution Michael had found. Knowing him as I did, I can say with confidence that the night he died, all he wanted was to be fresh for rehearsal the next day.

My brother Eddie flew directly to Los Angeles, to support Michael's kids and family. Randy, one of Michael's closest siblings, always steered clear of politics, and now he was again taking the lead for the Jackson family, graciously and efficiently overseeing the details. A week and a half later I flew to L.A., too. The memorial was held on July 7 at the Staples Center, where Michael had been in rehearsals for his concerts. In some ways, the funeral was just another big show, and this shouldn't have surprised me, since all of Michael's life had been a spectacle. Intimacy was impossible in such an existence. Many of the people who were present at the funeral truly mourned Michael's passing, but there were other people for whom it was an event that was comparable to attending the Academy Awards. But I know Michael would have loved to have everyone be a part of it. He was used to huge crowds. And all those faces were a reminder of how he brought people together and touched so many lives. All of us together in one room. Much as I wanted to say good-bye as a close friend, I recognized that Michael belonged to everyone.

There were many familiar faces—Rodney Jerkins, Frank DiLeo, Karen Smith, Michael Bush, and of course his family members. I hugged them and saw in their eyes the same feelings of shock and loss that I felt. There was Karen Faye—"Turkle"—Michael's makeup artist. When I saw her, I held her in my arms, both of us crying.

"Michael loved you, Frank," she wept. "You were like a son to him. He loved you, he loved you."

"Karen, he loved you, too," I sobbed back.

Michael's family had always been there for him. Whatever differences they might have had, they always united when one of them needed help, and now they were united in their grief. I gave Jackie a hug, as well as Janet, Tito, and his sons. I hadn't seen 3T for a while.

"I'm so sorry," I told them. "When things settle down, I'd really love to catch up with you guys." They were good people. I had looked up to them as a child.

Everyone seemed a little confused. It was so hard to believe that this was happening. Katherine, Michael's mother, was keeping it together—everyone tried, especially for the children—but nothing could change the fact that the person being buried was her very own son. Still, to this day, she hasn't been able to visit his grave at Forest Lawn Memorial Park. It's just too hard.

The service began, and much to my surprise, when the Reverend

Al Sharpton got up to speak, I found myself deeply moved by his words. He talked about how Michael had served as a force to unite people in a color-blind world, saying that he hadn't accepted limitations, and that he'd never given up. It was an uplifting speech. As I listened to the reverend's words, I heard something of Michael's own message, and I felt his radiant spirit fill the vast stadium. I believe that there is another world after this one—whether you want to call it heaven or something else—and I believe that Michael's energy and presence were so powerful that he still has a presence, both here on Earth and in that other world, wherever it may be.

I remember one winter night in Manhattan, soon after I'd started working for Michael, when, close to midnight, we got the urge to go down and hang out in Times Square. Without waking security, we slipped out of the hotel and took a cab. At the time, the Virgin Megastore was still in existence. It was open late, so we went there. Outside the store we noticed an old man. He had aluminum foil on his face and a fedora on his head, and he was dancing with great vigor. He must have been eighty years old, but he was dancing like a much younger man. Michael, who was just wearing winter clothes— no silly disguise—went up to him to get a closer look. Then he put twenty dollars in the ratty cardboard tip box on the sidewalk. The old fellow looked down, saw the twenty, and started dancing with an extra zing in his step. It was one of those moments—there wasn't much to it—but part of what made it special was that our cabdriver had had no idea it was Michael Jackson who was sitting in the back-seat of his cab, and the spirited old dancer hadn't had a clue that many elements of his movements had been inspired by the man who tipped him twenty dollars. We walked around the streets of Times Square, just the two of us, Michael experiencing a rare moment of being out in the world without having to deal with a frenzied mob. He was just a human being, out taking a walk, and his friend was beside him. The night was ours.

I had seen plenty of concerts, and now Michael the showman

was gone, a great loss to so many people. I would miss Michael the performer, Michael the musician, Michael the artist, but more than anything, I would miss Michael the person, the teacher, the friend, the family member. I missed and mourned that moment in Times Square, and infinite small moments that I wanted to preserve forever. That was my real loss. The funeral didn't give me closure, whatever people mean when they talk about closure, anyway. All I know is that time passes, and we have no other choice but to live on.

As the funeral came to an end, Jermaine sang Michael's song "Smile." He had chosen well: Michael loved that song.

After the memorial service, we drove from the Staples Center to the Beverly Wilshire hotel for a private wake. Paris, Prince, and Blanket were excited to see my family. They were in a cordoned-off VIP section of the room, and as soon as Prince saw us, he exclaimed, "The Cascios are here." We hurried forward to give them hugs, but security quickly stepped forward to block our path.

"Let them through," Prince said. "They're like our family." How many times can I say that Michael's children were always his top priority? No matter where he was or what he was doing, the kids always had access to him, and they knew it. If he was in a meeting and one of the kids needed him for something, he'd stop everything, attend to the child, then return. If they made a fuss about going to sleep, he stayed with them, talked to them, explaining why they had to go to sleep and what he was doing or where he would be. He soothed them if they were upset. He never handed off a crying child to Grace or a babysitter. He always had the patience to stay with his children until they were calm. He always took that time, no matter how late for an appointment it would cause him to be. He was never angry or frustrated. His patience was infinite, and the result was that his children were grounded, secure, and open to the world. But now, in their greatest hour of need, when he would have wanted more than anything to soothe and reassure them, he wasn't there, and there wasn't much that my family could say to comfort them. We just held them and shared our grief. In this moment, as always in Michael's life, his children came first.

I later found out that their mother, Debbie, was thinking the same thing. Marc Schaffel had arranged tickets for Debbie—he was going to escort her—but the night before, in the Westin Hotel near the Staples Center, they had a long talk about whether or not she should attend. Much as she wanted to pay her respects, Debbie didn't want to be a distraction for anyone. So, putting her own grief aside for the sake of propriety, she went quietly back to her ranch.

After the wake, my family and I headed to a private room. The kids got into an elevator, and it quickly filled up with people who happened to be in front of us. We wanted to be with the kids, but we also didn't want to be presumptuous.

"We want the Cascios to ride with us," Prince called out. So everyone else stepped out of the elevator and we rode with them. They were being very strong, but the sadness in their eyes was heartbreaking.

Later that day, my family went back to Katherine Jackson's estate, Hayvenhurst, to spend time with the Jackson family. At one point, while I was talking to Paris, she said, "Daddy told me all the crazy things you guys used to do together." Michael had told her about our trip to Scotland—the ghost, the creepy hotel. Talking to Michael's daughter, I knew that no matter what had happened between me and Michael, if he'd talked to his kids about it, then our past clearly meant as much to him as it meant to me. He never forgot that trip, and neither will I.

MICHAEL'S RELATIONSHIP WITH HIS FAMILY HAD BEEN complicated, and some of the power struggles that were always part of his world were still being waged at the time of his death. Jermaine told the press that he was Michael's backbone. The day after his death, Michael's father, Joe, would appear at an award show, promoting his new record label. His brothers—Jackie, Tito, Jermaine, and Marlon—shot episodes of a reality show. True, the show had already been in the works, but the impression these events left, perhaps unfairly, was that the family was rather tastelessly capitalizing on the spotlight Michael's death had thrown on them.

The following Christmas, Prince, Paris, and Blanket came to our house in New Jersey. They'd always spent Christmases with us, either at Neverland or in New Jersey. That's what they were used to doing, and their grandmother, Katherine, wanted to make sure to keep the traditions going so that the children's lives weren't any more disrupted than they had to be by the loss of their father. It was exactly what Michael would have wanted. Michael's nephew TJ, Grace the nanny, and Omer Bhatti came along with them.

For Christmas, my mother cooked her traditional turkey dinner, complete with all the dishes we knew were Michael's favorites. We tried to enjoy ourselves, relaxing, reading books, watching movies, and playing video games. But it was a hard Christmas for all of us. The person who'd brought us all together wasn't there. Michael had always played Santa, had always provided the energy to drive the whole event. He was the one who had stood under the tree, handing out the gifts. He was the spirit of our Christmases. Now my mother took the lead, as she tends to do in our family.

During those holiday nights in New Jersey, I had a lot of dreams about Michael. I talked to him in those dreams. We reminisced. I told him I loved him and vice versa. I felt his presence, and I know that I wasn't the only one. Various people reported that they'd caught sight of Michael walking the hallways of our house. My mother doesn't believe in supernatural phenomena, but late one night she was in the kitchen washing dishes when Michael walked past her and said, "Hi, Connie."

Eddie and I were brothers, and growing up, we'd been best friends. I'd quarreled with him just as I'd quarreled with Michael, but while Michael and I had made our peace long before, Eddie and

I had not. I couldn't really blame my brother for trying to do everything he could to defend and protect Michael. Hadn't I always tried to do the same? I had always been ready to talk our differences out, but this somehow never happened, and then, one day, Eddie had an eye-opening experience.

Eddie, like me, would have done anything for Michael. He was deeply loyal. But after Michael's death, John McClain and some Jackson family members started to turn on him, and Eddie found himself facing accusations as absurd as the ones that had been leveled at me—and that, I must repeat, Eddie had believed. It dawned on my brother that this was exactly what I had gone through, and with that realization, it was finally time for us to talk things out. Eddie said that he and Michael thought that I had betrayed him when they heard I wouldn't testify. Michael had doubted the very quality that I thought bound us forever: my loyalty. Eddie, in his own loyalty to Michael, had doubted me alongside him.

I explained to Eddie how untrue the accusation was and walked him through exactly what had happened, and now, at last, with his own experience of the malignant creatures that swam in the waters of Michael's organization, he believed me. I asked Eddie the question that still haunted me—"Who told Michael that I didn't want to testify on his behalf?"—and he couldn't answer it. So it looks like I will never know the answer, and I have to wonder if the person was none other than Michael himself . . . Michael, who, with his crippling doubts, some justified, some completely fabricated, and his paranoia, was compelled to believe that nobody—not even the person who was closest to him—could be trusted.

We talked about what Eddie was going through in his dealings with Michael's estate. He and Michael had recorded twelve songs together, three of which Sony and the estate had picked for Michael's posthumous album. But Eddie didn't understand the down-and-dirty politics and the treachery that surrounded Michael's business. Some people cast doubt on whether the songs Eddie had recorded with Michael were authentic. All of a sudden the word was that the Cascios were trying to cash in on Michael. I knew the personalities involved and had some idea of how to navigate through these shoals in order to help Eddie resolve his issues. Only now was my brother beginning to see how complex Michael's world was and how quickly those who lived in it could turn on one of their own.

Eddie and I talked for quite a while. In the end, he understood what I had been through and how it felt to have your intentions and actions so misrepresented. And I finally recognized where my brother was coming from. We should have talked much earlier. Life is too short to have unresolved issues with people you truly love. My brother had a newborn baby named Victoria Michael, the first grandchild in our family. I loved her and looked forward to being her uncle, and Eddie wanted me in her life. As a new parent, maybe he was seeing our relationship in a new light, realizing that he would want his own children to get along. Both Eddie and I had loved Michael, and both of us had a strong bond with him. We had shared this for many years as children, and we weren't going to let it come between us as adults. Michael was gone. Our hearts were broken. But there was really nothing left to fight about. These days my brother and I are as close as we ever were, all the more close for having realized how much we shared. We are both happy to be brothers again.

EPILOGUE

ON THE FIRST ANNIVERSARY OF MICHAEL'S death, a memorial gathering was held at his burial site. Family, friends, and fans went to his mausoleum at Forest Lawn cemetery. Outside, the crowds had gathered, but inside the mausoleum itself there were just a few people: Randy, Janet, Jermaine, Marlon, and some of Michael's cousins. A pastor spoke, and Michael's nephew Auggie said some words to remember his uncle that were both powerful and well delivered. They left us all impressed and deeply moved.

When the ceremony was over, I stepped forward. There was an aboveground tomb, and on top of it was a big golden crown. I tilted it up, as I had seen others do, and there I beheld a compartment full of Bazooka bubble gum. I smiled in spite of myself. It was a nice touch. Michael had loved that stuff. I said a prayer for Michael and took a moment to speak to him. I thanked him for everything he'd done for my family and for everything he'd given me. I promised him that I'd do everything in my power to preserve his legacy as he would have wanted.

Thank you, I said silently, *for the greatest adventure anyone could ever give to someone else. Thank you for opening my eyes to a whole world that, if not for you, I wouldn't have had the opportunity to experience. Thank you for the memories you left with me. I was truly blessed to have you in my life. I love you, and I miss you.*

Later, people told me that as I stepped away from the tomb, they saw a white petal come floating to the ground. It wasn't a windy day, and even if it had been, we were inside a building. There were no windows or doors open. I want to believe that Michael heard me and that the petal was his way of answering. You never know.

I HADN'T LIVED A NORMAL LIFE. WHEN MY FRIENDS were partying in college, playing beer pong, and going to bars, I was carving out a life in a wholly different world. Still, though, I was blessed. Beyond my warm, loving family, I had a teacher, a father, a brother, and a friend who happened to be massively talented, and because of that, he lived in the glare of a particularly bright spotlight. I saw the world from a megastar's perspective, from the inside out. I felt the glare of that spotlight, and I saw the dark shadows that beckoned and loomed beyond it. It was a life of unusual privilege and access, but it came with a burden of isolation and secrecy as well. I lived it first as a young boy, but as I grew into a more responsible role, I discovered its nuances and intricacies, good and not so good, and the challenges and hurdles that Michael had to face and leap over in order to nurture and sustain his work and art. From Michael himself I learned to explore the world through books; through him I was given the opportunity to appreciate the different people, places, religions, and cultures of the world. I fell in love with music, and with the business of entertainment.

Above all, though, I discovered the value and beauty of an open heart. There were hard personal lessons, too—the destructiveness of greed and ruthless self-interest, the painful wounds of betrayal, the struggle to balance love and self-preservation, the challenge of preserving a complicated and cherished friendship in a threatening and competitive environment.

I've spent the majority of my life so far in Michael's sphere, but God willing, I have a long life ahead of me. I believe that certain parts of life are predetermined, that things happen for a reason, but at the same time it is up to us to make the most of what we are given. I see my friendship with Michael, and the wealth of experiences it brought me, as important lessons for whatever I'm meant to do next. I intend to take hold of what I've learned and put it to good use, building my own legacy—whatever that might mean—from this point on. I don't take anything that I was given for granted. For me—for anyone who was moved by Michael's music, his being, or both—his message was simple and he said it often: it's all for love. I live by that principle.

Neverland, as far as I know, is deserted. The zoo is empty. The amusement park rides have been carted away. The pictures of the ranch that I've seen show it in a sad state of neglect: the once carefully groomed landscaping now overgrown in places and withered in others; the canopy over the bumper cars sagging and torn; the tepees collapsed in on themselves. The main house, empty for so long, must be full of stale air and ghosts. A place that was made for life, laughter, and children is now a haunted reminder of Michael's brilliant eccentricities.

The truth is, I don't miss Neverland's amusement park, or the zoo. I miss the little things: the way my whole family would bundle up and walk with Michael and the kids to the tepees for dinner. Little Prince talking his head off. Paris clutching her father, Daddy's little girl. Blanket in Michael's arms. I see it so clearly. The herd of bundled people walking along the train tracks. Music playing. The sound of the waterfall. Michael's laugh. His fedora. Even if Michael and I had continued as we'd been at the time of his death, either having made our peace and gone in different directions, or working together again on his concerts, I know we would have shared a nostalgia for our best years together. And I know that had he lived, we would have circled back to each other again and again over the years, to return to those memories; to talk, drink wine, and listen to music together well into old age.

Some evenings at Neverland, Michael and I would ask the chef to pack us a picnic basket for the next morning. At the crack of dawn, he and I would ride motorbikes a good ten or fifteen minutes up into the mountains. Then we'd spread blankets down and have breakfast while we watched the sun rise. We were still on his property, but we were so far away from everything that we couldn't even see the house. It was another world, mind-blowingly peaceful. I used to go up to the mountains all the time, even without Michael, and knew all the trails that led off the property, all the secret pathways and shortcuts, far away in the back of the property. Those mountains were our secret getaway, together and separately.

Those mountain trails were very narrow, so we had to be very careful. One false move, and we'd have fallen down a cliff. One time, Michael said, "Come on, Frank, let's go up the mountain." We jumped onto our motorbikes and drove up a path we'd never discovered before, spiraling up the mountainside. All of a sudden the road got narrower and narrower, like the tail of a snake, and disappeared into nothingness. Michael, who was ahead of me, stopped his motorbike just in time, and I stopped behind him. He looked back at me.

"Applehead, this is not good," he said. The path ahead was gone. There was a cliff on our left, a mountain wall on our right, and no room to turn our bikes around.

"Don't worry," I said. "I'm going to gently back up." I put my bike in neutral and started rolling it carefully backward. It was scary. If I looked down, I knew, I was dead. Dangerous as it was, though, I have to admit that I like stuff like that, and so did Michael. We rolled back to safety, then grinned at each other, turned our bikes around, and sped back down the mountain.

Every day something reminds me of my life with Michael. A

song, a Disney emblem, a gullible person who is ripe for a pranking. At night, I still dream about him, dreams about the old times. We're on tour, at an event, walking side by side, doing things we did for years and might have gone on doing for years if everything had gone differently.

I regret the way that our relationship suffered during and after the trial. I wish life hadn't gotten so complicated, but that's what life tends to do, particularly a life that was as success-driven and large scale as Michael's was. But we'd made our peace. From a young age, I understood that being friends with Michael meant sticking with him in good times and bad. I never stopped caring about him, loving him, and defending him. Someday, I like to think, we'll go up the mountain together again.

ACKNOWLEDGMENTS

To my parents, Dominic and Connie—I am forever grateful to you for loving and supporting Michael for over twenty-five years. If it wasn't for you, I would not have had the experiences am so blessed to have had. Thank you for supporting me, believing in me, and loving me unconditionally. Michael always called our family "the family of love," and I am truly blessed to be a part of it. I love you.

To my brothers, Eddie, Dominic, and Aldo, and my sister, Marie Nicole—I'm so proud of all of you, and I love you from the bottom of my heart.

To Freddy Todenhoefer—Thank you for all your love and support. If it wasn't for you, I would not have been able to write this book. I am forever grateful. Love you, Freddy.

To Matthew Guma—Thank you for having the faith, wisdom, and dedication to turn this book into a reality. I am forever grateful to you.

To Matt Harper—You believed in this story and in me, and brought absolute determination and commitment to the project. My deepest thanks.

To Hilary Liftin—Thank you for being so sensitive and understanding of me throughout this process. With all my heart, I thank you.

To Court Coursey and Derek Rundell—I am forever grateful for your friendship and support throughout the years. I love you guys.

To Frank "Tookie" DiLeo—First and foremost I want to thank you for loving and protecting Michael for all those years. He loved you very much. I miss our lunches by the pool at the Beverly Hilton Hotel and hearing your crazy stories and life experiences. Thank you for being a mentor and father figure to me. I miss you and I love you so much.

To Karen Smith—You are an angel. Thank you for being my shoulder to lean on, for guiding me through some tough situations, and for being the most loyal person Michael ever had working for him. I love you.

To my incredible friends Michael Piccoli, Vincent Amen, and Frank Barbagallo—I can't thank you enough for always being there for me, and for your help and guidance throughout the process of writing this book. I love you all so much. You are my family.

To James Porte—Thank you for your continued friendship and support. I love you.

To Shana Wall—I don't even know how to begin to thank you for all your love and support throughout this process. I am blessed to have you in my life. I love you with all my heart.

To Brad Buxer—Watching you and Michael work together was magical. You are a genius, with talents that are unparalleled. I love you.

To Valerie Todenhoefer—You have been a profound inspiration in my life. I will love you forever.

To Nathalie Todenhoefer—I adore you, and of course "Miha."

To Grace—Your loyalty to Michael was unparalleled, and I know how much Michael trusted you with his children from day one. I love you.

To Alex Farshchian—You were always there for Michael, and you helped him in a way no one else was able to. I thank you and love you dearly.

A very special thank you to Katherine Jackson—For over twenty-five years Michael told me again and again how much he loved you and everything you meant to him. He loved you more than life itself. Thank you for bringing such a special man into the world and for sharing him with us. Katherine, *you* are an inspiration to all of us. I love you.

To my HarperCollins family:

To Michael Morrison—I cannot thank you enough for making this book happen. You are amazing.

To Liate Stehlik, Lynn Grady, Seale Ballenger, Brianne Halverson, Laurie Connors, Juliette Shapland, and Beth Silfin—Thank you for all your hard work and dedication. I am forever grateful to all of you.

Special thanks to Bill Bray and family, Wayne Nagin, John Branca, Howard Weitzman, Al Malnik, and Karen Langford—You all were all so important to Michael and were always there for him.

Also, I want to thank my grandparents, Nicoletta and Edward Sottile, and Maria and Francesco Cascio; the entire Sottile family; and the entire Cascio family for all their love and support. My beautiful niece Victoria Michael Cascio, I love you. Françoise Todenhoefer, I love you. I would also like to acknowledge the entire Jackson Family, Miko Brando, Randy Jackson, Austin Brown, Rabbi Shmuley and family, Michael Prince, Marc Schaffel, Gary Hern, Big Al, Rudy the chef, Karen Faye, Michael Bush, Omer Bhatti, Samantha Rex, Eric Lerner, Bob and Lillian Wall, and the entire Neverland staff. Thank you and I love you all.